Communion in the Messiah

Studies in the Relationship between
Judaism and Christianity

Lev Gillet

With a Foreword by the Bishop of Cichester

WIPF & STOCK · Eugene, Oregon

השיבנו יי אליך ונשובה
חדש ימינו כקדם

Bring us back HaShem, and
renew us as before.

Wipf and Stock Publishers
199 W 8th Ave, Suite 3
Eugene, OR 97401

Communion in the Messiah
Studies in the Relationship Between Judaism and Christianity
By Gillet, Lev and Kinzer, Mark S.
Copyright©1942 James Clarke Lutterworth
ISBN 13: 978-1-62564-592-0
Publication date 1/15/2014
Previously published by Lutterworth Press, 1942

CONTENTS

                                                                Page

INTRODUCTION BY MARK S. KINZER iii

AUTHOR'S PREFACE ix

BIBLIOGRAPHICAL NOTE xiii

I. " DIALOGUE WITH TRYPHO " 1

POLEMICS AND DIALOGUE—JESUS AND THE PHARISEES—
PAUL AND JUDAISM—JUDÆO-CHRISTIANITY—JUDAISM
AND CHRISTIANITY IN PATRISTIC TIMES—JUDAISM AND
CHRISTIANITY IN THE MIDDLE AGES—RENAISSANCE
AND REFORMATION : THEIR RELATION TO JUDAISM—
JUDAISM AND CHRISTIANITY IN THE 17TH CENTURY—
THE PERIOD OF EMANCIPATION : LIBERAL JUDAISM—
" CONVERGENT SCHOLARSHIP "—ATTITUDE OF MODERN
JUDAISM TOWARDS JESUS.

II. THE PERMANENT VALUES OF JEWISH
TRADITION 41
TRADITION IN JUDAISM—THE JEWISH FATHERS—
SCRIPTURAL TRADITION—LEGAL OR TALMUDIC TRADITION
—MYSTICAL TRADITION.

III. JUDAISM AND THE CHRISTIAN CREED . . 71
JUDAISM, HELLENISM, CHRISTIANITY—CHRISTIANITY
AND JEWISH MONOTHEISM—THE WORD AND THE SON—
THE SHEKINAH—THE HOLY SPIRIT—THE ATONEMENT
—ELEMENTS COMMON TO JUDAISM AND CHRISTIANITY.

IV. THE MESSIANIC HOPE 100
JEWISH AND CHRISTIAN MESSIANISM—MESSIANISM AND
EXISTENTIAL THINKING—MESSIANISM AND SOCIETY.

V. THE JEWISH LIFE OF GRACE AND ITS RELATION
TO CHRISTIANITY 127
JEWISH WORSHIP—FROM THE INNER LIFE OF THE
JEWISH BELIEVER—HASIDISM.

VI. CHRISTIANITY AND THE EARTHLY PROBLEMS
OF ISRAEL 148
CHRISTIAN ATTITUDE TOWARDS JEWISH DIASPORA.
CHRISTIAN ATTITUDE TOWARDS ZIONISM.

CONTENTS

Page

VII. ISRAEL AND THE MISSION 172
CHRISTIAN MISSIONS TO JEWS—MISSION OF THE
CHRISTIAN CHURCH TO ISRAEL—MISSION OF ISRAEL TO
THE CHRISTIAN CHURCH—COMMUNION IN THE MESSIAH
AND THE ECCLESIASTICAL COMMUNITIES, JEWISH AND
CHRISTIAN—THE IDEA OF A JEWISH CHRISTIANITY.

VIII. CONCLUSION : THE MYSTERY OF ISRAEL . . 211

SPECIAL NOTES :

A. Jew, Hebrew, Israelite. 218
B. Martin Buber 218
C. Criticisms of Pharisees in the Talmud 219
D. Claude Montefiore 219
E. The *Qaraim* 220
F. The Samaritans 221
G. Was Jesus a Rabbi ? 222
H. Talmudic Dialectics 222
I. Jewish Creeds 223
J. *Bat Kol* 224
K. Jewish Messiahs 225
L. The Experience of the Shekinah and Christian Mysticism 226
M. The Seat of Moses 228
N. Jewish and Christian Priesthood 229
O. Baal Shem Tob 230
P. Judaism and some French Catholic Circles . . . 231
Q. Yiddish and neo-Hebrew Literature 233
R. Judaism and Philosophy in Modern Times . . . 234
S. Conversions to Judaism 235
T. Judaizing Movements within Christianity . . . 238
U. A Jewish Christian Liturgy 238
V. Jewish Learning for Christian Students . . . 240
W. Jewish and Christian United Worship in a Shelter . . 240
Y. Jewish Worship in a Camp of Internees . . . 241
Z. Judaism and Christianity as represented in Art . . 242

INDEX 244

Introduction to Lev Gillet's
Communion in the Messiah

by Mark S. Kinzer

LEV GILLET WROTE *COMMUNION in the Messiah* at a momentous juncture in Jewish and world history. Living in Britain in 1941, a Russian Orthodox Priest and a refugee from Nazi occupied France, Gillet looked with compassion on the suffering Jews of Europe, who were, as he knew well, "in danger of being exterminated" (page x). His humane concern was augmented by his awareness of the Church's sad record of cruelty and triumphalism in its dealings with the Jewish people, but even more by a profound appreciation for the spiritual riches inherent in the Jewish tradition, and by the conviction that Israel was still elect of God and entrusted with a mission in history.

How should Christians relate to Jews and Judaism? How can they explain their own faith in terms intelligible to Jewish ears? What do Christians have to learn from Jews and the Jewish religious tradition? How can Christians aid the Jewish people in fulfilling their mission in the world? How should Jews who believe in Jesus as Messiah relate to the Church and to the Jewish community? These questions are just as pressing now, at the beginning of a new millennium, as they were in the midst of the great European conflagration. Gillet's penetrating answers also have maintained much of their currency. In particular, his prescient discussion of "Jewish Christianity" deserves a careful hearing today among all concerned parties and offers valuable insight to the Messianic Jewish movement as it grows toward maturity.

One always encounters challenges when reading a work written three-quarters of a century past. It can no longer be assumed that educated people in the English speaking world have reading knowledge of Latin, Greek, French, and German, and so a few citations, allusions, and technical terms in *Communion in the Messiah* will lose their full force. For those accustomed to forms of Hebrew transliteration common in contemporary Jewish publications, Gillet's rendering of Hebrew words will make the familiar seem foreign. The difficult conditions for publication in wartime Britain prevented the elimination of numerous typos. The reader can easily overcome such obstacles, especially when the reward to be obtained is so great.

What in fact is that reward? One can only assess and appreciate the value of a book by reading it. Nevertheless, as the reader begins this task, he or she might be interested in what another, standing at a similar location in time and place, found to be of enduring worth.

Seven points in Gillet's work struck me as especially relevant. First, the author is an advocate for dialogue between Jews and Christians, but his understanding of dialogue is consistent with his notion of mission. According to Gillet, the essence of dialogue is reciprocity—the readiness of each partner to listen and learn from the other. Dialogue does not preclude all mission, but it does preclude unidirectional mission. "There is, and there ought to be, a mission of the Christian Church to Israel; but there is also a Mission of Israel to the Christian Church, and this (as we think) divinely appointed mission must not be overlooked" (172). When each learns from the other, each accomplishes its mission, and true dialogue is established.

Second, Gillet emphasizes the importance of taking Jewish tradition seriously. Many Christians think of Judaism as the religion of the Old Testament, as Christianity minus Jesus. Such views fail to take account of the ongoing development of Judaism. For Gillet, Judaism as a post-biblical reality constitutes a rich spiritual tradition superintended in its evolution by divine grace.

> … there is no form of Judaism which could be described as a pure Biblicism, devoid of tradition… Many Christian theologians and missionaries who have to deal with Judaism make a grave mistake in that respect. They imagine Judaism as being merely the religion of the Old Testament … They forget—or willingly ignore—that, between the Old Testament and our times, there lie more than nineteen centuries of Jewish thought … It is useless to approach Judaism without some knowledge of—and much sympathy for—the living tradition of the Jews. (43-44)

Introduction

Any attempt to explain the person, teaching, and work of Jesus the Messiah in Jewish terms must build not only on the Bible but also on this living tradition.

Third, Gillet finds in one strand of Jewish tradition a special contact point for fostering "communion in the Messiah": the heritage of Jewish mysticism. Messianic Jews and evangelical Christians appreciative of Judaism often treat Jewish mysticism with intense suspicion. This derives in part from the superficiality and faddishness of contemporary pop Kabbalah. Even more alarming is the perception that this tradition is riddled with superstition and occult influence. Caution, discernment, sound scholarship, and common-sense are all warranted, but wholesale dismissal would entail the loss of an immensely valuable resource in the fashioning of an authentic Messianic Jewish theology. As Gillet notes, Jewish mysticism provides the fundamental conceptual tools necessary for the articulation of a Jewish understanding of Jesus and of the Triune God.

Fourth, Lev Gillet recognizes the importance of this task—the development of what we might today call a distinctive Messianic Jewish theology. He also possesses much wisdom concerning the manner in which the task should be pursued. For example, he recognizes frankly the disjunction between traditional Jewish and Christian modes of thought, and the challenge facing the theologian who is seeking to articulate the insights of Christian tradition in Jewish terms. What is a Jew to make of the technical Greek terms (e.g, *hypostasis, ousia, physis, theotokos*) employed in the classical Christian creeds?

> In all these cases, a translation of words—even the most accurate—would be most inadequate. What is needed is a "translation of meanings." A re-thinking of Christianity in Jewish terms, i.e., not only in Hebrew words, but in Hebrew categories of thought … (73)

At the same time, the author refrains from pejorative characterizations of "Greek thought" and its baleful influences on Christian theology, and tendentious contrasts between it and an allegedly superior Jewish mode of thinking.

v

> This does not mean the violent elimination of the Greek formulas. They have been extremely useful for conveying the Christian faith to the Greek world and for keeping it unaltered .... Only these venerable words must not stand as an obstacle between Israel and the message of Jesus. There is no reason why a purely Jewish expression of the Christian faith could not be as adequate or become as venerable as the Greek one. But this cannot be achieved through a crude Judaizing process which would be lacking in understanding and appreciation of the Greek traditional values. (73)

All those engaged in the work of Messianic Jewish theology would benefit from an attentive reading of *Communion in the Messiah*.

Fifth, this volume makes an impressive case for the importance of what we now know as Messianic Judaism. When considering the path to be taken by the Jewish person who comes to faith in Jesus the Messiah, Gillet, though himself a Russian Orthodox priest, states that he is "very far from considering the adhesion of a Jew to one of the Gentile Christian Churches as an ideal solution" (191). Instead, he advocates the establishment of "Jewish Christianity." (In this, as in many other matters, he appears to have been influenced by his friend, Paul Levertoff, one of the most brilliant and learned Jewish Jesus-believing thinkers of the twentieth century.) He even entertains the possibility of what he calls "Synagogued Jewish Christianity," a movement of Jews confessing their faith in Jesus and yet participating actively in the wider Jewish community, to the point of maintaining membership in Reform, Conservative, or Orthodox synagogues. Regardless of the particular form it takes, Gillet is "convinced that a Jewish Christianity, under some form, is desirable for the good of the whole Christian Church" (209). He goes on to assert that "the development of a Jewish Christianity is inseparably linked with the development, among Christians, of a new ecumenical consciousness" (209). This breadth of vision makes *Communion in the Messiah*, written thirty years before the emergence of the Messianic Jewish movement, a work of prophetic force.

Sixth, Gillet both promotes and models a faith that is deeply devoted to Jesus and the truth he embodies, and also irenic and open to the best insights of modern scholarship and theology. He quotes with approval a writer who, commenting on a missionary conference he attended in 1927, holds that "it would be a disaster if Jewish missions were bound for the most part to a less progressive theology than is current among Christian scholars and thinkers generally" (187). He describes his friend, Paul Levertoff, in the following words:

> Himself a scholar, unable to conform to the obscurantism and weak pietism which have been regrettably favoured by some Christian missionaries to the Jews, he understood the importance of an intellectual appeal and the necessity of expressing the theological concepts of Christianity in Jewish terms (according to him, along the lines of the Shekinah teaching and the Hasidic mysticism) (203).

Like the missionary movements of the past and present, contemporary Messianic Judaism can also get mired in "obscurantism and weak pietism." On this topic as on many others, Gillet's reflections and recommendations still hit the mark.

Seventh, though writing seven years before the founding of the state of Israel, and by no means a dispensationalist, Gillet is an avowed Zionist. He perceives the sacred quality of the land of Israel and its importance for the Jewish people, and urges Christians to support the cause of a Jewish homeland. On this matter Gillet may have nothing substantially new to offer. However, his explicit Christian Zionism, at a time when many Jews themselves displayed indifference, ambivalence, or hostility to the Zionist project, once again reveals Gillet's clear vision.

Lev Gillet did not seek to write a book of groundbreaking scholarship. The volume reflects an impressive breadth of reading, and a good grasp of the best insights of his time. Nevertheless, he wrote before the discovery of the Dead Sea Scrolls, and his treatment of first century Judaism can no longer be affirmed without considerable modification. With a new appreciation for the diversity of Jewish life in that period, and a more vivid awareness of the problems inherent in using late rabbinic texts to depict first century realities, we can no longer say without qualification that "Pharisaism was the most characteristic manifestation of Palestinian Judaism in the time of Jesus" (4), or that "Hillel was the highest authority among the doctors of Jerusalem in the time of the first King Herod" (47). What is more striking, however, is that this occasional scholarly obsolescence detracts little from the essential argument of the work. Lev Gillet still has something to say to us, if we are willing to listen.

It is my sincere hope that this reprinting of *Communion in the Messiah* will bring Lev Gillet's work to the attention of many in the Messianic Jewish movement, the Christian Church, and the wider Jewish community, and that we might all attain that "communion" with one another in Messiah Jesus which Gillet envisioned and advanced.

Mark S. Kinzer (Ph.D., University of Michigan) is President Emeritus and Senior Scholar of Messianic Jewish Theological Institute (San Diego, CA) and Rabbi of Congregation Zera Avraham in Ann Arbor, Michigan. He is the author of *Postmissionary Messianic Judaism: Redefining Christian Engagement with the Jewish People* (Brazos 2005) and *Israel's Messiah and the People of God: A Vision for Messianic Jewish Covenant Fidelity* (Cascade 2011).

PREFACE

Currebant autem duo simul : sed Joannes praecucurrit citius Petro. Venit prior admonumentum, et ingredi non praesumpsit. Venit ergo posterior Petrus, et intravit. . . . Quid ergo per Joannem nisi synagoga, quid per Petrum nisi ecclesia designatur ? . . . Currunt ambo simul : quid, ab ortus sui tempore usque ad occasum, pari et communi via, etsi non pari et communi sensu Gentilitas cum Synagoga cucurrit. Venit Synagoga prior ad monumentum. . . . Homilia 22 sancti Gregorii Papae in Evangelia.

Loofty Levonian, as a Fellow of Woodbrooke, Selly Oak and later as a lecturer at the Selly Oak Colleges, wrote two books[1] on the relationship between Islam and Christianity, of which he said that " while they make no claim to be exhaustive in the study of their problems, they indicate a new direction and a new attitude." The present book, which also emanates from the Selly Oak Colleges, is an attempt of the same kind with regard to Judaism.

The author is not a Jew. He is not a rabbinic scholar. He has never taken part in any missionary work concerning the Jews. He has been, however, in close contact with them, not only through literature, but through many personal friendships. He owes his discovery of Jewish spiritual values mainly to Aimé Pallière, a Christian who became a Jewish preacher, and to Paul Levertoff, a Jew who became a Christian minister. The memory of the Jewish Refugee Students from Vienna, with whom he has spent the last two years in the East End of London, and from whom he has been separated by their internment in the Dominions, has never left his mind while these pages were written. If sympathy were a sufficient justification for writing about the Jews, this book would be amply justified. But there are other reasons. The opinion of somebody who (without having ever been a missionary) has attained, as an outcome of his own experience, very definite views about the Christian approach to the Jews, may seem the impertinent conceit of an outsider ; it may also possess some objectivity and originality and, if humbly offered, not be quite useless. Such is my hope. I am, moreover, a priest

---

[1] *Moslem Mentality. A Discussion of the Presentation of Christianity to Moslem* (London, 1928) and *Studies in the Relationship between Islam and Christianity* (London, 1940). The sentence quoted here is taken from the introduction to this last work.

ix

of the Russian Orthodox Church. The Orthodox Churches have a heavy historical guilt towards Judaism ; in the persecutions of the Jews, chiefly in Russia and Rumania, they have often sinned either by their silence or by their acquiescence or by their incitements.[1] I would here, as far as an individual can do it, atone for this guilt.

European Judaism is now (1941) in danger of being exterminated. Its present situation offers Christians a most serious opportunity for rethinking their relationship to Israel. It would be too early to discern in the vicissitudes of European Jewry any definite change of the religious or intellectual order. But the material changes have been so decisive that they are bound to have some spiritual repercussions. The recent hardships have purified and strengthened all that was best in Israel. To help the Jews in their plight is a necessary task, but other—and new—tasks of a religious order, lie in front of us. Could I say of the present book, as Levonian said of his own, that it indicates " a new direction and a new attitude " ? None of the ideas contained here is really new. Only they have always been the ideas of a small minority and they have never obtained a wide hearing among the Christian public ; they may therefore seem new to a certain number of people.

I am advocating two main ideas. One is the idea of a " dialogue " substituted for the idea of a one-sided " mission " to the Jews. By dialogue I mean that, if Christianity has a definite message to bring to Judaism, Judaism also has a message to bring to Christianity. The other idea is the " communion " of Jews and Christians either in the same personal Messiah (this total communion is a distant goal rather than an immediate possibility) or in Messianic values common to both of them (this partial communion can be reached to-day and progressively enlarged). It does not mean that the differences between Judaism and Christianity should be

---

[1] Some notable exceptions ought to be remembered. During the progrom of Tomsk (1905) a young monk ran to the progromists, raised a cross and said loudly : " Why do you beat my brother ? " The crowd turned aside. During the Kiev progrom of October, 1905, Bishop Platon organized a solemn procession through the streets of the Jewish quarter and, falling on his knees before the mob, begged them to spare the life and property of the Jews. Likewise, Bishop Parfenyi of Podolia told his priests to array themselves in their vestments and with their crosses to go before the mobs engaged in progrom and to calm their fury. See J. Shelton Curtiss, *Church and State in Russia. The Last Years of the Empire*, 1900–1917 (Columbia University Press, 1940), chiefly Ch. VI. Russia's great religious philosopher, Vladimir Soloviof (1853–1900) opposed the anti-Jewish attitude of the Slavophil Party and is said to have prayed for the Jews on his death-bed. (F. Getz, *Der Philosoph W. Solowjew und das Judentum*, 1927).

obliterated or minimized. Egerton Swan is perfectly right in saying " Judaism and Christianity are nearest to an agreement when Judaism is most unambiguously Jewish and Christianity most unambiguously Christian."[1] But Jews and Christians alike have to acknowledge and even to experience in their spiritual life the immanence of Israel in Christianity. A new and fruitful meeting between Judaism and Christianity implies a certain Judaization of the Christian's as well as a certain completion of the Jew's Judaism. I look forward to a revival of Jewish spiritual values among Christians ; and, if I had to express the trend of his book in terms of the New Testament, I would write here these two verses : " . . . and, as his custom was, He went into the synagogue on the sabbath day and stood up for to read " (Lk. iv. 16), and : " . . . they, continuing daily with one accord in the Temple, and breaking bread from house to house, did eat their meat with gladness and singleness of heart " (Acts ii. 46). The whole programme of the Christian approach to Judaism is there.

This is not a " learned " book. As far as scholarship is concerned, I have only tried to give some accurate information and up-to-date references. (Many defects or omissions are caused by the circumstances of the war which prevented me from using the London libraries.) The book is not written for scholars, but for ministers, theological students, and this fraction of the general public which may be interested in Jewish questions. Sometimes I have had to explain things which, to the specialist, may seem elementary. If I am read by Jews they will disagree with some (perhaps not many) of these pages. But they will recognize, I hope, that none of the problems raised is to be dismissed lightly. I hope also that they will perceive that the book was not written by a controversialist, but by a friend. I tried indeed less to impart knowledge, to expound concepts or describe history, than to enter sympathetically into the sentiments of Judaism, to feel its emotional undertone, and to enable the reader to realize, at least a little, " how it feels to be a Jew."

I wish to express my thanks to the Department of Missions of the Selly Oak Colleges, founded by Dr. Edward Cadbury, which granted me a research fellowship and made possible the publication of this book ; to Professor Godfrey E. Phillips, head of the department, whose personal friendship and interest

[1] Page ix of the symposium *In Spirit and Truth. Aspects of Judaism and Christianity*, edited for the Society of Jews and Christians by G. Yates, London, 1934.

in my subject have been a precious encouragement and stimulus to me ; to Dr. H. G. Wood, Professor of Theology at the University of Birmingham, whose initiative and suggestions opened me the way to Selly Oak ; and to Miss Helen Stevens, who kindly assumed the task of revising my foreigner's English.

In 1914 a Jewish rabbi named Abraham Bloch, serving in the ranks of the 14th French Army Corps, where I also was serving, happened, in the midst of the battle, to be mistaken by a wounded soldier for a Roman priest. The soldier asked the rabbi to give him a cross to kiss. The rabbi ran to find one, and then ran back to the soldier with the cross. When the ambulance people arrived they found the wounded man and the rabbi lying dead by his side.[1] With this " Jewish Christian " vision I shall close my foreword.

L. G.

Woodbrooke,
    Selly Oak Colleges, Birmingham

May, 1941 (*Rosh Chodesh Sivan* 1,5701).

---

[1] This episode was reported even by a remote newspaper like the Russian *Novoye Vremia.* W. Birkbeck (*Life and Letters*, published by his wife, London, 1922, p. 300) wrote that the rabbi's name " quite deserves to be remembered ".

BIBLIOGRAPHICAL NOTE

The bibliography (by no means exhaustive) of the various questions treated will be found within the book. Besides the special literature, we would mention the following works, which rather present a general interest:

H. Graetz, *History of the Jews*, translated by Bella Lowy, 5 vols., 1891–1892.

S. Dubnow, *Weltgeschichte des Jüdischen Volkes von seinen Uranfängen bis zur Gegenwart*, 10 vols., Berlin, 1925–1929.

Rabbi M. Goldstein, *Thus Religion Grows : The Story of Judaism*, London, 1936.

S. Baron, *A Social and Religious History of the Jews*, 3 vols., New York, 1937.

A. Ruppin, *The Jewish Fate and Future*, translated by E. Dikes, London, 1940.

Laurie Magnus, *Religio laici judaica. The Faith of a Jewish Layman*, London, 1907.

I. Abrahams, *Judaism*, London, 1907 ; and *Some Permanent Values in Judaism*, Oxford, 1924.

M. Friedländer, *Text-Book of the Jewish Religion*, London, 1896.

K. Kohler, *Grundriss Einer Systematischen Theologie des Judentums*, Leipzig, 1910.

H. Schoeps, *Jüdische Glaube in djeser Zeit*, Berlin, 1932.

M. Joseph, *Judaism as Creed and Life*, London, 1929.

L. Baeck, *The Essence of Judaism*, translated by V. Grubwiesera nd L. Pearl, London, 1936.

I. Epstein, *Judaism*, London, 1939.

H. Kosmala and R. Smith, *The Jew in the Christian World*, London, 1942.

As a work of reference, the *Jewish Encyclopædia*, edited by I. Singer, 12 vols., New York and London, 1901–1906, remains indispensable. It may be completed by the German *Encyclopædia Judaica*, edited by J. Klatzkin, 10 vols. (A–L), 1928–1934, and the *Jüdisches Lexikon*, edited by G. Herlitz and B. Kirschner, 5 vols., 1927. The *Yevreiskaya Enzyklopedya* (in Russian), edited by J. Kaznelson, 16 vols., St. Petersburg,

1908–1914, and the *Ozar Ysrael* (in Hebrew), edited by J. Einsenstein, 10 vols., New York, 1907–1913, are less accessible. *Valentine's Jewish Encyclopædia*, edited by A. Hyamson and A. Silbermann, London, 1938, is excellent for its size (vi + 696 pp.). The same can be said of the *Philo Lexikon Handbuch des Jüdischen Wissens* (vii + 831 pp.), Berlin and Amsterdam, 1937.

S. Shumani's *Bibliography of Jewish Bibliographies*, Jerusalem, 1936, contains 2,034 items with classified indexes.

PART ONE

DIALOGUE WITH TRYPHO

POLEMICS AND DIALOGUE

The whole Christian literature relating to differences between Jews and Christians falls under two possible headings. Such writings belong either to the type *Tractatus adversus Judaeos*, or to the type *Dialogos pros Tryphona*. They are either polemics against the Jews, or irenic conversations with them.

The first type has been largely prevalent. When A. Lukyn Williams wrote a history of the theological debate between Christians and Jews,[1] he entitled it *Adversus Judaeos*, and this title was quite justly chosen, for the book was the summing-up of a violent quarrel. Besides, the title " Against the Jews " is in accordance with a long tradition in the Christian Church. Tertullian opened the way with his *Adversus Judaeos*. Another *Adversus Judaeos* has been attributed to Cyprian (but it is a spurious work which comes perhaps from Novatian). Hippolytus wrote a *Demonstratio contra Judaeos*. Chrysostom preached homilies " against the Jews." Augustine also wrote a *Tractatus adversus Judaeos*. In comparison with this flood of polemic literature, the peaceful *Dialogue with Trypho* of Justin Martyr looks almost like an anomaly.

Justin's point of view, however, will be adopted and maintained here, and this is the reason why the title of his great work has been reproduced as a heading for this first part of the book. It seems useful that the present book should begin with a retrospect of the intellectual relations between Christianity and Judaism. But it would be fruitless merely to sum up the researches of Canon Lukyn Williams or James Parkes[2] on the Jewish-Christian " conflict." A more positive, more hopeful, standpoint may be taken. While it is impossible to set aside the persecutions and controversies, one can keep them in the background—a sad background, indeed—and place in the foreground the meeting points, the points of coincidence and penetration, of Judaism and Christianity.

Coming back to the title of Justin's book, and to the title of this section, the question is : when and how in history has a real dialogue between Christians and Jews been possible ?

[1] A. Lukyn Williams, *Adversus Judaeos. A Bird's Eye View of Christian Apologiae until the Renaissance*, Cambridge, 1935.
[2] J. Parkes, *The Conflict of the Church and the Synagogue*, London, 1934.

I

The answer to this question may help to solve another question : How can a real dialogue between Jews and Christians become possible in our days ?

There is for us, to-day, a special reason to go back to Justin's word and idea of a " dialogue " in regard to Jews and Christians. The reason is that, from the Jewish side, a strong emphasis has recently been laid on the same word and idea. Martin Buber, who is perhaps the greatest inspirer of modern religious Judaism and whose name will often reappear in these pages,[1] has placed the idea of " dialogue " in the very centre of his thought and applied it to Jewish-Christian relations. It may be useful and interesting to enter in some detail into Buber's ideology.

According to Buber, the relation of man to man can take two forms : *das Dialogische* and *das Monologische*, the form of dialogue and the form of monologue. There are three kinds of dialogue : the monologue disguising itself as dialogue, but remaining nevertheless a monologue ; the " technical dialogue," the aims of which are purely utilitarian ; and the " true dialogue," spoken or silent. In the true dialogue, " each interlocutor takes in earnest one or the other in their metaphysical and empirical being and turns to them with the intention of creating between himself and them a living reciprocity ".[2] And again : " The limits of the possibilities of the dialogue element are those of the process of becoming aware . . ."[3]

Buber asks next " whether, between the Church and Israel, there may be a genuine dialogue in which, indeed, the interlocutors do not agree, but understand one another for the sake of the one Being to whom the realities of faith refer."[4] We find often, between Christianity and Judaism, the monologue disguised as a dialogue : such generally are the discussions of the theologians. And often, too, we find the merely technical dialogue in which Christians and Jews may exchange ideas upon matters of knowledge or common social welfare. But the

[1] See on Buber special Note B—Buber's ideas on dialogue are expressed in his book *Zwiesprache*, Berlin, 1934.

[2] " . . . jeder der Teilnehmer den oder anderen in ihrem Dasein und Sosein wirklich meint und sich ihnen in der Intention zuwendet, dass lebendige Gegenseitigkeit sich zwischen ihm und ihnen stifte." *Zwiesprache*, p. 41.

[3] " Die Moglichkeitsgrenzen des Dialogischen sind die des Innewerdens." *Zwiesprache*, p. 23.

[4] " . . . ob es zwischen die Kirche " (und Israel) " einen echten Dialog geben kann, in dem man sich wohl nicht miteinander verständigt, aber einander versteht, um des einen Seins willen, das die Glaubenswirklichkeiten meinen." *Zwiesprache*, p. 163.

2

Jewish and Christian " genuine dialogue " has been a rare and beautiful event. To reopen and further the dialogue initiated by Justin is the common task of Jews and Christians.

These views on the dialogue are not restricted to Buber. Hans Schoeps has written a history of the debates between Jews and Christians during the last century, and he aptly entitled it : " The Jewish Christian Dialogue on Religion in the Nineteenth Century."[1] It is true that Schoeps does not use the word *Zwiesprache* or *Zwiegespräch* which are the exact equivalents of dialogue, but the more general word *Gespräch*, which means conversation or colloquy. The intention and the ultimate meaning are, however, the same. One of the best instances of the dialogue between a Christian and a Jew is afforded by the correspondence of Franz Rosenzweig (1886-1929), a disciple and friend of Buber, with the Christian convert Eugen Rosenstock.[2]

We shall now endeavour to discern some of the most positive and important moments in the history of the dialogue between Jews and Christians.

JESUS AND THE PHARISEES

The starting point of the study of relationships between Judaism and Christianity is necessarily the consideration of Jesus' attitude towards Judaism. Such a wide field cannot, of course, be covered here. A few remarks will be sufficient for the purpose of this book.

Modern research has confirmed more and more the truth of Wernle's assertion : " One thing is certain—that Jesus and His Gospel are intelligible from Judaism alone."[3] The attitude of Jesus towards the faith of Israel can be summed up in the *logion* of Matthew v. 17-18 : " Think not that I came to destroy the law or the prophets : I came not to destroy, but to fulfil. For verily I say unto you : till heaven and earth pass away, one jot or one tittle shall in no wise pass away from the law, till all things be accomplished." And in the *logion* of John iv. 22 : " Salvation is from the Jews."[4]

The highest moment in the relationships between Judaism and Christianity is the dialogue between Jesus and the

---

[1] *Jüdisch-Christliches Religionsgespräch in 19 Jahrhunderten*, Berlin, 1937.
[2] This correspondence forms a special section, entitled *Judentum und Christentum* in Rosenzweig's *Briefe ausgewäht und herausgegeben von Edith Rosenzweig, unter mitwirkung von Ernst Simon*, Berlin, 1935.
[3] *Beginnings of Christianity*, 1903, vol. I, p. 33.
[4] See T. Walker, *Jesus and Jewish Teaching*, London, 1922 ; B. Branscomb, *Jesus and the Law of Moses*, London, 1930.

Pharisees. Jesus originally belonged, not to the Pharisaic circles, but rather to the " poor of Israel," whose piety was nurtured by the Psalms, the Prophets and the Apocalyptic literature. Nevertheless it is through his meeting with Pharisaism that Jesus made His own position most clear, and this meeting assumes a quite exceptional importance. Why ? In the first place, Pharisaism was the most characteristic manifestation of Palestinian Judaism in the time of Jesus. Secondly, alone of all Jewish parties, Pharisaism survived the destruction of Jerusalem and, representing all that was left alive of Judaism, " shaped the character of Judaism and the life and thought of the Jew for all the future."[1] Thirdly, important as was the teaching given by Jesus to His disciples and to the surrounding crowds, He had to relate His message to the dominant theology of the time and to the atmosphere of Pharisaic dogmatism which the whole of Palestine breathed. Therefore the Pharisees occupy the foreground in the historical setting of the mission of Jesus.

The Christian usually views Pharisaism with not very friendly eyes. He takes too often for granted that hostility and rejection express the whole pharisaic attitude towards Jesus. He knows no more about the Pharisees than the denunciations throughout the Gospels and the traditional commonplaces of the Christian pulpit. Modern scholarship has, however, accomplished a largely justified rehabilitation of the Pharisees or, at least, a fairer presentation of their case. This is chiefly due to the works of R. Travers Herford, who sometimes idealizes Pharisaism and ought to be supplemented by Robertson ; one should also mention the admirable studies of Israel Abrahams.[2]

" There has seldom been for Christians the opportunity to know what Pharisaism really meant," writes T. Herford.[3] And he says again : " No one but a Jew . . . can fully realize the spiritual meaning of Pharisaism ; but sympathy can show even to a Christian much of that meaning."[4] If we try to approach the Pharisees with something of this sympathy and to read the Gospels with an unprejudiced mind, it will seem fair to note the following points.

[1] Rabbi K. Kohler, *Jewish Encycl.*, art. " Pharisees."
[2] T. Herford, *The Pharisees*, London 1924 ; *Pharisaism. Its aim and its Method*, London, 1912. A. Robertson, *The Pharisees and Jesus*,. London, 1920. I. Abrahams, *Studies in Pharisaism and the Gospels*, 2 vols., Cambridge, 1917 and 1924. D. Riddle, *Jesus and the Pharisees : A Study in Christian Tradition*, Chicago, 1928.
[3] *Pharisaism*, p. 331.
[4] *Pharisaism*, p. 3.

4

Not a few of the Pharisees are represented as being kindly disposed towards the person of Jesus. They treated Him with courtesy, at least in the beginning. They invited Him to dine. They gave Him advice about the hostility of Herod Antipas. It is quite certain that, in the manœuvres which incited Pilate to take action against Jesus, the priests and the Sadducees took a far greater part than the Pharisees.

Many of the Pharisees who, after a certain period of cautious hesitation, took up a position against Jesus, appear—at least most of them—to have done so in good faith, under the delusion that the teaching of Jesus was antinomian.

The rebukes by Jesus of the Pharisees are directed against a hypocritical section of narrow, exclusive and exacting men. What Jesus opposed in such Pharisees was not the fundamental element in Pharisaism, but rather a deviation from and a distortion of Pharisaism itself. " The impression is almost irresistible that the denunciations of the Pharisees occurring in the Gospels are directed primarily against a Shammaite section, and that the incident described in Mark vii. is an episode in the controversy between Jesus and the Shammaites."[1] The Talmud denounces as violently as the Gospels the perversions of Pharisaism.[2]

Some of the Pharisees were actually willing to accept the message of Jesus. A number of them secretly wished Him well. Others championed His cause and said : " These are not the sayings of one possessed with a devil. Can a devil open the eyes of the blind ? " (John x. 21). Others found after His death the courage to come out in the open on His side. Nicodemus and Joseph of Arimathæa then boldly took their stand for Jesus.

It is to be recalled also that Gamaliel, the most eminent Pharisaic member of the Sanhedrin in the time of Jesus, showed a kindly spirit towards the prosecuted apostles, Peter and John, and that some Pharisees espoused the cause of Paul against the Sadducees. C. Turner,[3] commenting on the words of Acts xv. 5 about " certain of the sect of the Pharisees who believed," says : " Though it was inconceivable that a Sadducee should believe without giving up his Sadduceeism, it was not inconceivable that a Pharisee should believe and still be known to be a Pharisee."

---

[1] G. Box, art. " Pharisees " in Hastings' *Encycl. of Religion and Ethics*, vol. ix, col. 835.

[2] See special note C.

[3] C. Turner, *Catholic and Apostolic*, p. 237.

5

But we come to a still more important point, which is this : Jesus himself was nearer to genuine Pharisaism than to any other religious school in Israel. He knew that the Pharisees were the *élite* of the nation. His own piety and teaching were often identical with theirs. On the two main questions on which they differed from the Sadducees, *i.e.*, the belief in the future life and their essentially religious, not political, concern, He agreed with the Pharisees.

Such are the remarks which an open-minded consideration of Pharisaism may suggest. To them we should like to add the following observations of Travers Herford :

" If it should appear . . . that the religion of the Torah as held by the Pharisees was a real expression of spiritual experience, the inspiration of holy living and holy dying, is the spiritual power of Christianity in any degree made less ? . . . Why should not the Christian be glad to own that the Jew, even the Pharisee, knew more of the deep things of God than he had supposed, and, after a way which was not the Christian way, yet loved the Lord his God with heart and soul and strength and mind—yes, and his neighbour as himself ? "[1]

Thus the meeting of Jesus with Pharisaism was not a fruitless encounter, but the assimilation by Jesus of what was best in the Judaism of his time and the elevation of this " best " to its utmost. Not only to the scribe who had " answered discreetly," but also to the genuine Pharisaic love of God and man, Jesus addressed the word recorded in Mark xii. 34 : " Thou art not far from the Kingdom of God."

PAUL AND JUDAISM

Next in importance to Jesus himself, in the dialogue between Judaism and Christianity, comes the Apostle Paul. Many religious historians of the last century would have considered Paul as an even more important factor in regard to the relationships between the two faiths. It was almost taken for granted, in Jewish as well as in liberal Protestant circles, that the theology of Paul differed widely from the Gospel of Jesus : that Paul fashioned a Christ and a system of belief of his own ; that Pauline Hellenism, from the beginning, came into radical conflict with Judaism ; and that from Paul dates the real parting of the ways between Jews and Christians and the

---

[1] *Pharisaism*, p. 333.

6

biased opinion of Judaism and its Law which took possession of the Christian world. These views have been greatly modified under the influence of recent scholarship.[1] It is impossible to enter here into a study of Paulinism ; but we find it necessary to underline and keep in sight a few points.

Paul never ceased to regard himself as a Jew. He called himself a " Hebrew of the Hebrews." He boasted of " our forefathers " and " fathers." He personally submitted to the observances of the Law. To show his Jewish orthodoxy, he took, and caused four other men to take, a vow which involved attendance at the Temple, where he was arrested.

The Christian Church accepted very one-sidedly the Pauline estimate of the Jewish religion. The Church Fathers insisted on the inadequacy of the Law and the forfeiture of the promises, but they seldom referred to the ultimate redemption of Israel on which Paul pinned his deepest faith.

Paul fought for the right of the Gentile Christians not to be bound by the Jewish Law. But he never questioned the legitimacy of Judæo-Christianity or the obligation of the circumcised Christian to keep the Law.

Then how are we to understand some apparently hard sayings of Paul concerning the Law ? In the first place, these passages ought not to make us forget the many other statements in which Paul is at pains to do justice to the Law. Secondly, we must remember the personal " catastrophe," the deep change which Paul experienced after his conversion. The religion of Paul became centred on a person, Jesus himself. This personality could by no means be expressed in terms of Torah. Devotion to a person is a mental attitude entirely different from devotion to a doctrine or an ideal. We find here, perhaps, the deepest explanation of the contrast between the New Testament and rabbinical literature. The latter expresses the steadfast devotion to a teaching ; the former expresses the vivid devotion—the " newly awakened devotion," as Travers Herford says—to a person. The spiritual fervour of the Rabbi becomes " study " of the Book, while the Christian

---

[1] On Paul and Judaism see H. St. John Thackeray, *The Relation of St. Paul to Contemporary Jewish Thought*, London, 1900 ; A. Deissmann, *St. Paul*, translated by L. Strachan, London, 1912 ; and *The Religion of Jews and the Faith of Paul*, translated by W.Wilson, London, 1923 ; C. Montefiore, *Judaism and St. Paul*, London, 1914 ; the symposium *Judaism and the Beginning of Christianity : a Course of Lectures delivered at Jews' College*, London, 1924 ; W. L. Knox, *St. Paul and the Church of Jerusalem*, Cambridge, 1925, and *St. Paul and the Church of the Gentiles*, Cambridge, 1939 ; J. Parkes, *Jesus Paul and the Jews*, London, 1936 ; J. Klausner, *From Jesus to Paul* (in Hebrew) 2 vols, Tel Aviv, 1940.

7

disciple finds a glowing rapture in the person of the Revealer. The personal relation to Christ takes the place of the Torah as the controlling factor of life. And, lastly, Paul never conceived this personal attachment to the Messiah as abolishing the Law, but rather as founding it and making it alive. Such an attitude is perfectly expressed by Romans iii. 31 : " Do we make then the Law of none effect through faith ? God forbid : nay, we establish the Law."

The true picture of Paul is the picture of a passionate Jew who, even when a Christian, would have gladly sacrificed himself for his people and who found in the total adhesion to his Master the fulfilment, not the destruction, of the Law. The constant " Jewishness " of Paul has been rightly affirmed by Deissmann : " The most genuine characteristics of the Jewish nature were preserved by Paul when he became a Christian. ' St. Paul the Jew ' does not mean that Paul was a Jew only before his conversion and afterwards no longer. Paul remained a Jew even when he became a Christian . . . In opposition to mechanical divisions of the Jewish and the Christian elements in him, we need not hesitate to call him the great Jew-Christian of the earliest age."[1]

A new attitude towards Paul is nowadays noticeable in certain Jewish circles. Paul has ceased to be merely the apostate and the enemy. One can grasp the importance of the recognition of Paul as expressed in the following words of C. G. Montefiore : " We can appreciate to some extent the doctrine of Paul as well as that of Jesus. We can perceive in it . . . a relative justification, and while not agreeing with it as a whole, and still less with its arguments and assumptions, we can, nevertheless, by ' putting ourselves above the documents ' (which is far removed from considering ourselves *superior* to the documents or their authors), find in them a certain suggestiveness, illumination and help."[2] And again Montefiore : " Jesus and Paul can help us as well as Hillel and Akiba. Let them do so."[3] Another striking instance of this new attitude towards Paul is afforded by a literary work to the inner meaning of which a Christian could fully subscribe—the drama *Paulus unter den Juden* of the Jewish-German writer, Franz Werfel.[4]

[1] *St. Paul*, p. 98.
[2] *The Old Testament and After*, London, 1923, p. 229.
[3] *ibidem*, p. 291.
[4] Translated into English by P. Levertoff : *Paul Among the Jews*, London 1928.

8

J U D Æ O - C H R I S T I A N I T Y

The first Christian believers continued to frequent the Temple ; they showed no hatred towards the priests and scribes who had contrived the death of Jesus ; they were not cast out from the Temple or synagogue.[1] These Jewish followers of Jesus constituted the group of Judæo-Christians, in contradistinction to the Samaritans converted by Peter and John and to the Gentiles admitted to the Church by the Antioch missionaries and, later on, by Paul and Barnabas. The history, as well as the present prospects of Judæo-Christianity, will be dealt with in Chapter VII, and the elements of a bibliography of the question will be given there. What we should now consider is the contribution of primitive Judæo-Christianity (*i.e.*, Judæo-Christianity of the first four centuries) to the dialogue between Christianity and Judaism.

There exists a widespread opinion that the whole of Judæo-Christianity was a narrow legalist sect which practically identified itself with the Judaizers who so often hampered the work of Paul. This is a complete mistake. The most important and the only official pronouncement of Judæo-Christianity has been the decree of the so-called " council of Jerusalem " (Acts xv). Now this decree represents a defeat of the Judaizing extremists and gives a very liberal decision concerning the duties of the Gentile Christians It promulgated, on the whole, this freedom from Jewish customs which Paul claimed for the Gentiles. It consecrated the existence with equal rights of the Gentile Church. Judæo-Christianity, later on, did not meet with a corresponding liberal treatment from the Gentile Christian side. When the numerical proportion of the believers was altered and Judæo-Christianity reduced to a nucleus, this nucleus was practically swallowed up by the Gentile Christian environment. The Church of the Gentiles, forgetting the broad-minded and large-hearted attitude of the ancient Church of Jerusalem towards the Greeks, disdained the Jewish Christians, supplanted them, and finally treated them as strangers and prohibited their old customs. The Gentile Christians proved to be narrower than the circumcised Christians.

Apart from the keeping of the Law, what were the chief characteristics of Judæo-Christianity ? We shall, in answering,

---

[1] See special note N.

9

follow Turner, whose views on the question are perhaps the most illuminating.[1]

First, Judæo-Christianity tended to lay more stress on ethics than on Christology.

Secondly, Judæo-Christianity looked back to the Twelve as authorities, putting Paul, to a certain extent, in the background and laying no special stress on Peter, while Gentile Christianity claimed predominantly to go back to Paul or to Peter and Paul.

As regards the first point, the elimination of Judæo-Christianity resulted in a victory of Greek intellectualism and a certain weakening of the ethical stress.

As regards the second point, Turner shows how Judæo-Christianity, by a slow and meritorious process, came nearer and nearer to the position of the Gentile Church, i.e., to the recognition of Paul as the equal of the Twelve. Here, again, liberalism is on the Jewish side. We witness an endeavour of the Jewish Church to disentangle itself from a purely " Jewish " view and to become more and more open to a " Catholic " view. This process expresses itself in four documents which have, in common, a Palestinian origin : the *Didache*, the *Apostolic Church Order*, the *Didascalia* and the *Apostolic Constitutions*.[2] In this last treatise, the process is completed and Paul, from being almost " boycotted," is raised to a position of full equality with the Twelve.

Turner may help us to get a clearer view of the council of Jerusalem. How are we to understand the attitude of the Church of Jerusalem towards Paul ? It was not a question of ritual or legal conversation, but rather of moral solicitude : " What happened, as I suppose, is that the Jewish Christians, James and his friends, did want to be reassured by Paul, that when he talked about faith in Christ as the one thing necessary, when he said circumcision, Sabbath and meats matter nothing at all—they did want to be reassured that when he thus threw over the ceremonial Law, he was not throwing over the moral

---

[1] See the two papers entitled *Jewish Christianity* in *Catholic and Apostolic Collected Papers*, by C. Turner, edited by H. Bate, London and Oxford, 1931.

[2] Many theories have been advanced concerning the birthplace and the authorship of the *Didache*. One of the latest theories suggests that the *Didache* is a pastiche of late origin (see F. Vokes, *The Riddle of the Didache*, London, 1938). Turner maintained the Palestinian origin theory, not only because of the Jewish elements in the *Didache*, but also for a topographical reason. The single indication of locality found in the *Didache* is that the wheat of the Eucharistic loaf has been grown " upon the mountains," which excludes Egypt or Antioch and throws us back on some mountainous district, such as the Transjordania of the Jewish Christian fugitives from Jerusalem.

Law as well. I do not think they suspected him for a moment of excusing immorality or anything of that sort ; but I do think they wondered whether he had enough basis of ethical discipline for his teaching to converts from Paganism."[1]

And next, how are we to understand, in the decree of the council, this strange mixture of purely ritual questions and fundamental questions of morals ? The decree prohibits, as on the same level, things sacrificed to idols, blood and fornication (Acts xv. 29, according to the text of the *Codex Bezae*). We understand better if we admit, with Turner, that " blood " means bloodshed and that " things sacrified to idols " means idolatry. " I have no hesitation in interpreting ' the defilement of idols and blood and fornication ' as a summary way of exposing the principal implications of the two halves of the Decalogue, the moral law in its most elementary form."[2] Here, again, the Jewish Christians are not so legally and unspiritually minded as is generally thought. Such an ethical-religious interpretation seems to be confirmed by the theory of *deuterosis* developed in the *Didascalia*.[3] According to this theory, the Mosaic Law had a double form, of which the first or original form is moral, the second and later, imposed for the sins of the people, is ceremonial. This ceremonial addition is abolished in Christ, while the Law proper, the Decalogue, is extremely valid.

The primitive Judæo-Christianity was far from having the narrow and sectarian character often attributed to it. The Church of the Jews sincerely tried to worship in spirit and truth and to collaborate with the Gentile Christians. It remains for us to say a few words about the three most precious gifts which Judæo-Christianity has made to the Universal Church : the Epistle of James, the Epistle of Jude, and the Odes of Solomon.

The general epistles of James and Jude " are sources from which a knowledge of primitive Palestinian Christianity can be drawn, and they represent a different line of development from that of the Hellenistic Christianity."[4] Between them and Paul, the epistles of Peter seem to occupy a mediate position. The letter of James—which Luther so much disparaged—describes the doctrine of joy in temptation, the

[1] Turner, *Catholic and Apostolic*, p. 249.
[2] Turner, *Catholic and Apostolic*, p. 251.
[3] See the translation of the *Didascalia* pubished by Dom Connolly, of Downside, at the Clarendon Press (1929), with an introduction of ninety pages,
[4] J. Ropes, *A Critical and Exegetical Commentary on the Epistle of St. James*. Edinburgh. 1916, p. viii.

exaltation of the lowly and the fading away of the rich, the delusion of hearing without doing, the unbelief involved in showing a worldly respect of persons among the brethren, the iniquity of respecting the rich and despising the poor, the sinful propensities of the tongue. Jude condemns the sins of the " ungodly men," either pagans or Jews. In both epistles one can hear an echo of the strong ethical teaching of the Prophets. Without these two letters " we should have known sadly little of the Mother Church of Jerusalem and of the teaching of the many early Christians who, while heartily embracing the Gospel of Jesus Christ, believed that they were bound to hold fast not only to the morality, but to the discipline of Moses."[1]

The Odes of Solomon are a collection of forty-two hymns recovered by Rendel Harris in 1908 from a seventeenth-century Syriac manuscript (containing also the eighteen so-called Psalms of Solomon). They were known to the writer of the gnostic *Pistis Sophia* and to Lactantius. Rendel Harris would date several of them between A.D. 75 and 100. He thinks that the author, though not a Jew, was a member of the Jewish Christian community of Palestine. Harnack considers that the Odes form a Jewish *Grundschrift* with several Christian interpolations.[2] These Odes are unmistakably Christian and constitute a link between the Jewish *Testaments of the Twelve Patriarchs* and Johannine, theology and piety. They are characterized by an extraordinary atmosphere of freshness and joy, of poetic beauty and radiant grace. Rendel Harris writes : " They are songs of the spring-time, too, as well as songs of the dark and of the dawn. When you hear them, instead of saying : ' That is the nightingale,' you will say : ' I hear a primitive Christian.' "

To have united the faith in Jesus with the most genuine Jewish piety, to have given their chart of freedom to the Gentile Christians, to have maintained among them the Jewish ethical stress, to have been the first bearer of the great hope and the singer of the Messianic song at sunrise : such are the achievements of this forgotten and misunderstood Judæo-Christianity of the first centuries.

---

[1] A. Plummer, *The General Epistles of St. James and St. Jude*, London, 1891, p. 10. See also A. Meyer, *Das Rätsel des Jacobusbriefes*, Giessen, 1930 (differs widely from Plummer).

[2] J. Rendel Harris, *The Odes and Psalms of Solomon*, London, 1909 ; *An Early Christian Psalter*, London, 1909 ; J. Flemming and A. Harnack, *Ein Jüdisch-christliches Psalmbuch aus dem ersten Jahrhundert*, Leipzig, 1910.

JUDAISM AND CHRISTIANITY IN THE PATRISTIC TIMES

The first Christian work concerning the debate between Judaism and Christianity was perhaps the dialogue of Jason and Papiscus, attributed to Ariston of Pella (after the Bar Kokba war) ; Celsus quoted this writing, which has perished. Next comes the question of the so-called *Testimonies*. The suggestion that extracts from the Old Testament had been drawn up by Jewish Christians for controversy with Jews was developed by Sanday and Headlam (1895). Rendel Harris accepted the suggestion and assumed that a collection of texts from the Old Testament, bearing testimony to Christ and hence called the *Book of Testimonies* (like the later *Testimonia* of Cyprian), was drawn up before the composition of our present Gospels, even before the Pauline Epistles. The original *Testimonia* of the Christian Church were collected by Matthew, the Apostle, and circulated first under his name. This book, gradually expanded and modified, would have continued in existence throughout many centuries, till the twelfth and perhaps even later. There is no evidence for the existence of one such *Book of Testimonies*, but there is a strong probability that several books of testimonies existed.[1]

It is unnecessary to epitomize here the history of the Patristic literature on Judaism. As has already been said, this task has been well performed in the *Adversus Judaeos* of Lukyn Williams and the *Conflict of the Church and the Synagogue* of Parkes, to which one should add the quite recent book of Filson.[2] But some essential points must be mentioned.

Till the fourth century there is—with the exception of Tertullian and the pseudo-Cyprian—no ill-feeling against the Jews. Besides the *Dialogue with Trypho*, the tone of which is quite irenic, the *Clementine Recognitions*, for instance, show no bitterness towards them. The *Acts of Philip*, a production of the third century, are almost friendly to them. It is true that the apocryphal *Epistle of Barnabas* warns its readers, with passion, against all compromise between Judaism and the Gospel, and even denies the historical connexion between the two, but it is not a piece of insulting polemics. After the fourth century the background becomes definitely hostile. In

---

[1] J. Rendel Harris, *Testimonies*, with the assistance of Vacher Burch, 2 vols., Cambridge, 1916 and 1920 ; C. Turner, *The Testimonies in the Early Church*, in the *Journal of Theological Studies*, 1905 and 1908.

[2] Floyd V. Filson, *Pioneers of the Primitive Church : with their Relations to Judaism*, New York, 1940.

eight sermons delivered in 387, Chrysostom accumulates
against the Jews bitterness, sneers and jibes.[1] He seriously
believes that the Jews, with their own hands, murder their
offspring to worship the devils. He gloats over their mis-
fortunes. He exclaims frankly : " I hate the Jews." St. Hilary
was so " orthodox " that he would not even answer the
salutation of a Jew in the street.[2] He asserted that " the Jews
were possessed of an unclean devil, which the Law for a time
drove out, but which returned immediately after their
rejection of Christ."[3] Sidonius Apollinarius sends letters by a
Jew " who would be dear to my heart if it were not for his
abominable religion."[4] *The Rhythm against the Jews*, falsely
attributed to St. Ephrem the Syrian, compares the synagogue
with a harlot and indulges in allusions suitable to this theme.
The apologetics of these Fathers are of a low intellectual level.
Ignorant of everything Hebraic, they brought out catenas of
texts in which words are everything, little account being taken
of historical reference or even of grammatical meaning. At
the very moment when they were elaborating a ritual and a
discipline as binding and almost as complicated as the priestly
code, they thought Jewish observances laughable and con-
temptible. Their conception of Judism was a parody. They
introduced an insulting anti-Jewish vocabulary : *flagitia
sacrilegi coetus, feralis secta, turpitudo*. While *judaica perfidia*
did not originally mean anything more than Jewish unbelief,
they gave to this term the significance of Jewish bad faith.
And acts began to correspond with the mental attitude.
Compulsory baptisms were initiated in the fifth century. In
355 the Bishop and the Christians of Dertona, in Italy,
destroyed the synagogue and erected a church on the site.[5]
The Bishop of Callinicum, in Asia, led a Christian mob to burn
a synagogue and, when the Emperor Theodosius ordered the
Bishop to rebuild it out of his own resources, St. Ambrose
protested indignantly.[6] The burning of synagogues by
Christians was widespread in the East during the fifth century.

Yet it seems that, in many places, the popular Christian
mind rather strangely kept some links with Judaism. From
the anti-Jewish sermons of Chrysostom at Antioch in 387, we
learn that some Christian groups still felt respect for the

[1] Migne *P.G.*, XLVIII.
[2] Migne *P.L.*, IX, 187.
[3] *Commentary on Matthew*, P.L. IX, 993.
[4] *Ep.* III, 4.
[5] *Acta Sanctorum*, April, vol. II, 483.
[6] Migne, *P.L.* XVI, 1101.

synagogue. From the prohibitions of the council of Elvira it appears that not only was intermarriage taking place between Christians and Jews, but that clerics and laymen accepted Jewish hospitality, and even that Christians had their fields blessed by Jews! The Syrian compilation of the fourth century called *Apostolic Canons* forbids the clergy to share in Jewish fasts or feasts, or to receive from the Jews unleavened bread. A council of Carthage, probably the fourth, expelled from the Church those " clinging to Jewish superstitions and festivals."[1] Still more significant is the fact that, under Gratian, conversion from Christianity to Judaism was prohibited.

But let us come to the question on which we are concentrating. Do we find, during the Patristic times, some privileged moments when the dialogue between Christianity and Judaism has been " genuine " and has given positive results ? We are happily able to answer yes. Without laying stress on the fact that Clement and Origen had learned from the Jews, we shall associate such moments with the names of Justin Martyr, Jerome and Augustine.

Justin, born in Samaria of pagan parents, was well acquainted with Jewish culture. Several references have already been made to his famous dialogue with the Jew Trypho and some other Jews of Ephesus, supposed to have taken place in that town between 135 and 161. The circumstances of the dialogue seem strictly historical. This *Dialogue with Trypho* deserves a special place in the history of the relationship between Judaism and Christianity, because it is a model of intelligent discussion and seemly demeanour. We hear Trypho saying to Justin[2] : " I know that the commands given you in what is called the Gospel are so admirable and great that I suspect that no one can keep them. For I took some trouble to read them. . . ." And near the end : " Now Trypho paused a little and then said : you see, it was not by design that we entered into a discussion over these matters. I acknowledge that I have been extraordinarily pleased with our intercourse. . . . For we have found more than we expected or that it was even possible for us to expect. And if we could do this more often, we should receive more benefit. . . . Do not hesitate to think of us as your friends." Before leaving, Trypho and his party prayed for Justin. And Justin " prayed also for

[1] Mansi, III, 958.
[2] See A. Lukyn Williams, *Justin Martyr*. *The Dialogue with Trypho*. Translation, Introduction and Notes, London, 1930.

them," and expressed the hope that they would follow the same way as the Christians. Lukyn Williams concludes : " Both were earnest and sincere, and neither shows any sign of desiring a merely verbal victory. . . . There is no Dialogue as such which is conducted on quite so high a level of courteousness and fairness until Gilbert Crispin's at Westminster at the end of the eleventh century."[1]

Jerome surpasses all the other Fathers in his Hebrew erudition. He sought his information among the educated Jews ; during his forty years in Palestine he had three Hebrew teachers, and the malicious Rufinus mockingly called him " the rabbi." He was conversant not only with the Hebrew language, but with the rabbinic tradition which, alone of all the Fathers, he admired and followed. He often rebuked the Jews in his writings, but no more than he rebuked his fellow-Christians. The importance of Jerome, from our point of view, is twofold. On the one hand, Jerome imposed upon all learned Christians the notion of the *hebraica veritas*. " *Nobis autem Hebraeorum opinionem sequentibus* . . .," says he,[2] and again : " *Hoc Hebraei autumant et sicut nobis ab ipsis traditum est, nostris fideliter exposuimus.*"[3] Since Jerome, the Hebrew text has been regarded as authoritative in all exegetical disputes. We must justly appreciate the magnitude of the revolution effected in the West by Jerome's Latin translation of the Hebrew Bible. The Greek Septuagint version was believed to have been made under the influence of the Holy Spirit ; Augustine saw in its errors inspired and subtle mysteries. The party in power at Rome was opposed to the new translation ; theological prejudices of every kind were aroused. The translation from the Hebrew had nothing to recommend it, except its scientific merit, and on this merit it won acceptance by the Latin Church. Another result, still more important from the spiritual point of view, was attained. Jerome was the first to show that Christianity and Judaism can engage in a common work of which the object is the Word of God.

Augustine was no Hebrew scholar, though he sought exegetical assistance from some African Jews. He wrote (as everybody !) a treatise *adversus Judaeos*, which, however, is not an attack against the Jews, but a defence of the right of the Christians to use the Old Testament, even if they do not

[1] *Adversus Judaeos*, p. 42.
[2] Commentary on Joel, IV, 11.
[3] Commentary on Amos, IV, 16.

keep the Law. Why give Augustine a place among the most important interlocutors of the debate between Jews and Christians ? It is because Augustine introduced in this debate a new spirit, a new tone. A few lines from Augustine will show his mind as regards the Jews : " Let us preach to the Jews, wherever we can, in a spirit of love, whether they welcome our words or spurn them. It is not for us to boast over them as *branches broken*. Rather let us consider by Whose grace, and with what loving kindness, and into what kind of Root it was that we were grafted."[1] Such an accent is unique in Patristic literature. Lukyn Williams says : " Chrysostom, when he thought of the Jews, was ecclesiastic ; Augustine was the Christian."[2]

JUDAISM AND CHRISTIANITY IN THE MIDDLE AGES

The ghettos, the Inquisition and the *autos-da-fé* express the darkest sides of the life of mediæval Jewry. The ghetto of Prague existed already in the tenth century ; those of Venice and Salerno in the eleventh ; the Roman ghetto dates only from 1556. The Inquisition against the Jews was introduced in Aragon in 1233 and in Provence in 1274. The first *auto-da-fé* including Jews took place in Troyes in 1288. It will be noticed that the Inquisition and *autos-da-fé* belong to the later Middle Ages. Till the end of the twelfth century the personal relations between Christians and Jews were not bitter. As late as the eighth and ninth centuries, certain Christians were present at Jewish religious ceremonies and observed the Sabbath in common with the Jews ; the Jews gave gifts to Christians on Jewish feasts and even on the festivals of the Christian Church ; a Jew would petition a judge, on a Jewish festival, to accept bail for the release of a Christian.[3] At Lyons, Christians used to go to the synagogue, preferring the sermons of the rabbis to those of the priests. In Provence, c. 1290, Christians made offerings in the synagogue and paid respect to the scrolls of the Law.[4] The business and the monastic developments of the 13th century marked a turning point. During the first Crusade the Rhineland Jews were either massacred or forced to accept baptism by the crusaders on their march.

[1] Quoted by A. Lukyn Williams, *Adversus Judaeos*, p. 317.
[2] *ibidem*, p. 312.
[3] I. Abrahams, *Jewish Life in the Middle Ages*, London, 1896, pp. 425 and 426.
[4] *Revue de l'histoire des religions*, 1888, vol. 17, p. 324 *sq.*

Popular prejudice against the Jews was an artificial creation ; there existed no natural animosity ; as always in history, anti-Jewish outbursts and massacres were not of popular origin, but resulted from the agitations of professional anti-Semites—to-day the politicians and journalists ; then, theologians and monks. The Dominicans constituted themselves the sword of the Church, and were in the forefront of every persecution. Among them Vincent Ferrer and Raymund Martini Peñaforte, author of the *Pugio fidei*, both canonized by the Roman Church, played a leading part. Even the disciples of St. Francis showed in many ways their antipathy to the Jews (John of Capistrano, Bernardinus of Feltre). In contrast to them, there stands out the noble figure of St. Bernard of Clairvaux, defender of the Jews.

What was the attitude of papacy ? The attitude of the Roman See towards the Jews seems to have been constantly inspired by three principles : first, that every effort should be made to convert the Jews ; secondly, that no facility must be allowed to Jews to rule or influence Christians ; thirdly, that lawlessness and violence should be avoided. But the Popes approved that the deicide Jews should live in subjection and degradation. For " Christendom " had decided that subjection and degradation ought to be the price of the Jews' loyalty to Judaism.

The popular polemics between Christians and Jews were coarse and violent. Public disputations with Christians were often forced on Jews. Such debates amounted to a disguised means of persecution, since Jews were permitted to use only arguments which could not give offence to Christian opinion.[1] The Jews retaliated by circulating among themselves literature which attributed to Jesus illegitimate birth, magic, and a shameful death. The Middle Ages saw the slanderous Jewish life of Christ, called *Toldoth Yeshu*, reach the height of its popularity. Hugh J. Schonfield has recently renewed the study of the *Toldoth Yeshu*, giving this document in a new translation based on a critical text, and compared with early Christian, Jewish and Islamic writings ; he holds the view that the *Toldoth* were a counterblast to the Gospel according to the Hebrews, published originally during the fourth century, and that they became more and more scandalous in the later

---

[1] See I. Loeb, *La controverse religieuse entre les Chrétiens et les Juifs au Moyen-Age*, Paris, 1888, and I. Ziegler, *Religiöse Disputationen im Mittelalter*, Frankfurt, 1894.

18

editions : their increased bitterness was a kind of thermometer of the hate between Jews and Christians.[1]

Notwithstanding all this, there did exist in the Middle Ages an exchange of thought, an interpretation, and even sometimes a genuine dialogue between Jews and Christians.

The first aspect of this change is the influence of Jewish philosophy on Western scholasticism. Greek thought, in its Aristotelian and Platonic sources, was transmitted to the West by the Hebræo-Arabic cultural tradition with which the names of Avicenna, Avicebron, Averroes, Maimonides are linked. William of Auvergne (1249) introduced Maimonides (1204) to the circle of Latin philosophers, and constantly relies on his *Guide for the perplexed ;* Alexander of Hales (1245) exhibits complete familiarity with the Latin translations of Maimonides. Albertus Magnus, the master of St. Thomas, was well acquainted with Jewish scholasticism ; he quotes even Jewish mathematicians and biologists. St. Thomas Aquinas is much indebted to Maimonides, whom he follows closely in his theodicy. He is strongly opposed to Avicebron and Averroes. In the altar-piece by Francesco Trairi, in Santa Catarina at Pisa, illuminating rays from Christ descend on Thomas, sitting between Aristotle and Plato ; Averroes lies prostrate, his *Commentary* transfixed by a lightning ray ; but, by some strange mistake, he wears the Jewish badge on both shoulders.

It is certain that a deep intellectual communion existed between Jewish and Christian scholasticism.[2] However, this communion was metaphysical rather than theological. Jewish and Christian philosophers met on a common Aristotelian ground ; their Jewishness and their Christianity did not penetrate each other. In contrast with popular debaters, these noble minds exhibited no hostility to beliefs divergent from their own. Thomas showed no personal feeling against the Jews, and was opposed to their baptism ; but he held that special taxation of the Jews was justifiable. One must admit that the great Jewish masters of the Middle Ages showed more appreciation of Christianity than the Christian doctors did

[1] H. Schonfield, *According to the Hebrews*, London, 1937.

[2] See M. Steinschneider, *Hebräische Uebersetzungen des Mittelalters*, Berlin, 1893 ; J. Guttmann, *Scholastik des dreizehnten Jahrhunderts in ihren Beziehungen zum Judentum*, Breslau, 1902. The final chapter of *Maimonides*, by David Yellen and Israel Abrahams (London, 1903), gives a summary of the influence of Maimonides on Christian philosophers, such as Aquinas, and Jewish such as Spinoza. See also D. Neumark, *Geschichte der jüdischer Philosophie des Mittelalters*, Berlin, 1907 (unfinished), and J. Husik, *A History of Mediæval Jewish Philosophy*, London, 1916.

of Judaism. Maimonides writes : " The teachings of Christ, and Mohammed who arose after Him, tend to bring to perfection all mankind, so that they may serve God with one consent."[1] Jehuda ha-Levi (12th century) said : " These religions (Christianity and Islam) are the preparation and the preface to the Messiah we expect."[2] The famous treatise, *The Duties of the Heart,* written by Bahya (11th century), extols Christian monasticism with hearty enthusiasm. Abravanel (15th century) quotes with respect Christian authorities such as Jerome and Thomas Aquinas. Caro (16th century) says in the *Shulhan Aruch :* " He who sees a Christian sage must utter the benediction : Blessed art Thou, O Lord, King of the world, who hast bestowed of Thy wisdom on man."[3] Jehuda Hadassi speaks " with much tenderness," as Israel Abrahams puts it,[4] of the person of Jesus.

The " Illuminated Doctor," Raymond Lull, seems to have penetrated deeply into the understanding of Judaism. He had a cabbalistic knowledge which he was able to fit into neo-platonic thought. He may be regarded as the spiritual father of Christian cabbalists.

Another aspect of the dialogue of Judaism and Christianity during the Middle Ages was the development of Jewish scholarship among Christians. It would be an error to think that Hebrew studies were then wholly neglected by Gentiles, and that our Hebrew scholarship dates from the Renaissance.[5] During the Middle Ages the Hebrew language stood for something strange, difficult, and vaguely magical. The Venerable Bede (+785) had some elementary, but real, knowledge of Hebrew. Stephen Harding (+1134), second abbot of Citeaux, revised for his monks the Latin text of the Bible with the help of some Jews who explained the Hebrew readings to him. The great Bishop of Lincoln, Robert Grosseteste (+1253), who introduced the study of Greek at Oxford, learned Hebrew. His best known pupil, the Franciscan Roger Bacon, laid special stress on Semitic languages, and wrote a Hebrew grammar, a fragment of which has survived ; the main motive for learning Hebrew was, according to Roger, the instruction and salvation of Jews, from whom " began the foundation of our faith," and whom " we ought to consider "

[1] *Mishne Torah, circa finem.*
[2] *Kuzari,* IV, 23.
[3] *Orach Chayim,* CCXXXIV, 7.
[4] Abrahams, *Jewish Life in the Middle Ages,* p. 416.
[5] See *The Legacy of Israel,* symposium edited by E. Bevan and C. Singer, Oxford, 1927, especially the richly documented essay of Singer, pp. 283-314.

as " the seed of the patriarchs, and prophets ; and, what is more, from their stem the Lord was born, and the glorious Virgin, and Apostles, and saints innumerable have descended."[1] Hebrew was the language in which God had imparted His Revelation.

In Hebrew books is to be found the source of all science. From Bacon was derived a Hebraist movement (William of Mara, and the learned unknown letter-writer of Toulouse). Raymund Martini read the Talmud in Hebrew, c. 1264, with some other Dominicans. In the 14th century, Hebrew, Arabic and Chaldean were taught at Oxford, while a remarkable intercourse between Christian and Jewish scholars was taking place in Southern France. The universities of Lunel and Narbonne were centres of Jewish and Moslem culture ; the Jews founded the famous Montpellier school of medicine where the teaching was given in Hebrew, till the 15th century. At the beginning of the 14th century, Armengaud of Montpellier and Arnald of Villanova worked with Jewish aid on medical and scientific texts. The French Christian, Nicholas of Lyra (+1340), devoted himself to Hebrew studies and taught at the Sorbonne. He worked on Biblical exegesis, laid stress on the literal sense, referred to the Hebrew text, and used rabbinic sources. He is an important link between the Middle Ages and the Reformation. His works, reprinted seven times, were well known at the University of Erfurt when the young Luther studied there. Luther calls Nicholas " a fine soul, a good Hebraist and true Christian," and a popular saying associated the piping of Lyra and the dancing of Luther : *Si Lyra non lyrasset, Lutherus non saltasset.* The convert Paul of Burgos (+1435) wrote *additiones* to the Commentary of Lyra.

On the whole Hebrew scholarship proved perhaps the most positive and fruitful common-ground of Christians and Jews during the Middle Ages.

A third aspect of Jewish-Christian " positive " contact in the Middle Ages is afforded by some particular cases of influence and friendship. Two Italians of the 10th century— the Jewish physician and scholar Donnolo, and the Christian abbot Nilus—were affectionate friends and, while holding literary converse, expressed a lively interest in each other's health.[2] Anatolio, the Hebrew translator of Arabic literature

[1] *Opus majus*, III, 13, translation by A. G. Little, *Studies in English Franciscan History*, Manchester, 1917, p. 210.
[2] Abrahams, *Jewish Life in the Middle-Ages*, p. 419.

at the court of the Emperor Frederic II, quoted most reverently the Christian savant, Michael Scot, as his master and friend.[1] But the most remarkable instance of literary intimacies between Jews and Christians is that of Dante and his Jewish imitator, Immanuel of Rome; on Dante's death, Bosone of Agobbio sent a sonnet to Immanuel to console him for the loss of the great poet.[2]

A. Guillaume has hinted[3] at Jewish influences in the greatest poem of the Christian Middle Ages. The funnel descending from Jerusalem to the bowels of the earth with its sevenfold strata ; the seven heavens ; the special strata in hell designed for certain categories of sin ; the ablutions in Purgatory ; the gigantic eagle formed of myriads of angels—these and other more subtle symbols are directly derived, as Asin y Palacios has shown, from Islamic Spanish writers, but may be found in the Talmud, in medieval *Midrashim* and in the *Cabbala* ; if the treatment of the material is Arabian, the substance and the genesis of the ideas are Jewish. Another scholar, G. H. Box, has raised the interesting question of the parallel between the seven heavenly hells (*hekaloth*) of the Cabbala and the seven halls of St. Teresa's " Interior Castle."[4]

Most of these close Jewish-Christian contacts occurred in Italy. Such a tradition of personal friendliness between Jews and Christians is hardly surprising in a country where rabbis introduced classical mythology into their sermons and where a certain David del Bene, at the end of the 16th century, referred in a synagogue oration to *quella santa Diana*.

RENAISSANCE AND REFORMATION : THEIR RELATION TO JUDAISM

As we have seen, Hebrew studies were not neglected in the Middle Ages. Nevertheless they had not become a recognized part of general culture. With the men of the " new learning " appears the idea of the complete humanist as a *trilinguis homo* who knows Hebrew, Greek and Latin. " A fair knowledge of the three languages is of course the first thing " wrote Erasmus in the prefatory remarks to his *Novum Instrumentum* (1516). But he himself so concentrated on Greek that he never found sufficient leisure to master Hebrew.

The Italian Renaissance witnessed a great development of

---

[1] *Jewish Encyclopædia*, vol. I, p. 563.
[2] Graetz, *Geschichte der Juden*, V, 289.
[3] *Legacy of Israel*, p. 170.
[4] *ibidem*, pp. 325–326.

Hebrew scholarship. Hebrew was taught at Bologna in 1488 and at Rome in 1514. Jewish rabbis penetrated into aristocratic Italian circles. Cardinal Guinani was instructed by Abraham de Balmes, Cardinal Sirleto by Lazarus of Viterbo, Guido Rangoni (who was not a cardinal, but a soldier!) by Jacob Mantino, Cardinal Egidio by Elias Levita. This thirst for Hebrew knowledge was not a mere fashion, but expressed a sincere desire to drink from the purest sources. Moreover, interest in the Cabbala was awakening, and Hebrew became the necessary key to it. As some Christians undertook the study of Hebrew with the object of providing themselves with weapons against Judaism, the Jews doubted whether it was lawful to teach a Christian the Cabbala. Maimonides had already taken his stand on the side of tolerance : " A Jew may teach the Commandments to Christians, for they admit that our Law is divine, and they keep it in its integrity."[1] When some rabbis blamed Levita for teaching the Law to a Christian, " Cardinal Egidio," says Levita, " came to me and kissed me with the kisses of his mouth, and declared : Blessed be the Lord of the Universe who has brought thee here ! Now abide with me and teach me, and I shall be to thee as a father . . . . Thus we took sweet counsel together, like iron sharpening iron. I imparted my spirit to him, and from him I learned excellent and precious things."[2] Some Churchmen went rather far. Cardinal Nicholas of Cusa (+1464) frequently quotes the Jews ; in his syncretist scheme of " one religion with many manifestations," he permits circumcision (and also idolatry!), provided that its symbolism is always kept in mind.

The Jews welcomed the craft of printing as " holy work." The first printed Hebrew Bible appeared in 1488 at Soncino, the Italian town which gave its name to a famous family of Jewish printers. The Christian printer, Daniel Bomberg (+1549), issued Hebrew works in Venice and employed Jewish scholars. Johann Froben (+1527) printed Hebrew in Basel.

Hebrew was widely taught in England from the time of Henry VIII onwards. In 1572, the boys of the Merchant Taylors School had to know not only Homer in Greek, but the Hebrew Psalter too.[3]

Giovanni Pico della Mirandola (1463–1494) was the first Christian student of the Cabbala. One of the famous 900 theses which he published at the age of twenty-three proclaimed that

[1] Maimonides, *Respousa*, ed. Leipzig, 58.
[2] Levita, *Masoreth Hamasoreth*, edited by Ginsburg, p. 96.
[3] *Memorial of the Guild of Merchant Taylors*, London, 1875, p. 408.

no science can more firmly convince us of the divinity of Christ than the Cabbala. He had received his cabbalistic training from a certain Jochanan Allemanno, who migrated from Constantinople to Italy. Pico translated into Latin several cabbalistic commentaries. But his greatest contribution to the Hebraic revival was his meeting with Reuchlin in Florence (1490) and his impressing the importance of the rabbinic studies upon the German scholar. This meeting, through its results, had a deep influence on the whole Christian world.[1]

Two years after the Florence meeting Johann Reuchlin (1455–1522) began the study of Hebrew, under Jacob Loans and Obadiah Sforno. In 1494 Reuchlin published at Basel his treatise *De Verbo Mirifico*, in which three scholars—a Jew, a Greek and a Christian—come to the conclusion that Jewish wisdom, expressed in Hebrew, must always come first. His *Rudimenta Hebraica* (1506) was the first Hebrew grammar by a Christian. From 1510–1520 he was involved in the famous Pfefferkorn controversy, which divided the universities, the humanists and the whole educated world. A baptized Jew, Pfefferkorn, had obtained from the Emperor Maximilian an order that all Hebrew books possessed by the Jews of Cologne and Frankfort should be destroyed. On Reuchlin's advice that the Talmud and the Zohar contained no heresy and were useful for theology, the Emperor rescinded his edict. The Dominicans started a violent opposition to Reuchlin for his *judaicus favor*, Reuchlin answered by his *Augenspiegel*, his *defensio*, and his *Clarorum virorum epistolae*. This last work was the occasion of the famous and anonymous pamphlet against clerical obscurantism, *Epistolae obscurorum virorum*, of which Reuchlin disclaimed the authorship. A process of heresy initiated against Reuchlin was decided in his favour by the Bishop of Speyer, but the Dominicans appealed to Pope Leo X who, although the Lateran Council took Reuchlin's side (1516), decided finally against him in 1520.

Meanwhile, Reuchlin published the Hebrew text of the penitential psalms with explanations, the manual from which Luther partly learned his Hebrew ; the treatise *De accentibus et orthographia linguae hebraicae*; and in 1517 his most important work, *De arte cabalistica*. Not only does Reuchlin display an extensive knowledge of the cabbalistic tenets, but he admits that the primeval revelation made to Adam was continued by

---

[1] I. Abrahams has described the Hebrew activity of Pico della Mirandola in the *Hebrew Union College Jubilee Volume*, Cincinnati, 1925.

an unbroken tradition down to the time of the men of the Great Synagogue and afterwards transmitted to the Talmudic teachers. At the University of Ingolstadt he taught Melanchthon, Œcolampadius, and Johann Forster—men distinguished not only as theologians, but also as Hebraists. Erasmus sent a copy of the *De arte cabalistica* to Bishop Fisher and Dean Colet, who dared not express an opinion on matters so mysterious.

Abbot Trithemius of Spanheim (+1516), famous in Benedictine history, was connected with Reuchlin. He built a library containing an almost unique collection of Greek and Hebrew works, and wrote some mystical books which seem influenced by the Cabbala. As often happened, Hebrew scholarship led him to friendship for the Jews, whom he defended in 1510 against the charges of profanation and ritual murder.

Among other Christian scholars who took a lively interest in the Cabbala, we should mention Agrippa of Nettesheim (+1535), Paracelsus (+1541), Hieronymo Cardano (+1576), and van Helmont (+1644). The extraordinary influence of the Cabbala at the time of the Renaissance and Reformation was due partly to the reaction against medieval scholasticism, partly to the revival of Hebrew learning, and partly to the general growth of mystical movements in Germany (Boehme and others). This enthusiastic discovery of Jewish mysticism by the Christian Hebraists was a very " genuine dialogue " with Judaism. Cabbala was not for them a kind of mystical art. They considered ethics as an essential part of Cabbalist doctrines, and they taught that love for God transcends knowledge. For Reuchlin the central doctrine of Cabbala was the Messianology. The Cabbalist, they thought, must first of all purify his soul from sin, and only then does he become open to divine illumination and inspiration.

The spirit of Jerome revived at the time of the Renaissance and inspired a great Biblical effort along Hebrew lines. Jews and Christians took part in it. Several manuscript translations of the Old Testament direct from the Hebrew into Castilian have survived. Thus the manuscripts of the Escorial (date?) and of Evora (1429). The best known Castilian version was the *Bible of the House of Alba* (1430) ; the translator, the Jew Moses Arragel, received the aid of certain Franciscans, and quoted Jewish authorities as well as Christian scholars. At the beginning of the 16th century Pope Clement VII wished a new Latin translation of the Old Testament to be made, in which Jews and Christians were to co-operate ; but his scheme

25

was not executed. Tyndale's Old Testament was rendered direct from the Hebrew. In Spain the great Complutensian Bible of Cardinal Ximenes (dated 1514–1517) gave the Hebrew text of the Old Testament and Targums. The German Protestant, Sebastian Münster (+1552) and the Spanish priest Arias Montanus (+1598) must be mentioned, the first for his grammatical works on Hebrew and Aramaic, the second for his edition of the Antwerp Polyglot Bible.

In Luther's attitude towards the Jews we ought to distinguish two periods.[1] During the earlier—until about 1537—he speaks highly of the Jews. They are the children and, in comparison with them, Christians are the guests, the strangers, the dogs that eat the crumbs which fall from their master's table. Had he been a Jew, he would never have accepted Christianity as it is prosecuted by bishops and monks. He begs everybody to deal kindly with the Jews. It seems that Luther expected a general conversion of the Jews to the reformed Church. Being disappointed, he changed his attitude and spoke of the Jews with bitterness and coarseness. In the writings of his last years he urges the burning of synagogues, the prohibition of Jewish worship, the avoidance of the slightest intercourse with Jews, and he wishes that, if the most prominent Jews assembled could not defeat the Christians in a disputation, their tongues should be torn out through the backs of their necks. Finally, he advises his reader to strike the Jews in the jaw. Luther's authority may rightly be quoted by modern Nazis. His knowledge of Hebrew was scant.

Calvin was a careful Hebraist, but had no interest in Judaism. Zwingli was, of all the Reformers, the most interested in Hebrew studies. He learned Hebrew at Basel, and later on studied the speculations of Pico della Mirandola. His disciple Bullinger (+1575) compared the text of the Old Testament with Jewish commentaries.

On the whole the Reformation furthered Hebrew scholarship and appeared to have a kind of Jewish flavour, owing to the stress it laid on the Old Testament. But there was no deep inner approach to Judaism. None of the Reformers penetrated the heart of Jewish piety as Pico della Mirandola and Reuchlin had done.

---

[1] Luther's pro-Jewish and anti-Jewish views may both be found in his *Briefe*. The pamphlet *Dass Jesus ein Geborner Jude sei* (1543) is an attack on the Catholic opponents of the Jews rather than an *apologia pro Judaeis*. In the following year (1544), Luther published two violent anti-Jewish books: *Von Juden und Ihren Luegen* and *Shem Hamphoras*.

JUDAISM AND CHRISTIANITY IN THE 17TH CENTURY

The time of the Renaissance had been marked by the Christian discovery of Cabbalist mystical literature. The 17th century discovered Talmudic and rabbinical literature. Johannes Buxtorf (+1629), professor of Hebrew at the University of Basel, opened up the subject of rabbinics to Christians (rabbinical Bible of Basel, *Tiberias*, *Synagoga Judaica*, *Lexicon Talmudicum*, *Bibliotheca Rabbinica*). His son and successor was also a Hebrew philologist. The French Hebraist Plantavit (+1651), published a *Florilegium rabbinicum*. In England, Pococke (+1691) edited rabbinic commentaries on the Bible ; John Lightfoot (+1675) contributed his important *Horae Hebraicae et Talmudicae* ; Selden (+1654) and Spencer (+1695) studied Hebrew law. The Jewish scholar, Isaac Abendana, translated the entire Mishna into Latin at Cambridge, between 1663 and 1675 ; this version was never printed, but Abendena gave an impetus to Jewish studies in Oxford and Cambridge, edited eight Jewish calendars containing miscellaneous information, and wrote a comprehensive treatise on Jewish culture. The Dutch Campegius Vitringa (+1722) produced an important *De synagoga vetere*. Another Dutchman, Reland (+1718), published his *Analecta Rabbinica*. Michælis, Schulteus, Wetstein, Kennicot, Lowth, were other contributors to Biblical studies. J. C. Wolf (+1739), of Hamburg, collected much rabbinic material in his *Bibliotheca Hebraica*. But the most extensive and monumental work on Jewish culture was the *Thesaurus Antiquitatum Sacrarum* in 34 vols. by the Italian, Blasio Ugolino (+1700).

The 17th century saw the rise of modern Biblical criticism. Spinoza's *Tractatus theologico-politicus* was its first sign-post. The French Oratorian, Richard Simon (+1712), in his *Histoire critique du Vieux Testament* (which provoked a storm, was attacked by Bossuet and suppressed) anticipated the 19th century theories about the composition of the Pentateuch. Walton (+1661) and Castell (+1685) prepared the London Polyglot Bible.

All this learning was very different from the Jewish passion of the humanists. Hebrew knowledge assumes the form of mere erudition and becomes divorced from living religious enthusiasm ; it is no more the burning flame of the Renaissance, but rather an afterglow. Buber would say that the 17th century witnessed, between Christianity and Judaism, a "technical," but not a "genuine," dialogue.

An important phenomenon of the 17th century was the artificial and partial Judaization of Protestant England through the channel of the Old Testament. What the revival of Hebrew learning had done in a small intellectual minority was accomplished among the English masses by Puritanism. England became the people of a book—the Bible. Milton knew Hebrew and blended the Greek and Hebraic geniuses. The Puritans found an analogy between their fortunes and those of ancient Israel. The Lord of Hosts would help them to smite the Amalekites and Philistines ; they rejoiced in the punishment and plagues of the " idolaters " ; they had a strong feeling of their own election. In their moral stringency, they failed to discriminate between use and abuse. They fell into a sour legalism, far stricter than the synagogue tradition which they ignored. The " joy of the commandment," the Jewish happiness in the Sabbath and Torah remained alien to them. The Psalms became their spiritual food. The ills of this crude, one-sided Israelitism are still felt. It was, if we may risk this term, a Jewish " pseudo-morphose," not a real assimilation of the soul of Judaism. Nevertheless, says W. B. Selbie, " it played a noble part in shaping our history and moulding the character of our people. . . . The legacy of Judaism was to them a real inspiration, and they have handed it on to their posterity in an intensity of religious devotion and a passion of moral fervour for which the whole world is still in their debt."[1]

In the American colonial days, the Jewish " Law of God " had an influence on the legislation of Massachusetts, Connecticut, New Haven and West New Jersey.

The person of Spinoza, not his system, belongs to the Jewish and Christian " dialogue." Excommunicated by the Synagogue, Spinoza felt a sympathy for the teaching of Christ (though he was never received into any Christian community) but rejected the notion that God took upon Himself the nature of a man, and lived and died in the greatest spiritual isolation. But his philosophy is as foreign to Judaism as to Christianity. Educated under Manasseh ben Israel and Saul Morteira, influenced by Maimonides and Hasdai Crescas, he was nevertheless, in his thought, very far from being a typical Jew. The analogies between his monism and the monism of the Cabbala are merely apparent. No conciliation is possible

---

[1] In *Legacy of Israel*, p. 431. See also L. Newman, *Jewish Influence on Christian Reform Movements*, Columbia University Press, 1925.

between Spinozist metaphysics and the profoundly personalist Jewish conception of the world.[1]

The personal attitude of some scholars towards Judaism was not hostile, as two anecdotes would suggest. Buxtorf was fined a hundred gulden for having attended the naming of the son of a Jew who had helped him in his edition of the Basel Bible.[2] Johann Christoph Wagenseil attended the Synagogue in Vienna, in 1650 ; as a burning candle fell during the Saturday service, he hastened to extinguish it, knowing that Jews were not allowed to touch fire on the Sabbath.[3]

Manasseh ben Israel (+1657), the Dutch polyhistor, was instrumental in the re-admission of Jews into England. The title of one of his books, *El Conciliador*, could be applied to himself ; he is remarkable not so much for his books as for his astonishingly wide correspondence and friendships with Christian scholars or statesmen and his general activity as a link between Christians and Jews.

THE PERIOD OF EMANCIPATION: LIBERAL JUDAISM

With Moses Mendelssohn (1729–1796) there began a new era in Judaism.[4] This proficient self-taught man from Berlin, friend of Lessing (whose writings *Die Juden* and *Nathan der Weise* he inspired), himself the author of widely read books—*Phädon, Jerusalem, Morgenstunden,* and a translation of the Bible—initiated a great movement for securing the civil and political emancipation of the Jews, as well as a kind of religious readjustment of Judaism. This movement almost coincided with the rise of the *Judenkunde* or " Jewish Science," fruit of the philological and historical investigations of Leopold Zunz. The establishment of the Temple Congregation at Hamburg and of the Reform Union in Frankfort-on-the-Main, the convening of the rabbinical conferences (Brunswick 1844, Frankfort 1845, Breslau 1846, etc.) and the activity of the Breslau rabbinical seminary under Frankel (1854) were instrumental in the development of Reformed Judaism or Liberal Judaism. The movement gained ground in America from 1840 onwards (Einhorn, Adler, Hirsch). In Eastern Europe a similar movement began about the end of the 18th century under the neo-Hebrew name *haskalah* (" enlightenment ") ; its adherents

[1] See special note R.
[2] Schechter, *Studies in Judaism*, p. 354.
[3] Kaufmann, *Die letzte Vertreibung der Juden aus Wien*, p. 69.
[4] See Kayserling's *M. Mendelssohns Leben und Wirken*, 1887.

were called *maskillim* ("scholars"). It led, especially in Russia (Isaac Bär Levinson), to a certain Westernization of the Jews, but also to the creation of a neo-Hebrew literature.

Reformed Judaism assumed four aspects. Doctrinally it aimed at a break with rabbinical Judaism and a return to primitive Mosaism. The belief in a personal Messiah and in the Resurrection was relinquished. In the sphere of discipline, it drew a distinction between the moral and the ceremonial laws, retaining from these only the Sabbath, circumcision (for the time being) and, in certain circles, the dietary laws. As regards ritual, there were many innovations such as the use of the vernacular language, the organ and mixed choirs, and the introduction of regular sermons ; the text of the services was revised and shortened. In the matter of nationalism, the idea of an earthly restoration was given up and assimilation recommended.

Among the most prominent modern leaders of the Reform movement, the names of K. Kohler, Emil Hirsch, Stephen Wise should be mentioned. But from the point of view of Jewish-Christian relationships, none of these has the significance of Claude Montefiore.[1]

The Rabbinical Conference of Pittsburg (1885) has given the following summary of the beliefs of Liberal Judaism :

(1) Recognition in every religion of an attempt to grasp the Infinite, Judaism presenting the highest conception of the God-idea.

(2) Recognition of the Bible as the record of the consecration of the Jewish people to its sacerdotal mission, and interpretation of the Bible in the light of modern scientific research.

(3) Recognition in the Mosaic religion of a training for Jewish national life, the Mosaic moral laws only being accepted as binding.

(4) Rejection of the rabbinical regulations concerning diet, purity and dress.

(5) Recognition in the modern era of the approaching realization of Israel's Messianic hope, and declaration that neither a return to Palestine nor the restoration of sacrificial worship is a part of the expected kingdom of justice.

(6) Recognition in Judaism of a progressive religion, striving to be in accord with the postulates of reason.

(7) Re-assertion of the doctrine of immortality of the soul, but rejection of the beliefs in bodily resurrection and in Gehenna and Eden.

[1] See special note D.

(8) Proclamation of the duty of participation in the great modern task of solving social problems.

Jewish opinions concerning the value of Liberal Judaism differ widely. If we listen to C. Montefiore, Liberal Judaism will constitute the religious unity of the world. It is not, says he, a particularist creed. The essential doctrines of Judaism are universal in character. The world will ultimately adopt them. Even the festivals of the synagogue can become catholic and universal; they can be made to celebrate certain broad human conceptions which transcend race and nationality.[1] On the other hand, the Chief Rabbi of London, J. H. Hertz, writes: " Liberal Judaism is dry rationalism—irreverent and disintegrating."[2] Heine, in a letter to his friend Moser, had already criticized Liberal Judaism as being " a narrow evangelical Christianity with a Jewish label."

It is true that some interpreters of Liberal Judaism convey the impression that the Reform movement is sliding towards a humanism vaguely tainted with theism. This is, for instance, the conception advocated by Rabbi Kaplan, of the Theological Seminary alongside Columbia University, New York : "Jewish religion should ally itself with the modern orientation toward religion as the spiritual reaction of man to the vicissitudes of life, and as the expression of the highest needs of his being. . . "[3] Rabbi Vivian Simmonds remarks in the course of a sermon that " religion is but another name for the highest expression of the best in human nature."[4] A small Swiss periodical has tried to achieve a kind of synthesis between Liberal Judaism and Unitarianism.[5] The Rabbinical Conference of Pittsburg (1885) declared: "We recognize in the modern era of universal culture of heart and intellect the approaching of the realization of Israel's great Messianic hope for the establishment of the kingdom of truth, justice and peace among all men." The foundation of the *Society for Ethical Culture* by Felix Adler in America may be regarded as an extreme development of Reform Judaism.

Liberal Judaism has opened a new chapter in the dialogue between Judaism and Christianity, but it is rather difficult to draw the conclusions of this chapter. The Reform movement has undoubtedly approached Christianity with an open mind

[1] These views are developed in Montefiore's book *The Place of Judaism Among the Religions of the World.*
[2] *Affirmations of Judaism*, London, 1927, p. 176.
[3] Kaplan, *Judaism as a Civilization*, last chapter.
[4] Quoted by Olga Levertoff in *The Wailing Wall*, London, 1937, p. 56.
[5] *L'espoir Messianique*, edited by T. Grin, Lausanne.

and a friendly tone. To quote once more the Conference of Pittsburg : " Christianity and Islam being daughter-religions of Judaism, we appreciate their providential mission to aid in the spreading of the monotheistic and moral truth." This is the very language of Maimonides. Montefiore goes much further : " Outside it is right for Liberal Jews to read the New Testament ; it is their duty, and it is within their power, to appraise and estimate it correctly. . . ."[1] Again, Montefiore says : " If Judaism does not, as it were, come to terms with the Gospels it must always be, I am inclined to think, a creed in a corner, of little influence and with no expansive power."[2] On the other hand, the same Montefiore writes : " The Liberal Jew is in some respects still further removed from orthodox Christianity than the Conservative Jew. Such an assertion may seem odd, but it is nevertheless true."[3] And he explains why. A Liberal Jew no longer believes in the miracles of the Old Testament ; is he likely to accept the miracles of the New ? In spite of a certain advance towards a due appreciation of the teaching of Jesus, Liberal Judaism holds that the refutation of orthodox Christianity by modern scholarship is complete and triumphant.

We can perhaps sum up the situation thus :—In so far as the Reform movement deviates from a revealed faith in order to become humanitarian idealism, and in so far as it adopts towards the Christian facts a negative historical standpoint, the distance between Liberal Judaism and Christianity will be greater than between Christianity and orthodox Judaism. But, in so far as Liberal Judaism has broken barriers which seemed unshakable, as it has sought and acquired a true knowledge of the Christian teaching, as it approaches the person of Jesus with respect and sympathy, it will find a hopeful and friendly answer in Christian hearts.

" CONVERGENT SCHOLARSHIP "

A most important factor in the modern relationship between Judaism and Christianity is what we might call " convergent scholarship," *i.e.* close contact and intellectual interpenetration due to the unbiased work of Jewish and Christian scholars in the same fields of research. In order to know the consequences and extensions of Judaism, Jewish scholars had to meet Christianity. In order to understand better the person of

[1] *Liberal Judaism*, London 1903, pp. 180–181.
[2] *The Synoptic Gospels* p. 906.
[3] *Outlines of Liberal Judaism*, London, 1912, p. 313.

Jesus and the origins of his message, Christian scholars had to discover the Jewish antecedents and surroundings. This has been highly beneficial both to Jews and Christians. Such was the opinion of the eminent Jewish scholar, Israel Abrahams: " The very causes which make Christian commentaries useful for the Jew, if he would understand the Old Testament, make Jewish commentaries helpful to the Christian for understanding some aspects of the New Testament."[1] It has happened, in modern times as in the time of the Renaissance, that pairs of Jewish and Christian scholars have been linked together in intimate collaboration. Herbert Loewe, the Cambridge rabbinic scholar, said that he was supremely conscious of the lifelong association and mutual influences for good typified in such pairs of friends and scholars as Schiller-Szinessy and Peter Mason, Schechter and Taylor, Abrahams and Burkitt, the Christian and the Jew benefiting each from the other.[2]

The Christian exploration of Jewish sources was largely the work of converts from Judaism. Ferdinand Christopher Ewald (+1874) published a translation of the talmudic treatise *Abodah Zarah.* Johann Neander (+1850), whose name, prior to his baptism, was David Mendel, wrote a *Leben Jesu.* He denounced the " mediæval lie " when the Jews of Damascus were persecuted on account of a blood accusation (1846). But two men especially—Edersheim and Chwolson—were originators along the " back to the Jewish sources " line of research.

Alfred Edersheim (1825-1889) was a Jew who became a Christian and wrote, besides other Jewish studies, a commentary of more than 1,500 pages on the four Gospels.[3] It is a pious, rather conservative " harmony " of the evangelical narratives, full, to a greater extent than any previous book, of interesting and reliable pictures of Jewish life in the time of Jesus. But the book chiefly repays attention because of Edersheim's intimate and detailed knowledge of rabbinic literature ; he reproduces a great number of texts from the Talmud and constantly interprets the Gospels in this Jewish light. The drawbacks of the book are a tendency to exaggerate the contrasts between the teaching of Jesus and the teaching of the Pharisees, and a frequent lack of discrimination in the use and dating of rabbinic sources. Nevertheless, Edersheim has opened new horizons to Christian readers, and even to Christian scholars.

[1] *Studies in Pharisaism and the Gospels,* First series, p. vii.
[2] Foreword to *Jesus, Paul and the Jews,* by J. Parkes, London, 1936.
[3] *The Life and Times of Jesus the Messiah* 2 vols., London, 1883.

Daniel Chwolson was a Russian Jew who embraced Christianity in 1855 and dedicated himself to Oriental studies. His book on the date of Jesus' death[1] is more than the discussion of a chronological problem. Chwolson makes a critical examination of the deep-rooted belief that Jesus was crucified by Jews and points out that the proceedings of the trial were in violation of the rabbinical laws. He considers that Jesus throughout behaved as a true Pharisee. As well as the Jewish religion, the Jewish race was defended by Chwolson (blood accusation of Saratov, 1857).

The important works of another convert, Paul Levertoff, will be mentioned later on with precise references, when we consider the history of Jewish mysticism and the contemporary endeavours to restore a Jewish Christianity. It will be sufficient now to say that Levertoff, besides an English translation of the Zohar and a Hebrew version of St. Augustine's *Confessions*, has written also the first life of Jesus in modern Hebrew.[2]

It would be impossible to give here even a bird's-eye view of modern Christian scholarship in the field of post-Old Testament Judaism. More will be said when talmudic literature is considered. But there are two kinds of work which should be mentioned at this point.

In the first place, there is the bulky Commentary of H. Strack and P. Billerbeck on the New Testament according to rabbinic sources[3]—a book which has become indispensable to the exegetists.

Secondly, there are the writings of Gustav Dalman, in particular *The Words of Jesus considered in the light of post-biblical Jewish Writings and the Aramaic Language* and *Jesus-Jeshua*.[4] These titles give immediately an idea of the author's purpose. Dalman himself has explained in what frame of mind he approached such subjects. " The mere fascination of linguistic activity in connexion with a dialect which has long been dead, and the supposed 'genuine' colouring in expression and sound of the words of Jesus gained in the process, would not alone have justified my work of the last

---

[1] Translated from Russian into German: *Das letzte Passamahl Christi und der Tag seines Todes*, St. Petersburg, 1892.

[2] *Ben-ha-Adam* (The Son of Man), London, 1905.

[3] *Kommentar zum Neuen Testament aus Talmud und Midrasch*, 4 vols., Munich, 1922–1928.

[4] *The Words of Jesus* has been translated from the German by D. Kay, Edinburgh, 1902. *Jesus-Jeshua* has been translated, also from the German, by P. Levertoff, London, 1929.

thirty years upon the structure of the language of our Lord. It is the examination, as such, of how the thoughts of Jesus, the formulation of which has been transmitted to us in Greek, were expressed in the original idiom, that I consider of importance. But this cannot be separated from the consideration of the conceptions and thoughts which the Jewish sources offer for a comparison as regard subject-matter and the relation of the thoughts and words of our Lord to them. . . . The real problem is, how our Lord, Whose portrait is preserved to us in a Greek form, looked among the ' Hebrews.' "[1]

Just as Christian scholars have explored the Jewish field, the Christian field has been explored by the Jewish scholars. C. Dodd writes : " It is certain that the contributions of devout Jewish scholars to our understanding of the Gospel in recent years have earned our gratitude."[2] Not only those who have dealt directly with the comparison between rabbinic literature and Gospel teaching, like Claude Montefiore and Israel Abrahams, or with the history of Christian origins, like Samuel Krauss and Kaufmann Kohler, but also those who have specialized in the study of Jewish thought in the first century of the Christian era, like S. Schechter and J. Abelson— these have contributed, with understanding and irenic minds, to our better knowledge of Christianity. We shall meet some of these names again and give a more precise idea of their work and tendencies. And there is also the phalanx of Jewish historians, G. and M. Friedländer, Eschelbacher, Klausner, etc., who have concentrated on the *Leben Jesu-Forschung* and so deeply modified the current Jewish appreciation of Jesus. This last aspect of Jewish scholarship is so important that it requires separate treatment.

THE ATTITUDE OF MODERN JUDAISM TOWARDS JESUS

It is still possible to find traces of the old Jewish hostility towards the person of Jesus, or, at least, of the conviction that the thought of Jesus must never even cross a Jewish mind. S. M. Melamed, a Liberal Jew, writing in *The Reflex*,[3] said : " There is nothing more undignified than for a Jew to flirt with Jesus, whatever the attitude of a Jew may be to the positive Jewish traditions, whether he is a believer or not,

---

[1] *Jesus-Jeshua*, transl. Levertoff, pp. xi-xii.
[2] *The Epistle of Paul to the Romans*, London, 1932, p. 181.
[3] June, 1930, p. 21.

interested or uninterested in Jewish life and doctrine, he ought to steer clear of Jesus and of Christ. . . . It is something that the Jew must never discuss, either with his fellow Jews or a Gentile." This attitude and tone, however, are unusual nowadays. Most educated Jews sincerely try to know the person of Jesus and understand His message ; they show respect towards Him and often sympathy.[1]

Already in Joseph Salvador's book, *Jésus-Christ et sa doctrine: histoire de la naissance de l'Eglise, de son organisation et de ses progrès pendant le premier siècle*,[2] written more than a century ago, one notices a remarkable effort to understand and interpret Jesus. Salvador finds the whole of the ethical teaching of Jesus in the Prophets ; he emphasizes the great difference between Pharisaic Judaism, endeavouring to secure men earthly happiness as well as spiritual life, and Jesus, who adopted a negative attitude to the life of this world ; he sees in historical Christianity the outcome of a compromise between Judaism and Paganism.

Graetz discussed Jews in a work entitled *Sinai and Golgatha* ; the author did not publish it, but embroidered it in his *History of the Jews*[3] ; but it was separately translated into French by Moses Hess (1867). According to Graetz, save for the cases of spiritual healing, Jesus was simply a teacher honoured in His circle, just as Hillel was in his. Christianity arose out of Essenism. Abraham Geiger, in his lectures on the History of Israel,[4] agrees with Graetz in thinking that there is nothing new or striking in Jesus' teaching, but he sees in Jesus, instead of an Essene, a Pharisaic Jew.

Diametrically opposed to the views of Graetz and Geiger are those of M. Friedländer. According to him, Jesus and John the Baptist were popular prophets of the same type ; Jesus, in the late period, was influenced by Hellenistic Judaism, tended to set aside the ceremonial laws, perfected the universalistic teaching of the Prophets and wholly spiritualized it.[5]

[1] On the evolution of Jewish opinion with regard to Jesus see : T. Walker, *Jewish Views of Jesus. An Introduction and an Appreciation*, London, 1931; J. Bonsirven, *Les Juifs et Jesus, Attitudes Nouvelles*, Paris, 1937 ; Gösta Lindeskog, *Die Jesusfrage im neuzeitlichen Judentum*, Leipzig, 1938. It is in this last book that the most detailed account of the Jewish utterances about Jesus are to be found.
[2] 2 vols., Paris, 1838.
[3] III, 5, Leipzig, 1905, pp. 271–313.
[4] *Das Judentum und seine Geschichte*, 1854.
[5] *Die Religiösen Bewegungen innerhalb des Judentums im Zeitalter Jesu*, Berlin, 1905.

A comparative study of Judaism and Christianity by Rabbi J. Eschelbacher[1] has been translated from German into Hebrew. Claude Montefiore has written much about Jesus, always in a spirit of deep sympathy.[2] On the one hand, much of the substance of the Gospels is to be found in the talmudic literature. On the other hand, the Gospels are generally superior to the Talmud and should be accepted by the Jews as a part of their Hebrew message. Montefiore's views elicited a violent reply in an article of the famous Zionist writer Ahad-ha-Am (Asher Ginsberg) and a more scholarly rejoinder in a book where G. Friedländer[3] tried to show that the teaching of Jesus was either borrowed from the Old Testament or, in its original parts, inconsistent, and incompatible with social life.

The best known Jewish work on Christ is probably the book of Joseph Klausner, *Jesus of Nazareth. His Life, Times and Teaching*.[4] Klausner is a Jewish scholar from Jerusalem whose literary output in German and Hebrew was already considerable before he published this book. His purpose was to write, in modern Hebrew, " a book which shall tell the history of the Founder of Christianity along the lines of modern criticism," and to " give Hebrew readers a truer idea of the *historic* Jesus, an idea which shall be alike far from that of Christian or Jewish dogma."[5]

Klausner's conception of Jesus may be summarized as follows :—Jesus was a Jew and a Jew he remained to his last breath. His one idea was to implant within Israel the idea of the coming of the Messiah and to hasten the "end." More Jewish even than Hillel, Jesus sacrificed national life to an extreme, one-sided ethic. Jesus' ideals imbibed from the Prophets and Pharisaism, brought Judaism to such an extreme that it became, in a sense, non-Judaism, the negation of everything that had vitalized Judaism. Jesus sacrificed the God of justice and righteousness to the God of mercy ; he sacrificed the God of social order, the God of the nation, the God of History. However lofty a conception Jesus' teaching may represent for the individual moral conscience, it stands

---

[1] *Das Judentum und das Wesen des Christentums*, (Hebr.) translated Vilna, 1911.
[2] See chiefly *The Synoptic Gospels*, 2 vols., London, 1909, and *Some Elements of the Religious Teaching of Jesus*, London, 1910 ; also *Rabbinic Literature and Gospel Teachings*, London, 1930.
[3] *The Jewish Sources of the Sermon on the Mount*, London, 1911.
[4] Translated from the original Hebrew by H. Danby, London, 1925.
[5] P. 11.

D 2

for ruin and catastrophe for the social and national conscience. Judaism is not only a religion ; it is the sum-total of all the needs of the nation, placed on a religious basis. Jesus annulled Judaism as the life-force of the Jewish nation. His over-emphasis on self-abnegation was not Judaism and can make its appeal only to the more spiritually minded among individuals, whose sole interest is religion. Hence two-fold misapprehensions : the nearness of the kingdom and His Messiahship. To the Jewish nation He can be neither God nor the Son of God ; neither can the Jews regard Him as a lawgiver or even a rabbi. He did nothing to strengthen the national life or Israel. He is for the Jewish nation a great teacher of morality and an artist in parable. His extremist ethical code has become a *Zukunfts Musik* for the isolated few, an ideal for the end of the old world and the days of the Messiah. It is no code for the nations of to-day. But in this ethical code there is a sublimity and originality of form unparalleled in any other Hebrew ethical code. Stripped of its wrappings of miracles and mysticism, it is one of the choicest treasures of Israel for all time.

Rabbi J. L. Levy, of Pittsburg, who often chose his texts from the New Testament and was even offered the pastorate of a church in Scotland, declared : " Side by side with Moses and the Ten Commandments, we are willing to place Jesus and the Nine Beatitudes."[1] Rabbi G. H. Enelow wrote *A Jewish View of Jesus.*[2] According to him, Jesus taught nothing that was not already to be found in Judaism, but he presented it in a more striking fashion and left the impress of a unique personality. Although the Jews cannot see in Him either a God or a Messiah, they should look upon Him as an exceptional teacher who influenced humanity more than any other man.

Rabbi Abba Hillel Silver would not have Christians abandon their exalted view of the Lord Jesus : " Quite apart from the question of the divinity of Jesus, it is an indisputable fact that the personality of Jesus has been a luminously radiant fact in the life of Christianity. To ask of Christianity to reduce and attenuate this personality so as to make it acceptable to others would be to deprive it of that which is its prime distinction and its specific contribution to mankind."[3]

The German Jewish writer, Constantin Brunner, published in 1921 a large volume entitled *Our Christ.* He does not share, of

---

[1] See Chief Rabbi Hertz, *Affirmations of Judaism*, p. 179.
[2] New York, 1920.
[3] *Religion in a Changing World*, New York, 1931, p. 110.

course, the Christian faith. But he sees in Christ " the last word of Judaism : never man so spoke." He addresses Christ thus : " I loved none so tenderly as Thee, O Christ. We need Thee ; without Thee we cannot live."

Hans Schoeps, in his book on the controversy between Judaism and Christianity during the last century, acknowledges the New Covenant within the full meaning of the New Testament as an inscrutable divine mystery, but only outside Judaism. The Incarnation is called a "cruel blasphemy."[1]

According to J. Cournos, Jesus must be rediscovered not only by the Jews, but also by the Christians, and, when so discovered, He may link Jews and Christians in a great religious crusade for righteousness. Unprepared to acknowledge the Messiahship of Jesus, Cournos does not deny categorically the possibility of such Messiahship and seems to leave the question open.[2]

Einstein has declared : " I am enthralled by the luminous figure of the Nazarene."[3]

Certain books, written by Jews, are on the border between Judaism and Christianity. In a scientifically worthless book called *Jeshua the Classical Jew*,[4] De Jonge tried to " destroy the ecclesiastical image " and " reveal the Jewish image " of Jesus. The author was Christian for a while and tried to revert to Judaism. More will be said about his case in another place.

It would be very unfair to put Hugh Schonfield's book about Jesus[5] on the same level with De Jonge's. The common point is that Schonfield, like De Jonge, endeavours to unite in himself Judaism and Christianity ; but he is a quite definite Jewish-Christian, and it is perhaps a mistake to mention his book in this section, instead of giving it a place among the works of Christians of Jewish origin. Although Schonfield is a historian, he sometimes gives us a strange mixture of history, unwarranted assumptions and religious enthusiasm.

Half-way between history and fiction, far from Christian orthodoxy, but sympathetic towards Jesus, the *Son of Man* by Emil Ludwig, *Jesus as Others saw Him* by Joseph Jacob, *The Crucified Jew* by Max Hunterberg, and, more recently, *The*

[1] *Jüdisch-Christliches Religionsgespräch in 19 Jahrhunderten*, Berlin, 1937.
[2] *Hear, O Israel! An Open Letter to Jews and Christians*, New York, 1938.
[3] Quoted by J. Conning, *Religion and Irreligion in Israel*, in *International Review of Missions*, vol. 19, 1930, p. 544.
[4] *Jeschua, der Klassische Jüdische Mann*, Berlin, 1904.
[5] *Jesus. A Biography*, London, 1939.

Nazarene by Sholem Asch[1] ought to be recognized as important manifestation of the Jewish change of attitude to Christ.

A rather strange but interesting movement has taken form in America, under the direction of Solomon Schwayder, of Denver, to have the action of the Sanhedrin that condemned Jesus reviewed by a new accredited Sanhedrin of Jewish leaders.

If we wish to summarize the modern Jewish attitude towards Jesus and his message, it is best perhaps to reproduce what Martin Buber says in *Dei Reden über das Judentum* : " Only *Galuth* (= exile) psychology is responsible for the fact that we have allowed such a movement as Christianity, which originated in our midst, to be torn out from our history. It was a Jewish evil that this spiritual revelation burst into flame ; Jewish men carried the movement far and wide. We must overcome the superstitious terror with which we have regarded the Nazareth movement, a movement which we must place where it properly belongs—in the spiritual history of Israel."

Such an attitude may be diversely appreciated. On the Christian side, one sometimes finds the avowed suspicion that the Jewish writers who acknowledge the greatness of Jesus only seek thereby to emphasize the greatness of Judaism. A veteran of the Christian Missions to the Jews, Otto von Harling, who was the head of the *Institutum Judaicum Delitzchianum* of Leipzig, speaking of the trend of ideas represented by Buber, says : " This Judaism is all the more dangerous just because it unites with true piety and great spiritual power a recognition of Christ, divesting Him of His majesty as Saviour and degrading Him *in majorem Judaeorum gloriam* to one of the great Jewish race leaders."[2] Of course, it would be naïve to interpret this new Jewish " recognition of Christ " as boding an adhesion to Christianity. But if the old hostility and bitterness disappear, if even a mere human sympathy sincerely moves so many Jewish hearts towards Jesus, what Christian ought not to rejoice ?

---

[1] Translated from Yiddish by M. Samuel, London, 1939. It is the only one of the above-mentioned books originally written in Yiddish.

[2] *International Review of Missions*, vol. 19, 1930, p. 349.

PART TWO

THE PERMANENT VALUES OF JEWISH TRADITION

TRADITION IN JUDAISM

The treatise *Pirke Aboth*, which is read during the closing service of the Sabbath in summer, begins with these words : " Moses received the Torah from Sinai and he delivered it to Jehoshua, and Jehoshua to the elders, and the elders to the prophets, and the prophets delivered it to the men of the Great Synagogue."[1] Although this passage is not to be taken too literally, we find in it the foundation of the Jewish oral law and traditional teaching. The tradition of the elders, *midrash zekenim*—this " fence made to the Torah " (according to a rabbinic expression) in order to protect the written law— correspond exactly to the *paradosis tōn presbyterōn* of the primitive Christian Church. Another Jewish technical term designing the tradition is *Torah shebe al peh* ; it means the law given orally, and it includes all the conclusions, interpretations and regulations deducted from the written Torah. Later rabbinical statements imply that God Himself imparted to Moses all the traditional teachings developed in the course of time. Such fundamentalism is no longer admitted, even by the most conservative Jews ; but the traditional teaching remains an essential part of orthodox Judaism. The expression " the two laws," *i.e.* the written and the oral law (the latter being later crystallized in rabbinical writings), is ascribed to Hillel and Shammai, who spoke of both as equally authoritative. The Talmud says that the oral law is the " seventh day " through which the world was completed " and the whole is preserved."[2]

What is the content of Jewish tradition ? Its substance may be divided into the following three groups :

In the first place, the Scriptural tradition. We must give to this term a very wide meaning. It includes not only the fixing of the biblical text and its direct exegesis, but also what the rabbis called *debar Torah* (regulation of the Torah), *i.e.* all

---

[1] C. Taylor, *Sayings of the Jewish Fathers comprising Pirke Aboth in Hebrew and English*, Cambridge, 1897 ; W. Oesterley, *The Sayings of the Jewish Fathers*, London, 1919 ; R. T. Herford, *Pirke Aboth. Introduction, Translation and Commentary*, New York, 1925.

[2] *Bereschit* 47b.—On Jewish oral law in general, see Gotthard Deutsch, *The Theory of Oral Tradition*, Cincinnati, 1896.

the interpretation deduced from the Scripture by logical conclusions or hermeneutical rules. Many of them have but a very artificial connexion with the Scripture.

Secondly, there is the legal tradition. This term covers statutes which are not connected with the Scripture, but are ascribed to Moses, or to the elders, or to the scribes. The part played by the scribes or scholars (*Soferim*) in the introduction of new customs and observances explains why many regulations are called *dibre Soferim*, "words of the Scribes." Under the heading of legal tradition fall also the regulations decreed by the Sanhedrin and courts of law, and sometimes also the statutes of foreign countries in which Jews are living.

Thirdly, there is the mystical tradition. This last is generally not mentioned as a part of Jewish tradition. Sometimes the historians oppose Jewish mysticism to the *de-rabbanan* or rabbinical regulations. They oppose the Zohar to the Talmud. This is an entirely mistaken view. It is true that the mystical Hasidic movement, in the 18th century, took an attitude of reaction and protest against a narrow legalist rabbinism. But the most ancient manifestations of Jewish mysticism were closely linked with rabbinic tradition. The same man could be a Talmudist and a mystic. The mystical writings ought to be interpreted into the great historical Jewish tradition. The very word Cabbala means " tradition."

These three aspects of the Jewish tradition will be separately considered later on. But we must now raise an important question. Have we the right to assert that tradition is essential to Judaism, when considerable Jewish groups reject the orthodox oral law ? What about those Jewish communities which proclaim their independence of what is called "rabbinism" or rabbinic Judaism ?

The reader will immediately think of Liberal Judaism. The attitude of the Reform movement towards the oral law is more complex than it may seem at first sight. If there are many aspects of Judaism which Liberal Judaism does not teach from its pulpits, this does not mean that it repudiates them. If Liberal Judaism denies the necessity of certain practices, *e.g.* circumcision or abstention from pork meat, this does not mean that it requires their abandonment. It is true that the Liberal communities refuse to regard the talmudic rules as the last word and seal of Judaism. But Herbert Loewe points out that Liberal Judaism " asserts the continuation of rabbinic tradition as a living force."[1] What can this mean ? Loewe

[1] Art. *Judaism* in Hasting's *Encycl. for Rel. and Eth.*, vol. 7, p. 608.

himself gives a deep and two-fold explanation of this sentence. First, Liberal Judaism, as well as orthodox Judaism, maintains that religious teachers have the power to bind and loose. But, instead of limiting this power to the teachers of the past, it insists on the power of the teachers to bind and loose to-day as of old (orthodox Judaism would not deny it ; it is rather a question of emphasis). Secondly, Liberal Judaism does not limit to a recognized synod or to a rabbi with a *facultas docendi* the right to sanction any change or new development, but gives the same right to the individual members of the communities. Thus Liberal Judaism modifies the exercise of traditional teaching, but does not abolish it. As Loewe says : " In this respect (Liberal Judaism) is something positive, not a mere negation of orthodoxy."

Then comes the case of Qaraitism.[1] The *Qaraim* (" adherents ") or Qaraites are a Jewish sect which arose in the eighth century A.D., and which numbers about 15,000 people in Russia and in the East. They also call themselves the *bene mikra*, " sons of the writing " ; this designation expresses the central idea and watchword of Qaraitism, which is : " Back from tradition to Scripture." They reject the Talmud. Here again the reality is far more complex than appearances. Although Qaraitism may seem to be a kind of Jewish Protestantism, it has simply substituted for rabbinic tradition a tradition of its own. The Qaraites are very careful to avoid the word " tradition," but they speak of the " yoke of inheritance," and hold, as obligatory and binding, some doctrines and practices which are not taught in the Bible. Their " yoke of inheritance " seems to correspond to the Muslim notion of *ijma* or *consensus*.

Although the Samaritans are, strictly speaking, not Jews, this little remnant—to a certain extent—belongs to Israel[2]. They have evolved a strong tradition of their own, an oral interpretation of the Pentateuch. They call this tradition *hilluk*, " the way." Their tradition, doctrinal, liturgical and mystical, is rich and impressive. The sun of the Samaritans may be setting fast, but there are " rays which still light up the holy Mount Gerizim."[3]

Thus there is no form of Judaism which could be described as a pure Biblicism, devoid of all tradition. There are, as we

---

[1] See special note E.
[2] See special note F.
[3] M. Gaster, *The Samaritans*, 1925, p. 158.

have shown, several Jewish traditions,[1] but the rabbinic tradition is undoubtedly the most important. A layman wishing to be initiated into the spirit of the rabbinic tradition could not find a better guide than the work of C. G. Montefiore and H. Loewe, *A Rabbinic Anthology*.[2]

We have strongly insisted on the existence and importance of tradition in Israel because their recognition is the first condition of a fruitful approach to Judaism. Many Christian theologians and missionaries who have to deal with Judaism make a grave mistake in that respect. They imagine Judaism as being merely the religion of the Old Testament. They come to the Jews with the New Testament in hand and wonder why it does not " fit in " easily. They forget—or willingly ignore—that, between the Old Testament and our times, there lie more than nineteen centuries of Jewish thought. We could compare them with non-Christian theologians or propagandists who would engage in a theological conversation with Christians, while firmly determined to take no account whatever either of the Church Fathers, or the Scholastics, or the Reformers, or the exegetes of the last century. The Old Testament is the foundation of Judaism, but the house built upon it has been edified with the stones of Jewish tradition. The Christian who pretends to " crown " the Jewish building by simply superimposing the New Testament on the Old is like a man who would try to put a roof directly on the foundations, instead of on the top of the house. It is useless to approach Judaism without some knowledge of—and much sympathy for—the living tradition of the Jews.

And one should not think that the dialogue with orthodox Judaism is necessarily more difficult just because this is " orthodox." While fully acknowledging the readiness of Liberal Jews to find a common ground with Christians, we may discover that the most conservative Jew of Ukraine or Galicia, just because he has cultivated a mental habit of reverence and obedience towards revelation and tradition, will lend a docile ear to a message in which he can detect their genuine echo. A sentence from the Talmud may be quoted here : " If you have heard, you will continue to hear ; if you have not heard,

---

[1] It seems unnecessary to speak here of the 40,000 Yemenite Jews (Arabs converted to Judaism), of the 70,000 Caucasian Jews (also converted) or the 10,000 *Bene Israel* of the region of Bombay. They all have their traditions, but they do not present the same interest as the Samaritans or the Qaraites.

[2] London, 1938.

44

you will not hear. If you have heard the old, you will also hear the new : if you have turned your heart away, you will hear no more."[1]

THE JEWISH FATHERS

The bearers and interpreters of the Jewish tradition have been the " Fathers." The Jews used that word in the plural (*Abboth*) to designate famous men of Israel's history, especially the three patriarchs (Abraham, Isaac, Jacob), and also the wise and learned men. The Mishna calls Hillel and Shammai, Akiba and Ishmael " fathers of the world."

In the book (already mentioned) *Pirke Aboth* or *Sayings of the Fathers*, the word " father " is practically synonymous with " rabbi." Before examining the history and substance of the rabbinic tradition, we ought to know something about the rabbis themselves.

The Jewish doctors were called by three names : *rab, rabbi, rabban*. The term *rab* means originally " master " in opposition either to pupil or slave. *Rabbi* means " my master." *Rabban*, " our master," was a title given only to the presidents of the Sanhedrin.

The rabbis were teachers and judges. They invariably had some manual work or trade, with which they busied themselves for a third of the day, studying during the remainder Hillel was a wood-chopper, Shammai a builder, Hanina a shoemaker. Anyone could qualify as a rabbi : the famous rabbi Resh Lakish was originally a gladiator. They preached in synagogues. The question whether Jesus was a rabbi is still discussed.[2] The honour paid to the rabbis, " elders in knowledge," exceeded that paid to the parents, " elders in years."

The history of ancient rabbinism after A.D. 70 may be divided into three periods : the talmudic period, the geonic period, the mediæval period.[3]

The talmudic period includes the times during which the many constituent elements of the Talmud were gathered together. This period may itself be divided into three sub-periods :

(a) The tannaitic times (*tanna*, plural *tannaim*, means " teacher "). The *tannaim* belonged to the Pharisaic party.

[1] *Berakoth*, 40a.
[2] See special note G.
[3] See W. Oesterley and G. Box, *A Short Survey of the Literature of Rabbinical and Mediæval Judaism*, London, 1920.

After the destruction of the Temple, A.D. 70, Titus authorized the Pharisees to establish a new Sanhedrin at Jabne, near Jaffa, under the presidency of Jochanan ben Zakkai. An Academy founded also at Jabne was later on removed to Sephoris and afterwards to Tiberias. But, finally, Babylon became the authoritative centre of Judaism ; the political head of the Eastern Jews was called *resh Gelutha*, " head of the captivity," just as the leader of the Jabne Academy had been called *nasi*, " prince." Gamaliel II and Akiba are the greatest names of this time.[1]

(b) The time of the *amoraim*. Approximately between A.D. 200 and 500. *Amoraim* is the plural form of *amora*, " speaker " or rather " interpreter," because the *amora* was a commentator on the writings of the *tannaim*. After the death of Judah I, the principal seats of Babylonian Judaism were the Academies of Nehardea and Sura. Arika and Ashi are the most prominent *amoraim*.

(c) The time of the *saboraim*. This short period (500–550) closes the talmudic period. The scholars called *saboraim* (from *sabora*, " decision ") gave the final touch to the Babylonian Talmud.

After the talmudic period comes the geonic period (6th–11th centuries), or period of the *gaonim*, plural of *gaon*, "excellency," the title given to the presidents of the Academies. Two great events mark this period : the rise of Mohammedanism and the schism of the Qaraites ; the latter we have already discussed. The most distinguished *gaon* was Saadya (+942), who lived in Egypt, Palestine and Babylonia, and who united Arabic culture with Judaism as Philo had united Judaism with Hellenism.

We turn now to the medieval period. From the 8th to the 13th century the Jewish settlement in Spain was the Golden Age of modern Judaism. Avicebron (Ibn Gebirol, +1070) introduced neo-platonism into Europe. Bahya (+1100) wrote the beautiful ethical treatise *The Duties of the Heart*. Judah ha-Levi (+1140) was great as a philosopher (*Sepher ha-Kuzari*, 1140), but greater still as a poet. Abraham Ibn Ezra (+1167) wrote on exegesis and philosophy. Of Moses Maimonides (1135–1204) the Jews said : " From Moses to Moses there has arisen none like unto Moses." His " Guide to the Perplexed " set aside traditional rabbinism and spiritualizes Judaism on Alexandrine lines. During the 13th century the great centres of Jewish learning were rather France and Germany, though

[1] See G. F. Moore, *Judaism in the First Centuries of the Christian Era. The Age of the Tannaim*, 2 vols., London, 1927.

eminent spiritual writers like Azriel (+1238) and Nahmanides (+1270) were Spaniards. In France lived the talmudic commentator Rashi (+1105), and the Aristotelian philosopher Levi ben Gerson or Leo Hebraeus (+1344) ; Germany produced the Cabbalist, Eleazar of Worms (+1237). The last great voices heard from Spain were those of Hasdai Crescas (+1410) and Joseph Albo (+1444), who tried to liberate Judaism from the influences of Aristotle and Maimonides and to come back to the root-principles of revealed faith. Though Joseph Caro, who was born in Spain and died in Palestine (1575), lived in the 16th century, he belonged spiritually to the Middle Ages, and was the last great codifier of rabbinical Judaism. His *Shulhan Aruk* was for centuries, and in part still is, the ritual and legal code of orthodox Jewish life ; it is ultra-rigorous and scrupulous, but it embodies a high ethical standard. We may close this bird's-eye view of ancient rabbinism with the name of the eminent mystic Isaac Luria, founder of the modern Cabbala, who was born and died in Palestine (1572).

After this dry enumeration of names and dates it will perhaps be refreshing to look more closely at some of these figures of saints and masters in Israel.

Hillel was the highest authority among the doctors of Jerusalem in the time of the first King Herod. He had to overcome many difficulties and hardships in order to be admitted, notwithstanding his poverty, to the schools of the rabbis Shemaiah and Avtalion. His own teaching and school stood in opposition to the rigorist school of Shammai. The first of Hillel's maxims recorded in *Pirke Aboth* mentions Aaron as the model to be imitated in his love of peace and of man. Love of man was considered by Hillel as the kernel of the whole Law. He said : " Do not unto thy fellow man what is hateful unto thee ; this is the whole Law ; the rest is mere commentary."[1] It may be assumed that Hillel's formulation of the Golden Rule was not without influence on the Gospel teaching.[2] Among his other sayings recorded in the Mishna, we should quote these : " Judge not thy neighbour till thou art in his place. Trust not thyself till the day of thy death. If I am here, says God, every one is here ; if I am not here, nobody is here. If thou comest to my house (says God), I come to thine." The meekness and mildness of Hillel became proverbial : " Let a man be always humble and patient like

---

[1] *Shabath*, 31a.
[2] F. Delitzsch, *Jesus and Hillel*, Erlangen, 1879. See also A. Büchler, *Types of Jewish-Palestinian Piety from 70 B.C.E. to 70 C.E.*, London, 1922.

Hillel and not passionate like Shammai."[1] He himself had said : " My humility is my exaltation ; my exaltation is my humility." At his death such lamentations were uttered as : " Woe for the meek one ! Woe for the pious one ! "[2] One day, while Hillel and other rabbis were sitting together, a voice from heaven is said to have exclaimed : " Among those here present is a man upon whom the Holy Spirit would rest, if only his time were worthy of it."

Gamaliel (not to be confounded with his grandson of Jabne) was the grandson of Hillel. He presided over the Sanhedrin of Jerusalem, where he spoke in favour of the disciples of Jesus who were threatened with death (Acts v. 34 sq.). He was the teacher of Paul. As a consequence of this he became a subject of Christian legends : the Talmud was attributed to him by a German monk of the 12th century. Jewish tradition held him in high honour : " When he died the glory of the Torah ceased, and purity and piety became extinct."[3]

Among the saintly rabbis, some martyrs must be specially mentioned. Jewish tradition names ten great teachers who suffered martyrdom under Hadrian for having taught the Law : Ishmael ben Elisha, Simeon, Ishmael, Akiba ben Joseph, Hananiah ben Teradion, Huzpit, Yeshebab, Eliezer ben Shammua, Hananiah ben Hakinai, Judah ben Baba. The midrash gives us no details about the death of Akiba and Hananiah ben Teradion. While Akiba underwent the torture, he recited the prayer *Shema Ysrael* with a peaceful smile on his face. He said that he rejoiced that he was permitted to love God " with all his life," and he died pronouncing the last words of the *Shema* : " Adonai is One." Hananiah was wrapped in a scroll of the Law and placed on a pyre. Wet wool was placed on his chest to prolong his agony. When the fire reached him he said : " I see the parchment burning, but the letters of the Law soar upward." The martyrdom of the " ten teachers " is commemorated in one of the services of the Day of Atonement. The desire for martyrdom was frequently expressed by the later rabbis. Joseph Caro, in 1532, was filled with a longing to be " consumed on the altar as a holy burnt offering."[4]

---

[1] *Shabath*, 31a.
[2] *Toseftah*, Sotah XIII, 3 ; 48b.
[3] *Sotah*, XV, 18. See Büchler, *Das Synedrion in Jerusalem*, pp. 115-131.
[4] The Jewish martyrs of the Middle Ages (who suffered at the hands of the Christians) are commemorated in many Jewish martyrologies, the most famous of which is the memor-book of Nuremberg (1296). Since anti-semitism has been rampant in Central and Eastern Europe, in our own times, such memor-books could be published again.

48

The most beautiful figure of the late rabbinism is perhaps Isaac Luria (1534–1572). At the age of twenty-two he adopted the life of a hermit, removed to the banks of the Nile and secluded himself in meditation. He spoke seldom and only in Hebrew. He visited his family each Sabbath day. On the Sabbath he dressed himself in white and wore a fourfold garment to express the four letters of the name of God (Tetragrammaton). He believed that he had a special spiritual intercourse with the prophet Elijah, and his followers looked upon him as a saint who had the power to perform miracles. When he settled at Safed, the circle of his disciples (Moses Cordovero, Joseph Caro, Hayim Vital, etc.) widened and became a kind of congregation or rather monastic novitiate. They met every Friday and confessed their sins one to another. Isaac did not write anything except for a few poems, but his disciples circulated under his name about twenty works, mostly concerning mystical Judaism.

The modern rabbi—a preacher and a social worker, fully conversant with the lay culture of his own time—has little in common with the ancient type of rabbi, which still survives in the East and in some Hasidic circles of Poland and Rumania : the rabbi who has nothing in the world but the Talmud, who is ready to sacrifice himself for the Torah. (This ancient type, in its turn, is very different from a still more ancient type : the hellenized Pharisee or the cultivated Spanish rabbi of the Middle Ages.) But the disappearance of the " Carpathian " rabbinic type, the death of an old form of Judaism, has something pathetic and sad about it which the great neo-Hebrew poet Bialyk has beautifully expressed in his poem *Alone*. A young rabbinic student sits alone with his books : " I was left by myself, in utter loneliness, but the Shekinah[1] set upon my head her broken and trembling right wing. My own heart knew her heart : she was sore grieved for me, her only son." And yet, nevertheless, the student looks to the window ; the space beneath the wing of the Shekinah becomes too strait for him ; he feels a longing for the outside light and the open air. Then the Shekinah " leant her head against my shoulder, and her tears fell upon the open page of my Talmud ; she wept in silence because of me, she clung to me, she wanted to spread out her broken wing over me, saying : All have flown away, and I am left alone, alone. . . . It was a prayer of pleading and fear which I heard in that subdued sobbing, in these hot tears."

[1] The personified presence of God.

49

Herbert Loewe, speaking of the work of the Pharisees, has
said : " It should . . . be equated with the Patristic
literature."[1] What has gone before in this present work
should be considered as a plea for the Christian re-appreciation
of the " Jewish Fathers," and the pages which follow,
concerning the work of rabbis, will perhaps better explain and
justify that plea. We really think that a Christian may, in
some way, speak of the " Jewish Fathers " as he speaks of the
Church Fathers. He may, as a Christian, feel himself a son
and pupil of Hillel, meditate with Isaac Luria, pray with the
hymns of Juda-ha-Levy ; he may receive great help and
benefit from the rabbinic interpreters of the Old Testament.
St. Jerome did not hesitate to use the Jewish Haggadah
methods of *gematria* and *notarikon* in his Biblical exegesis.
He refers to the rabbinic tradition as " *arcanae eruditionis
Hebraicae et magistrorum synagogae recondita disciplina.*"[2] He
says : " *Haec ab eruditissimis gentis illius didicimus.*"[3] Reuchlin
found in the Jewish mystical tradition traces of divine
inspiration. Jerome and Reuchlin have not been widely
followed. It is time for the Christians to acknowledge the
treasures of learning and piety contained in the tradition of
the Jewish Fathers and to approach those men with respect
and affection, for, of many of them, we can truly say : " Saints
and sages they were, who served God faithfully and found in
the Torah His full and perfect word."[4]

SCRIPTURAL TRADITION

What is the debt of the Christian Church to the Scriptural
tradition of the rabbis ? What kind of interest may this
tradition offer us nowadays ?

In the first place, we should never forget that the Bible
(*i.e.*, the Old Testament) was handed to us by the rabbis.
We have received our Scripture from Israel. " The Bible
might not be the heritage of the world to-day if scrupulous
care had not been taken to guard its every letter and its every
particle."[5] Let us remember with gratitude the labours of the
innumerable Jewish scholars who, as far back as pre-Maccabean

---

[1] *Judaism and Christianity.*
[2] On *Zech*, VI, 9.
[3] Epistolae, lxxiii, 9 (i, 443).
[4] T. Herford, *Pharisaism*, p. 334. See special note M.
[5] E. Levine in *The Parting of the Roads. Studies in the Development of
Judaism and Early Christianity*, edited by F. J. Foakes Jackson, London, 1912,
p. 310.

times, dedicated themselves to the *Masorah*, the fixation of the Biblical text with critical notes.[1] Words, letters, dots, marginal readings—all this was religiously weighed and fixed by them. If we wish to get a just idea of the care with which the rabbis applied themselves to the text of the Bible, we must read the talmudic treatise *Soferim* (" Scribes ") ; it deals, in twenty-one chapters, with the rules relating to the preparation of the holy books and to their reading. It enters into such detail as the space between letters, the width and height of the scrolls, the capital and final letters, but it speaks also of the qualifications for preparing the books, of their respectful handling and of their sanctity : through such work we can enter into communion with the deep piety of Israel towards the Word of God.[2]

The rabbis fixed not only the text of the Bible, but also the order of reading the books throughout the year. It is only in recent times that Christian scholars have begun to see what new light this scriptural-liturgical calendar can throw on the New Testament problems.

P. Levertoff, in the New S.P.C.K. Commentary, advanced a theory of the connection between the teaching of Jesus and the Synagogue reading. He suggests that the " document Q " is a parallel to the Mosaic Deuteronomy and that the sequence of events and speeches in Matthew's Gospel corresponds chronologically with the Jewish liturgical seasons. Many of the problems connected with the Sermon on the Mount solve themselves when duly related to this liturgical factor : the Beatitudes, for instance, are a transposition of the " blessings " from the Law ; the parable of the builders on the rock corresponds to the *haphtarah* (prophetical lesson) from Ezekiel xiii, 1–14, which itself completes the *parashah* (Pentateuch lesson) from Deuteronomy xiii, 2–6. Many other instances could be quoted.

R. Finch[3] has considered the problem more generally. He thinks that the three-year cycle of readings from the Law and the prophets brings an important contribution to New Testament chronology, especially to the dating of the events and discourses of Jesus' life.

V. Burch has especially considered the Epistle to the Hebrews in connection with the liturgical scripture readings. The

---

[1] C. Ginsburg, *The Messorah*, London, 1880–85.
[2] See Müller, *Masseket Soferim, der Talmudische Traktat der Althebräischen Graphik, der Masorah, und der Altjüdischen Liturgie*, Vienna, 1878.
[3] *The Synagogue Lactionary and the New Testament*, London, 1939.

sources of the Epistle are to be found in the Synagogue lectionary. Isaiah ix is the prophetical lesson ; and Exodus xviii, 19 and 20, provide the readings from the Torah for the fourth Sabbath, according to the talmudic treatise *Shebath*. These lessons explain the contents and order of the Epistle. A very fruitful field of research is open in that direction. Burch writes : " We shall never get things straight in the first century, until we learn that the transmutative handling of the lectionary of the Synagogue by the revelation of Jesus Christ is one of the great creators of the New Testament writers and writings."[1]

The Christian theologians (we say " theologians," not only exegetes and orientalists) should turn to the *Targums* with special attention. Aramaic translations or rather paraphrases of the Bible, the Targums belong to the time of the Second Temple and the first centuries of the Christian era (Targums of Onkelos, of Jerusalem, of Jonathan ben Uzziel, etc.). A characteristic of the Targums is that they avoid everything that might savour of anthropomorphism or simply a direct communion between God and men. They constantly paraphrase, in order to attain this result. The *Memra* and the *Dibbura*, or " Word," and the Shekinah, or " Indwelling," seem to take up an intermediate position between God and man ; these words are used instead of the word " God " whenever the author wishes to avoid the idea of a direct relationship between God and man. From this fact it has generally been concluded that the Targums teach an extreme transcendentalism. " The thought of the divine working in the hearts of men directly seems to be almost entirely eliminated," says Oesterley.[2] But there is another side to the question. The Targums date from a time when the Alexandrine thought had introduced the conception of divine immanence even into Jewish circles. It was the classical time of the theology of " intermediaries " (angels, Logos, Wisdom, etc.). Does the multiplication of beings between God and man mean necessarily or exclusively, in the Targums, the distance and " otherness " of God ? Cannot it mean, perhaps, or also, the coming down of God to man, the closeness of their mutual link ? Whatever may have been the intention of the writers of the Targums, the notions of the Word, of the Indwelling or Presence of God among men, are not without analogies in certain

---

[1] *The Epistle to the Hebrews*, London, 1936.
[2] *A Short Survey of the Literature of Rabbinical and Mediæval Judaism*, p. 46.

Christian ideas. They might serve as many bridges which could open communications between Judaism and Christianity. Thus the Targums constitute a source and a witness of a particularly interesting phase of Judaism, when Jewish theology was not yet stereotyped and hardened and, being more plastic, could lend itself to many influences and interpretations. They are therefore extremely important for Christian theology.[1]

The Christian Church received from the Synagogue not only the text of the Bible, but also methods of interpretation. The four methods of exegesis recommended by Bahya ben Asher and the Zohar are perhaps inspired by the theory of the fourfold sense—literal, moral, allegorical, anagogical—formulated by the Venerable Bede in the eighth century and Rhabanus Maurus in the ninth ; but the general principles underlying these methods had been conceived and applied long before by the Jewish Fathers of Palestine and Alexandria. The four kinds of Jewish traditional exegesis distinguished : *peshat*, historical or literal sense ; *remez* and *derasch*, allegorical senses ; and *sod*, secret or mystical sense. The initial letters of these four words form the word *pardes*, " paradise, garden of pleasure," which designates the whole of the Jewish exegesis and of which the culminating point is the final *s* representing *sod*, the mystical sense. All this is more or less common to Jewish and Christian exegesis. But the rabbis evolved techniques of allegorical interpretation which are much more precise and complex than the Christian methods. One of them is the *gematria*, a cipher method which enables one to interpret the meaning behind some number. This was well known to the writers of the New Testament : the number of the Beast (Rev. xiii. 18) is clearly a case of *gematria*. The quest for numerical cryptographs in the Old Testament is not a mere fancy. Genesis xiv. 14 mention the 318 " trained men " of Abraham ; now 318 is the numerical equivalent of Eliezer, a servant of Abraham mentioned in Genesis xv. 2 ; it seems difficult to admit that this should be a pure coincidence, and therefore the rabbis applied Genesis xiv. 14 to Eliezer. In Deuteronomy xxxii. 1–6, the initial letters of these six verses give the number 345, which is the value of the name of Moses ;

[1] See Maybaum, *Die Anthropomorphein bei Onkelos und den späteren Targumim*, 1870 ; Ginsburger, *Die Anthropomorphismen in den Targumim*, Braunschweig, 1891. Etheridge has published an English translation of the Targums to the Pentateuch (1865). In the rabbinical Bibles, the Targums are printed by the side of the Hebrew text.

E 2

in manuscripts, the first letter of verse 6 has an abnormal form calling the reader's attention to the acrostic. Many instances of *gematria* could be found in the Old Testament. Eliezer ben Jose (*c.* 200) formulated thirty-two rules of gematric exegesis. They imply some highly complicated notions : cyclical, square, cubic, decadic, quaternion, involution and integration values of words, permutations of letters, etc.[1] Another method is the *notarikon*, a technique of abbreviation obtained by writing the initials of words. Jerome knew and used these methods. We suggest that, if the attention of the Christian exegetes were turned again to them, this attempt would not be fruitless for our understanding of the Old Testament and, more generally, of Hebrew religious thought.

Rabbinical exegesis is often the key to the exegesis of St. Paul. Only the dependence of Paul on the Haggadah can explain the view that the Law was given not by God Himself, but by the angels (Gal. iii. 19), or the mention of the number 430 (Gal. iii. 17), or the story of the rock which followed the Israelites and gave them water in the wilderness (1 Cor. x. 4).

The exegesis of the Jewish Fathers was predominantly allegorical and mystical. Everything is represented as being at once this thing and the covering of another thing. Every outward meaning veils an inward meaning. It is the sacramental method applied to the sacred text. For this reason, many will consider the old rabbinical hermeneutics as valueless. On the contrary others will appreciate in them a true and deep spiritual intuition, an inestimable gift, and a still living source of inspiration to Christians themselves. Deissmann, speaking of Paul, says : " The Jewish habit of allegorizing, which has so often lent crutches to the small masters of theology, here gives a religious genius wings to soar aloft like an eagle."[2] And the modern voices are found to declare that spiritual exegesis " requires more consideration than it has recently received," and that we feel " the need for a fresh treatment of mystical interpretation which shall distinguish between its arbitrary and its rational use."[3] The study of ancient Jewish

[1] See the article *Gematria* by Caspar Levias in vol. V of the *Jewish Encycl.*, and the article *Number* by Ed. Konig in Hasting's *Dictionary of the Bible*, vol. III.

[2] *St. Paul*, p. 106.

[3] C. Harris in a note appended to Darwell Stone's note on " The Mystical Interpretation of the New Testament," *New Commentary* by Gore, Goudge and Guillaume, 1928, p. 687.

hermeneutics may powerfully contribute to such a spiritual revival in exegesis.[1]

If we are patient enough to assimilate and overcome the subtleties of the rabbis, we shall be rewarded by the perception of some deep beauties. A few instances may illustrate this assertion.

Here is Rabbi Jose ben Hanina in his allegorical interpretation of the narrative of Jacob's arrival in Haran (Gen. xxix. 4f.). It was : " The shepherds say : We are from Haran. It means : We flee from the wrath (*haron*) of God. Jacob says : Do you know Laban ? It means : Do you know him who will make your sins white (*labben*) as snow (Is. i. 18) ? Jacob says : Is it well with him (*shalom*) ? The shepherds answer : It is well. Jacob says : By whose merit ? The shepherds say : Behold, Rachel comes with the sheep."[2] The Rabbi alludes here at the same time to the successful propitiation of Rachel, who " weeps for her children " (Jer. xxxi. 14), and to the name of Rachel (*rahel*, ewe). This word *rahel* is used by Isaiah (liii. 7), speaking of the " sheep dumb before the shearers."

One of the writers of the Mishna meets in the Bible the expression " bundle of myrrh." Myrrh or camphor is expressed by the Hebrew word *kofer*. But *kofer* means also ransom or atonement. Hence our writer says : " This refers to Isaac who was tied up like a bundle upon the altar. . . . He is *kofer* because he atones for the sins of Israel."[3]

In one of the rabbinical commentaries[4] the words of Boas to Ruth (Ruth ii. 14) are referred to the Messiah. " Approach to this place " refers to the Kingdom. " Eat from the bread " refers to the bread of the Kingdom. " And dip thy bread in vinegar " refers to the sufferings of the Messiah. Here the Rabbis quote Isaiah liii. 5 : " And He was pierced for our sins." Thus the bread of the Messianic Kingdom must be eaten with the vinegar of the Messiah's pangs.

Such passages as the three we have just mentioned are deeply interesting—nay, moving—to the Christian. Could we not say of them : *spirant crucem* ?

Another question presents a special interest to the Christian : the question of the parallels between the rabbinical teaching—

---

[1] On Jewish exegesis in general, see I. Abrahams, *Jewish Interpretation of the Old Testament*, in the symposium *The People and the Book*, edited by A. Peake, Oxford, 1925 ; and S. Rosenblatt, *The Interpretation of the Bible in the Mishnah*, Baltimore, 1935.

[2] Gen. R. 70 (151b). Quoted in Dalman's *Jesus-Jeshua*, p. 195.

[3] Quoted in Montefiore and Loewe, *A Rabbinic Anthology*, p. 220.

[4] *ibid.*, p. 206.

which is always a kind of marginal annotation to the Old
Testament—and the Gospels, or, in other terms, the question
of the rabbinic sources of the Gospels. Much has been written
on this subject, which is the particular purpose of Strack and
Billerbeck's Commentary on the Gospels as well as Dalman's
Jesus-Jeshua. The question of these parallels in general has
been excellently treated, from the Jewish point of view, by
C. Montefiore in the introduction to his *Synoptic Gospels*. We
shall not insist on the innumerable rabbinic elements of the
Gospels ; we shall rather, as an illustration, give (though not
textually) two rabbinic parables which belong to the Scriptural
tradition, since they are *midrashim* on books of the Bible, and
may have some connexion with two Gospel parables.[1]

The Lost Sheep. When Moses fed the sheep of Jethro in the
wilderness a kid went astray. Moses went after it and found
it drinking at a spring. As the kid was weary, Moses laid it
on his shoulder and brought it back. God then told Moses
that, because of his compassion for the sheep of a man, he
would give him Israel, His beloved sheep, to feed.[2]

The Prodigal Son. A king sent a tutor after his son who
had left home with this message : " My son, come back ! "
The son replied : " I am ashamed ! With what face can I
return ? " The father sent another message : " Can a son be
ashamed to return to his father ? Thou shalt come back."
So God has sent Jeremiah after Israel, with the call to return
from their sin to their Father.[3]

The spirit and methods of modern exegesis, already present
in Maimonides and Spinoza, become predominant in Judaism
with Moses Mendelssohn, who not only translated the
Pentateuch into German (1773), but wrote commentaries in
which he endeavours to restore *Peshat*, the natural and
historical meaning, to its rights. For this reason his collabor-
ators and disciples (Dubno, Wessely, Iaroslav, Homberg)
were called " biurists," from the Hebrew *biur*, " exposition."
Among the Jewish exegetes of the last and present centuries,
one can find radicals and conservatives. The Hebrew
commentary on Genesis published (1903) in Russia by Abraham

---

[1] Midrash on the Book of Ruth, 15a.
[2] On the subject of the rabbinic and Gospel parables, see Fiebig, *Die
Gleichnissreden Jesu im Lichte der rabbinischen Gleichnisse des neutestament-
lichen Zeitalters*, 1912 ; Rabbi Asher Feldmann, *The Parables and Similes
of the Rabbis, Agricultural and Pastoral*, Cambridge, 1924 ; W. Oesterley, *The
Gospel Parables in the Light of their Jewish Background*, London, 1936.
[3] *Shemoth Rabba*, midrash on Exodus iii. 1.
[4] *Debharim Rabba*, midrash on Deuteronomy iii. 25.

Cahana is frankly " critical," as well as Geiger's *Urschrift*, while the commentary on Leviticus published (1905) in Germany by David Hoffmann, is rather conservative. Segal (on Samuel) and Hoschander (on Esther) occupy an intermediate position. S. Schechter was afraid that " higher criticism " might sometimes express a " higher anti-Semitism."

There is a revival of essential Old Testament thought among the Jewish younger generation. It began, perhaps, in England, with Montefiore's *Bible for Home Reading*. In Germany and Austria it has somewhat caught fire with the appearance of the combined work of Martin Buber and Franz Rosenzweig : their German translation of the Hebrew Bible (1925). With this work something new became manifest in modern Judaism : an endeavour to listen to God speaking in the Scriptures. " Must we not bow in awe before the Word of God ? " asked Rosenzweig in a pamphlet, in accents which remind us of Barth.

But why speak of Barth ? It is rather a return to the love of the Jewish Fathers for the Scripture. When Rabbi Hanina ben Teradyon was burned, wrapped in the scrolls of the Law during Hadrian's persecution, he was only expressing, by this utter self-surrender to " the Book," the heroic and constant devotion of Israel to the Word of God. Is this not a fidelity in which we can experience a full communion with Israel ?

LEGAL OR TALMUDIC TRADITION

The greatest part of rabbinic tradition is expressed in the talmudic literature, *i.e.*, in the text of the Talmud itself, the work of generations and centuries, or in the commentaries (*e.g.*, Rashi) on this text. For a long time Christian scholars have recognized in the Talmud[1] one of the highest products of the religious culture of mankind, but such an acknowledgement has still to overcome much ignorance and prejudice in the general—even the enlightened—Christian public. From the Middle Ages to our days, the Talmud has been the bogey of anti-Semitism. Even philo-Semites may show a strange ignorance in speaking of the Talmud. In his book *Where now, Little Jew ?*[2], the Swedish writer, Magnus Hermansson, himself a Christian, moved by compassion for the tragic fate of Jewry, advocates entire assimilation and exhorts the Jews to " give up the Talmud, their diabolical hatred of Jesus Christ "[3] and their arrogance, fed by Talmud study. To tell

[1] See A. Lukyn Williams, *Talmudic Judaism and Christianity*, London, 1933.
[2] Translated by G. Djurklou and M. Weisman, New York, 1938.
[3] p. 230.

the truth, the greater part of modern Jewry no longer knows anything about the Talmud or cares for it. But it is to be wished that they were able to read it intelligently and to draw from it still a religious inspiration. If world Jewry were more conversant with the Talmud, its moral tone would be considerably higher. In any case, no Christian wishing to approach the Jews on religious ground can dispense with some knowledge of the Talmud and some genuine sympathy for many parts of it.

As these pages are not intended for scholars, it may perhaps be useful to remind the reader of—or to introduce him to—the contents of the Talmud. Such mystery still enshrouds this section of Jewish literature that very few people, among non-specialists, have any exact notions when speaking of the Talmud.[1]

The word *Talmud* (" teaching ") does not designate a book, but a *corpus*, or, still better, a kind of library. In this library we shall distinguish two collections which both bear the name of Talmud : the Palestinian Talmud, or Talmud of Jerusalem, and the Babylonian Talmud. We have already described the process of their formation.[2]

The two Talmuds have essentially the same composition. They juxtapose three elements: (1) a fundamental text or *Mishnah*; (2) a commentary on that text, the *Gemara*; (3) some additional elements.

Mishnah. This term means " learning by (oral) repetition." It is supposed to be an interpretation of the Scripture. The text of the Mishnah is arrayed in six " orders " (*sedarim*) ; each order is divided into tractates, each tractate into chapters, each chapter into paragraphs. We have thus six orders containing sixty-three tractates as follows :—(i) " Seeds ": eleven tractates on blessings, agricultural laws, tithes, first-fruits. (ii) " Festivals ": twelve tractates on Sabbath, Passover, Temple-taxes, Day of Atonement, Tabernacles, New Year, Fasting, Purim (feast in remembrance of Esther), minor feasts, pilgrimages. (iii) " Women ": seven tractates on

---

[1] Besides *A Short Survey of the Literature of Rabbinical and Mediæval Judaism* (Chap. III) by Oesterley and Box, already mentioned, see Chaps. I and III of the *Short Story of Jewish Literature* by I. Abrahams, London, 1906, and *Einleitung in den Talmud* by H. Strack, Leipzig, 1908. *A History of the Talmud* constitutes the introductory volume of the translation of Rodkinson, New York, 1896. See also T. Herford, *Talmud and Apocrypha*, London, 1933.

[2] H. Danby, *The Mishnah translated from the Hebrew with Introduction and brief explanatory notes*, Oxford, 1933 ; W. H. Loewe, *The Mishnah on which the Palestinian Talmud rests, edited from the unique Manuscript preserved in the University Library of Cambridge*, 1883.

Levirate marriage, marriage-settlements, vows, Nazirites, adultery, divorce and betrothals. (iv) " Damages " : ten tractates on damages, property, trusts, usury (prohibited), law-courts, punishments, oaths, idolatry, maxims of the Fathers, legal decisions. (v) " Holy Things " : eleven tractates on sacrifices, meals, slaughter of animals, first-born, persons; and things dedicated to the Temple, excommunications, sacrileges, burnt-offerings, dove-offerings. (vi) "Purifications": twelve tractates on sacred furniture, Levitical uncleanness, leprosy, the red heifer, baths, menstruations, other defilements.

Gemara. This word is the Aramaic for "learning." According to another etymology, it means "perfectioning." The Gemara is a running commentary on the text of the Mishnah. It has the character of an amplification. Most times it is identified with the two first of the additional elements in such a way that one can hardly separate them.

Additional Elements. They are : (*a*) The *tosephtah* ("supplement"), a kind of parallel to the Mishnah proper, and covering the same ground, often illustrating it with anecdotes ; (*b*) the *baraithas* ("externals"), traditions not incorporated in the Mishnah and perhaps having the same relation to it as the apocryphal books to the canonical Scriptures ; (*c*) the " minor tractates," of which there are seven in the Babylonian Talmud and seven others in the Palestinian Talmud, the chief of these books being the *Aboth de Rabbi Nathan.*[1]

As the words *midrash, halakah, haggadah,* are frequently met in connexion with talmudic literature, it may be useful to give their exact meaning. *Midrash*=investigation, inquiry. A *midrash* designates a non-literal interpretation of the Scripture. There is a vast midrashic literature of which the oral origins date from the Old Testament times and which is broadly divided into two classes : *midrash halakah* (hal=binding

---

[1] The *editio princeps* of the Babylonian Talmud was published in Vienna, 1520–1523 : the *editio princeps* of the Jerusalem Talmud in Venice, 1523. The Jitomir edition of the Jerusalem Talmud, 1860–1867, is one of the best. Complete translations of the Talmud are rather rare. See M. Schwab, *Le Talmud de Jerusalem traduit pour la première fois,* 11 vols., Paris, 1878–1889 ; a new English translation of the Babylonian Talmud (abridged) has been made by M. Rodkinson and edited by a " New Talmud Publishing Company," 16 vols., New York, 1896–1903. There are many excellent translations of isolated tractates of the Talmud, e.g., in English *A Translation of the Treatise Chagigah from the Babylonian Talmud with Introduction, Notes, Glossary and Indices* by A. Streane, Cambridge, 1891, and the already mentioned translations of the *Sayings of the Fathers ;* and, among recent works, *The Babylonian Talmud (Seder Nezikim and Seder Nastuim),* translated into English with notes, glossary and indices under the editorship of Rabbi Dr. I. Epstein, London, 1935–1936.

law), or legal rules of practice, and *midrash haggadah* (hag= telling), homiletic and anecdotic explanation. Much midrashic material may be found in the Talmud, but there is an independent midrashic literature : *e.g.*, the tractates *Mekilta Sifre*, to Numbers, *Pesikta, Pirke de Rabbi Eliezer, Midrash ha Gadol*, etc. Midrashic books were still written in the 6th century A.D.[1]

These data may seem rather complicated, but, in reality, they are grossly simplified here.

We should now consider a few questions : Is the Talmud anti-Christian ? Is the talmudic literature the expression of a mere narrow legalism ? Has the Talmud any permanent value ?

The charge of being " blasphemous " has been brought forward against the Talmud by erstwhile Jews like Geronimo de Santa Fe (15th century) and Pfefferkorn (16th century). The Talmud has been burned many times under that charge, even as late as in 1757 (in Poland). Nevertheless all passages which could appear derogatory to Christianity were expunged in 1264, under Pope Clement IV, and, between 1546 and 1581, by the censors of the Venice and Basel editions ; the Venice edition was personally revised by the Inquisitor Marco Marino, who affixed his name to every page. Many talmudic references to ancient idolatry were misinterpreted as attacks on Christianity.[2] Reuchlin and modern scholars have seen justice done on these baseless attacks against the Talmud.

Now is the Talmud, as Christians too often think, a wearisome collection of formal rules ? This question affords us a good opportunity of making our minds clear about the meaning of the " Law " for the Jews.

It would be a mistake to consider that Paul's argument on the failure of the " Law " gives an exact representation of what is to be understood by the word " Torah." The Greek word *nomos*, " law," always used by Paul and so loaded with juridical meaning, is no equivalent of *torah*. The term *torah* is less precise and more dynamic than *nomos*. It means " instruction " and also " direction." For the Jews the Torah was very different from a legal code. It was the revelation and coming down of God to man, the communion

---

[1] Weber, *Jüdische Theologie . . .*, pp. xxiv–xxx, 1897 ; Hoffmann, *Zur Einleitung in der Halachischen Midraschim* (1886).
[2] See *Jesus Christ in the Talmud, Midrash, Zohar, and the Liturgy of the Synagogue*, texts and translations by G .Dalman, together with an introductory essay by H. Laible, translated and edited by A. Streane, Cambridge, 1893.

of God with man, the very expression of God's nature. Only in that light can we understand the rabbis when they say that all the world is not equivalent to a single word of the Torah and that God looked upon the Torah when He created the world. They said also that God Himself studies the Torah every day ; this may sound sheer extravagance to non-Jewish ears, but it will appear a powerful symbol if we grasp the fact that the Torah is the very communication of the mind and heart of God, of His essential truth and power, goodness and love. The Jewish attachment to the Law does not imply a slavish obedience to a written rule. One should rather, with Parkes, speak of the Torah as an " Incarnation " of the Divine. Travers Herford, with whom Montefiore fully agrees on this point, writes : " It is near the truth to say that what Christ is to the Christian, Torah is to the Jew."[1] And Israel Abrahams : " Those who tell the Jew that he has nothing to love with the passion which a Christian feels for Jesus forget Israel's passion for the Law."[2] " An only daughter was Mine, and I gave her unto you," says God to Israel (in the Talmud), speaking of the Torah.[3]

If we understand this Jewish attitude to the Torah, we begin to see that the Talmud is not a petrified legalism. Every precept has a deep spiritual significance. Let us take, for instance, the dietary laws. Do they merely reflect a narrow superstition ? No, they foster a spirit of self-surrender, a continuous restriction placed on the appetites for the sake of duty ; they are part of the price to be paid for the privilege of belonging to Israel. If a Christian pours scorn on the dietary laws, what about Christian fasting and asceticism ?

But is not the Talmud full of casuistry and hair-splitting ? It is true that there is a very special talmudic dialectic, which is worth serious attention ;[4] it is also true that there is a Christian casuistry not less complicated than the Jewish,[5] and besides, casuistry (which means the application of the law to individual cases) is not necessarily an evil thing. We should keep in mind, too, the remarks of Montefiore and Loewe in the introduction to their *Rabbinic Anthology*. They suppose, between an ancient rabbi and a modern reader, a conversation which may be summarized like this : " Listen, rabbi, you said

[1] *Pharisaism*, p. 171.
[2] *Some Permanent Values in Judaism*, Oxford, 1924, p. 73.
[3] *Op. cit.*, p. 83.
[4] See special note H.
[5] H. F. Stewart has written a comparative study of Jewish and Jesuit casuistry, *Judaism and Christianity*, vol. II, pp. 299–331.

such and such a thing.—Oh, did I ? Well, if you say so . . .—
But now you say opposite things !—Well, I have forgotten.
Moreover, it was so long ago. And, you know, there are many
things we said just because we loved to argue. If one said A,
the other said B. You must not take it too seriously. We
never thought of it in that way. . . ." Of course, this should
be taken *cum grano salis.* In everything which the rabbis
said there was some definite intention ; they never totally
disbelieved their assertion of the moment ; nevertheless one
should not read into each one of their sayings a very deliberate
and constant conviction. Rabbinic discussions had something
lighter and more supple than the disputations of the Scholastics
or of the Puritans.

There are contradictions in the Talmud ? Yes, but " the
very incoherence of the Talmud, its confusion of voices, is an
index of free thinking," as said Israel Zangwill.[1]

What is the permanent value of the Talmud ? The Talmud
aims at the penetration of the whole of human life by God's
presence. It does not confine worship to the hours of prayer,
but sanctifies the home and its daily round of duties. So wide
is its range that arts and sciences, agriculture and cooking,
medicine and worship, jurisprudence and building are equally
inspired by its spirit, which is the hallowing of life. This
universality of the Talmud, this interconnexion of religion and
every phase of life, saves the talmudic student from stagnation
and keeps him fresh-minded ; the intelligent reading of the
Talmud gives a perpetual contact with actualities and constitutes a liberal education in many disciplines. Far from being
final and crystallized like a code, it reflects the continuity, the
manifold steps, the progress and freedom of an organic evolution. Is it great literature ? It is certainly lacking in artistic
form—though often intensely poetical ; but, as surely as the
Homeric poems and Greek tragedy, it is the unique expression
of a people and a culture. It bears the mark of a supreme
originality, for that people and that culture are above all
theocratic. It expresses all the dreams and hopes, all the
pangs and joys of Israel. As such it is not only a masterpiece
of Jewish literature, but one of the summits in the history of
the human mind.

Reformed Judaism does not give to talmudic literature the
same place as does orthodox Judaism. Montefiore has explained
how Reformed Judaism puts prophecy higher than Law. The
Liberal Jew cannot regard the Law as the centre of Jewish

[1] *Chosen Peoples*, p. 24.

belief and practice. If he were founding a new public worship, he would not make the reading of the Law its most important feature. If he were building a synagogue, he would not put scrolls of the Law into an ark; he would put in it the prophecies of Amos, Hosea and Isaiah, for the Prophets are more essential than the Torah. This does not mean that Liberal Judaism has rejected the talmudic tradition. In fact, as it has adapted the ancient worship and not founded a new one, it keeps the scrolls of the Law in the ark. The Liberal Jews have rebelled against a slavish acceptance of the Talmud's authority, but they retain respect and affection for its spirit.

Frug,[1] in his fine and pathetic Yiddish poem on the Talmud, compares its old leaves, yellow, spotted and worn, to a disused cemetery. But the Talmud "is not, never was, a cemetery; it was, it is, a moving sea on which sail the ships of living men."[2]

The Basel editor of the 16th century said (and his words then implied that he had courage as well as a fine spiritual perception) that the Talmud may be read by Christians not only without reproach, but even with profit—*etiam cum fructu a nobis legi potest*.

MYSTICAL TRADITION

The view that Jewish mystical literature is an authentic part of the tradition of the Jewish Fathers has won acceptance since a relatively short time ago. Several factors stood strongly against that view. It was a prevailing opinion that Judaism and mysticism were a glaring contradiction in terms; the exclusively transcendent character of the Jewish God was a kind of unquestioned assumption; the Jew could not have an inward experience of God similar to the Christian one. Another erroneous assumption was the stamping of Judaism as unrelieved legalism. Most people saw in the Jewish God a mere lawgiver and in Jewish piety an outward mechanical routine. Then many Jewish writers themselves, chiefly the historian, H. Graetz (+1891), categorically asserted that Jewish mysticism was an exotic and, in reality, un-Jewish importation. Whether congenitally or by mental training, these scholars had no sympathy with religious emotion. Lastly, the mystical movement which arose under the name of " Hasidism " among the Jews of Poland in the 18th century took up a position against rabbinical Judaism, and this fact falsely

---

[1] Jewish Russian poet who wrote at the end of the last century.
[2] Abrahams, p. 83.

led to the belief that, since the very beginning, the legal and mystical traditions in Judaism had been agnostic. But none of these assumptions holds good in the light of modern scholarship.[1]

Jewish mysticism is as old as the Old Testament. The mystical current flowed uninterrupted from the Bible into the rabbinical era. Jewish mysticism can be traced to a very early date : let us remember the *Hasidim* (" pious ones ") of the pre-Maccabean age, the Essenes and the Therapeuts (of these last Philo wrote that, if they did not offer animal sacrifices like the priests, they were anxious to keep their minds " in a priestly state of holiness "), the treatise of Philo himself on contemplative life, and some little groups of esoteric teachers mentioned by the early rabbis, like the *Hashaim*, who kept silence and secrecy, the *Vatikin*, " men of firm principles," who insisted on the prayerful mood, the *Zenuim*, " lowly ones," who loved modesty and purity and claimed to know the secrets of the alphabet letters.

It seems that the first chapter of Ezekiel played a determinant part in the origins of Jewish mystical speculation. The *Merkabah*, or chariot on which Yaweh rides, became the symbol of the mystic way and the instrument by which one may be carried into the heavenly " halls." To be a " Merkabah-rider " became the hope of the elect, and a " science of the Merkabah " developed : a high moral level was the indispensable condition of this recondite knowledge ; fire consumed a certain young man, while he busied himself with the Merkabah lore, because this youth had not yet attained the necessary maturity.[2] Fire is always mentioned in connexion with the chariot, for it symbolizes the brightness of the illumination which comes to man as well as the red-hot state of the soul held in the grip of God. Rabbi Akiba, hearing that fire played round about Ben Azzai while this man explained the Law, asked him whether he was then engaged in unravelling the secret chambers of the Merkabah.[3] Rabbi Eliezer ben Arach was once expounding the mysteries of the Merkabah when fire came down from heaven and encompassed the trees of the field, which burst into the song of Psalm cxlviii, 9 : " Fruitful trees and all cedars, praise ye the Lord," and then an angel cried out from the fire : " Truly these are the secrets of the Merkabah "[4] Certain early Jewish

---

[1] See J. Abelson, *Jewish Mysticism*, London, 1913.
[2] *Talmud Babyl., Haggigah* 13a.
[3] *Midrash Rabba* on *Canticles*, i, 12.
[4] *T. B. Haggigah* 14b.

mystics seem to have been able to enter a state—auto-hypnosis or divine ecstasy?—in which they declared that they saw heaven and its mysteries open before them ; this was called Ascension or Merkabah-ride.

Hellenistic Judaism, as distinguished from the Palestinian, had its own mystical elements : the *logos*, and the *logoi* or angels (they were, too, words of God), *Metatron*, the Wisdom, etc. These notions possess a great doctrinal importance and, as such, will be dealt with later on. But they are also important from the mystical point of view, for through these agencies the human soul could attain union with God.

There was also a story of Shekinah mysticism. It is not yet time to indicate the capital importance of the idea of the Shekinah (=divine indwelling, Presence) in the comparative theology of Judaism and Christianity. This idea is probably the shortest and best established bridge between the two faiths. But, keeping to the strictly mystical standpoint, the Shekinah appears as a door flung wide open to every man, the condescension of God continually offered to His creatures. On His own initiative and uninvited, God, in the Shekinah, seeks union with us.

The oldest mystical work in the Hebrew language is the book *Yetsirah* (" creation "). It probably dates from the sixth century A.D.[1] The question of authorship had better be left open. In this work, the letters of the Hebrew alphabet are pressed into the service of cosmogony. The Hebrew letters *aleph* (h), *mem* (m), and *shin* (s), which may be considered as the " mothers " of the other letters because they represent the aspirates, the mutes and the sibilants, correspond to the three primal substances : water, fire, and air. *Aleph* symbolizes the air because this aspirate *h* has an airy and empty pronunciation. *Mem* symbolizes water because fish, the chief product of water, represent the mute creation just as *m* represents the mute letters. *Shin* symbolizes fire, because both fire and the sibilant *s* or *sh* have a hissing sound. The correspondence between letters and elements suggests that God has founded the world upon the Hebrew letters, and this is quite natural, for with these Hebrew letters His holy Name is written. The seven " double " letters express the " contraries " in the cosmos (seven days and seven nights, etc.). The twelve " simple " letters are emblematic of the twelve

[1] Reitzenstein, in his *Poimandres*, suggests that *Yetsirah* is a Hebrew production of the second century B.C., influenced by Gnosticism. But certain elements of thought found in the book belong to many centuries later.

signs of the Zodiac, the twelve months of the year, etc. Thus the cosmos is ideally embraced in the twenty-two Hebrew letters, which reflect the mind of God.

We find here—for the first time in Jewish thought—the idea of emanation : all things are conceived as outflowings of God ; they are radiations from the One to Whom they will finally return. It is true that the correspondences between letters and elements could be explained by exemplarism and not necessarily by emanationism, but the doctrine of the ten *Sephiroth*, developed in the same book, confirms the emanationist interpretation. The idea of the *Sephiroth* originated with the Talmud, which says :[1] " Ten agencies through which God created the world : wisdom, insight, cognition, strength, power, inexorableness, justice, right, love, mercy." *Yetsirah* enumerates the *Sephiroth* in the following way : the number. *one*, which is the spirit of the living God ; the number *two*, which is the air coming from the spirit)*ruah* means both spirit and wind) ; the number *three*, which is water coming (as vapour) from the air ; the number *four*, which is fire, the substance of God's glory, throne and angels ; and then north, south, east, west, height and depth.

We have spoken of emanation ; but we must be careful not to give to this word the pantheistic meaning it has in neo-platonic philosophy. In the book *Yetsirah*, emanation is not a communication of, and sharing in, God's substance ; it is a derivation from the unit, *one*. The *Sephiroth*[2] are the categories or moulds of the universe ; they are the prime cause of form as the twenty-two letters are the prime cause of matter. Now *Yetsirah* is more than a theoretical cosmogony. It is a deeply mystical book, giving the impulse to an intimate union of man with that God Who, though He remain transcendent and not identical with the universe, unfolds Himself in all the essences derived from Him. The speculations about letters and numbers may seem strange to us ; but, underlying them, is the question of relationship between God and the world, the most poetical question of God's otherness and nearness ; and the *Yetsirah* answers this question in a not unworthy manner.

Isaac ben Abraham of Posquières, a French rabbi of the 12th and 13th centuries, has been called the father of the

---

[1] *T.B. Haggigah*, 12a.
[2] The etymology of the word is dubious : it may mean " lights," or " spheres," or " numbers."

Cabbala.[1] He wrote a mystical dialogue called *Bahir* (" Brightness "). But the text-book of the Cabbala and generally of the whole of Jewish mysticism has been the *Zohar* (" Shining "), which belongs to the 14th century ; its author (or authors) remain unknown.

Like the Talmud, the Zohar is an unsystematic medley of ideas and facts, truth and fiction, covering a development of many centuries. Some foreign elements (from neo-platonism, gnosticism, even perhaps Persian Sufism) have found entrance into it. But it proceeds mainly from the *midrashim* and Talmud. The *Zohar* claims to be a commentary on the Pentateuch. However, it neglects the " garments " and the " body " of the Law in order to reach the " soul," *i.e.* the mystical sense.

We shall try to summarize some of the Zohar's main ideas—

(*a*) The term *En-Sof* (literally " no end ") is applied to God, in order to emphasize His boundlessness and endlessness.

(*b*) The world, material expression of God's immanent activity, is made up of four worlds or component parts, which are :

i. the world of *Azilut* (emanation), domain of the *Sephiroth* ;

ii. the world of *Beriah* (creative ideas), where are the Divine Throne and also the souls of the pious ;

iii. the world of *Yetsirah* (creative formations), place of the heavenly halls (*hekalot*) guarded by angels, and where the souls of ordinary men gain admission ;

iv. the world of *Asiyah* (creative matter), where the *Ophanim,* or lower angels, minister.

One has already noticed that the position of man, in this gradation, is far superior to that of the angels.

(*c*) Evil, sin and the demons are only the coverings or wrappings (*kelifoth*) of all existing things. They are only imperfect external aspects of creation. Evil is a mere state of absence, symbolized by the primeval chaos, void and formless, of which Genesis speaks.

(*d*) The process of creation is a process of " contraction " (*tsimtsum*) of the Divine. This contraction or limitation of the

[1] The origin of the word *Cabbala* is the Hebrew verb for " to receive." *Cabbala* means " received lore," " tradition." On Cabbala, see A. Waite, *The Doctrine and Literature of the Kabbalah*, London, 1902, and S. Hirsch, *The Cabbalists*, 1922. G. Scholem's *Bibliographia Kabbalistica* (Leipzig, 1927) gives an annotated list of all available material. A publication of *Quellen und Forschungen zur Geschichte der Jud. Mystikhad* begun in Leipzig, the first work edited being *Bahir.*

Infinite makes possible the production of the finite world of phenomena.

(e) In order to descend towards us, God uses as a chariot the " Heavenly Man " (*Adam Ilaa*), also called the " original Man " (*Adam Kadmon*) and the " terrestrial Presence " (*Shekina Tataa*). This first man was pre-existent, and through him was the earthly man created. Thus God has created man in His own image. The mystery of the Heavenly Man is the very heart of creation : " For, inside man, there is the secret of the Heavenly Man."[1]

(f) The ten Sefirot are Names of God, at the same time, a copy of God's activity. They are :—

i. The Crown, first emanation of the transcendent *En-Sof*, thought of God, in which everything was originally embraced ;

ii. Wisdom ;

iii. Intelligence ;

iv. Reason.

We must stop here to consider a capital feature of the Zohar mysticism, namely, the trinitary principle and even the metaphysical application of the idea of sexual relationship. The Crown stands alone ; but Wisdom, Intelligence and Reason constitute a triad. Wisdom is the " father," the active, masculine and engendering principle. Intelligence is the " mother," the passive, feminine and receptive principle. Reason is the " son," their offspring. Wisdom represents " knowledge," Intelligence " the knower," Reason " that which is known." The remaining Sefirot also fall into triads.

v. Mercy ;

vi. Justice ;

vii. Beauty.

Mercy and Justice form a dyad which rules the universe and corresponds to a rhythm of expansion and contraction of God's will. Mercy (and not Justice) is the active masculine principle. Before being just, God is life-giving and ever-forgiving. Justice is not an impetus like Mercy ; it is a passive and immanent, and therefore feminine, principle, whose passivity necessarily opposes and somewhat holds back the outflowing of Mercy. The product of the union of Mercy and Justice is Beauty, *i.e.* the moral order of the universe. The first triad is rather an interpretation of its metaphysical order.

viii. Victory ;

ix. Glory ;

x. Foundation.

[1] *Zohar*, ii, 76a.

This third triad explains the physical order of the universe, its dynamic aspect and ceaseless changes. The idea of Victory is associated with the idea of force and army ; this self-realization of force constitutes the active, masculine principle. Glory, as the passive radiance of Victory, constitutes the feminine principle. In their union is implied all the reproductive power of nature, and from it results Foundation, *i.e.* the building up of the world.

We finally come to Royalty, which—like the Crown—stands outside the triads and indicates the sum and harmony of the Sefirot. In the classical expositions, Royalty is called the tenth of the Sefirot ; then Reason (the fourth of the Sefirot on our own list) is not counted with an independent number though maintained as the son of Wisdom and Intelligence; and Mercy becomes the fourth of the Sefirot. We have risked a modification of the traditional numeration, on this point, in order to make clearer the succession and meaning of the three triads. It is rather difficult to understand why Reason is not independently counted ; the explanation seems to lie in the idea of Wisdom and Intelligence forming a triad with the Crown ; but, in this case, the very notion of the triads of Sefirot is altered, as, instead of a male and a female principle uniting to produce a son, we have an original principle producing two parallel emanations. Moreover, the function of Royalty is not very apparent and its inclusion in the Sefirot may be due to the desire of artificially making up the number ten.[1]

(g) The Zohar expounds an elaborate theology of the soul. Individual souls are fragments of an " oversoul " of the universe. The soul is a trinity comprising : the vital element (*nefesh*), which emanates from Foundation ; the moral element (*ruah*), which emanates from Beauty ; the rational element (*neshamah*), which emanates from Wisdom. A heavenly pattern or image of our soul was pre-existent. The idea of a transmigration of souls, before their ultimate return to God, seems to be admitted. The soul cannot, on this earth, enter into the presence of God without the ecstatic emotion of love, which is a divine kiss. Whosoever serves God out of love and really prays to Him reaches union with Him—*itdabak*.

We must not forget that the Zohar is not a systematic

---

[1] The Hebrew names of the Sefirot are : *Keter* (crown), *hokmah* (wisdom), *binah* (intelligence), *daat* (reason), *hesed* (mercy), *din* (justice), *tifereth* (beauty), *nezah* (victory), *hod* (glory), *yesod* (foundation), *malkut* (royalty). Some authorities invert the order of Foundation and Royalty. We sometimes find slight variations in the naming of the Sefirot, but the varying names imply the same meanings, even when this does not appear at first sight.

F 2

treatise, but a commentary on the Pentateuch. Such an abstract analysis of the Zohar's theology as we have just given fails to render the freshness and poetry of the book, and the deep spiritual impression often produced by these sometimes strange speculations around the words of the Scripture. How far the Zohar has penetrated orthodox Judaism appears from the fact that a hymn of the Sabbath-morning service produces the whole theory of the Sefirot.[1] The understanding of that hymn would be impossible without some knowledge of the Cabbala. Abelson says of the Zohar : " It mirrors Judaism as an intensely vital religion of the spirit. More overpoweringly than any other book or code, more even than the Bible, does it give to the Jew the conviction of an inner, unseen, spiritual universe—an eternal moral order. . . . A modified and modernized adoption of a little more Zoharic sentiment to the Jewish liturgy of to-day would be a welcome improvement."[2]

Modern Hasidism, being foreign and often hostile to the main rabbinic tradition (of which the Zohar is a part as well as the Talmud), will be separately considered.

The study of Jewish mystical tradition may help the Christian to understand certain elements of his own belief. He will, for instance, perceive some connexion between the idea of *Adam Kadmon* and the teaching of Paul concerning the Second Adam. Moreover, it is easy to see why Christian cabbalists—a Pico della Mirandola, a Reuchlin, a Paracelsus, a Knorr von Rosenberg—were so eagerly drawn to the Zohar : in the trinitarian trend of the book, they found some prefiguration of the Christian dogma. But, independently of this point, Jewish mysticism deserves approach for its own sake. It is full of joy and warmth. Beneath a certain crudeness and clumsiness of expression, it offers a symbolical—nay, a sacramental—view of the universe with which a Christian can fully sympathize. The author of the pseudo-Areopagitic writings, or Ruysbroek, or Julian of Norwich would—each for his own reasons—have felt quite at home in certain parts of the Zohar. There are many pages of this book which, if they were meditated upon by Christians, could illuminate and inflame them, give them a new vision of the Old Testament and prepare them for the Gospel. Who more than the writer of the fourth Gospel could be said to have a " Zoharic soul " ?

---

[1] See the *Authorized Daily Prayer Book*, ed. Singer, p. 129.
[2] *The Zohar*, translated by H. Sperling, M. Simon and P. Levertoff, with an Introduction by J. Abelson, 5 vols., London, 1931–1934. The quotation is from the Introduction, pp. xii and xxii.

PART THREE

JUDAISM AND THE CHRISTIAN CREED

JUDAISM, HELLENISM, CHRISTIANITY

The early Church had to interpret Jesus to the Gentile world. Hence a prevalence of Greek forms of thought and Greek terminology in Christianity. Hence also a difficulty for Christianity—once Hellenized—to find a common ground and a common tongue with Judaism.[1]

The general categories in which Jews and Greeks moulded their religious thoughts were very different and often opposed. We will recall some of these differences.

The Greek was primarily interested in the physical world around him. The Hebrew mind, on the other hand, was not interested in the sun and the moon and the stars, but in distinguishing good from evil and knowing the one, abiding God. It is the deep difference between a naturalistic-philosophical and a purely religious frame of mind.

When thinking of God, the Greek remained an intellectualist. He tended to an abstract philosophy, by which he could understand the relation of the One to the many. To the Hebrew, religion was emotional and ethical. It was the personal—not metaphysical—relation of man to his Creator, King and Father. Not only is the word " theology " a Greek one, but the very conception of theology is purely Greek. To a Jew it would have seemed the dissociation of reflection from action, the substitution of philosophy for revelation, prophecy, experience.

Greek religious thinking is static, while the Jews' is dynamic. The God of the Hebrews is primarily a worker. History is the act of God. He enters into our storms and conflicts ; he struggles and advances ; he loves and suffers. In Greek thought, God always appears as an aristocrat. The idea of progress was equally foreign to the Greek and Roman mind. For both, the idea of perfection could not be separated from stability and permanence. The essence of the Divine excluded the idea of change : God's life is eternal and changeless contemplation. The Greeks would never have conceived the

---

[1] See G. Macgregor, and A. Purdy, *Jew and Greek : Tutors unto Christ,* London, 1936 ; and J. Macmurray, *The Clue to History,* London, 1938.

history of the world as a single action which realizes an intention of God.

Christian ethics, inspired by the Greeks, provide us with a philosophical theory of the " good " and rest on the basis of a dualism between " spiritual " and " material." For the Jews " good " is simply submission to the will of God. It is on this basis that the Hebrews were looking for a practical rule of life. Moreover, the Hellenistic imagery, its cosmic import, its opposition between spirit and matter, are distant from, and alien to, Jewish comprehension. The consequences of the Greek dualism were far-reaching. The body became the prison of the soul and the source of evil. As a corollary, the conception of the immortality of the soul occupied the foreground and relegated to the background the Jewish idea of the resurrection of the body.

These are general aspects of the Greek-Jewish conflict of thought. The opposition becomes greater and more precise if we look at some particular details. One knows the importance of the notions of " nature," " essence," " substance," " person," in the elaboration and formulation of the Christian dogmas of Incarnation and Trinity. Such notions had no equivalents in Jewish intellectual categories ; there were not even words in Hebrew to translate them adequately. The difficulty in thought was doubly aggravated by a difficulty in words.

The case of the Monophysites may help us to grasp the seriousness of these difficulties. Words unhappily translated played a considerable part in early Church conflicts. Certain technical Christian words, which underwent a sufficiently tangled development in their original Greek, have no real equivalent in Syriac. Thence arose abundant opportunity for misunderstanding among people already disposed each to think the other wrong. For instance, *hypostasis* was translated by the Syriac word *Qnuma*, which has no exact equivalent in Greek. *Theotokos* was rendered by the misleading *Yaldath Alaha*. These questions had much to do with the genesis of the Jacobite and Coptic "separated Eastern communions."[1]

The difficulty with regard to the Jews is still greater. To translate to them such terms as *physis*, *ousia*, *hypostasis* seems an almost impossible task. And how can we present to them the word *theotokos*, which has such a *prima facie* blasphemous aspect ? It seems that Paul himself, on the question which is central in Christian dogmatics, felt that kind of difficulty. Dodd remarks that, though he ascribes to Christ

---

[1] See W. Wigram, *Separation of Monophysites*, London, 1923.

functions and dignities which are consistent with nothing less than deity, yet he avoids calling Him God ; this explanation is suggested : " The reason why Paul could not do so, while the theologians who followed him could, was not that they differed from him in their belief about the person of Christ, but that they were Greeks and he a Hebrew ; though he spoke Greek, his religious terms always bore their Hebrew colouring : and the Greek *theos* is not the precise equivalent of the Hebrew *elohim*."[1]

In all these cases, a translation of words—even the most accurate—would be most inadequate. What is needed is a " translation of meanings." A re-thinking of Christology in Jewish terms, *i.e.*, not only in Hebrew words, but in Hebrew categories of thought, constitutes the first task of the Christian who wishes to interpret his own belief to the Jews.

This does not mean the violent elimination of the Greek formulas. They have been extremely useful for conveying the Christian faith to the Greek world and for keeping it unaltered ; and, though many modern Christians claim that creeds have lost any intelligible meaning, many other Christians still find in the old words of Nicæa and Constantinople the most precise, most satisfactory and most adequate intellectual expression of their faith. Only these venerable words must not stand as an obstacle between Israel and the message of Jesus. There is no reason why a purely Jewish expression of the Christian faith could not be as adequate or become as venerable as the Greek one. But this cannot be achieved through a crude Judaizing process which would be lacking in understanding and appreciation of the Greek traditional values. As Burkitt said[2] : " Our abstraction and separation of the Jewish and non-Jewish elements in a living Christianity must not be thought of as a surgical operation, but rather as the tracing of features in a child characteristic of each parent." Montefiore insists[3] that the comparative study of these two forms of thought " would need large knowledge and large sympathy ; it would need a fervent admiration both of the Greek and the Hebrew genius, together with a recognition of their limits."

How far may Jesus have had contact with Hellenism ? The thesis of the Hellenism of Jesus has been expounded in rather an attractive way by Professor Eduard Wechssler, of the University of Berlin. Though his book[4] has won universal

---

[1] C. Dodd, *The Epistle to the Romans*, London, 1932, p. 152.
[2] In the *Legacy of Israel*, p. 71.
[3] *The Old Testament and After*, London, 1923, p. 469.
[4] *Hellas im Evangelium*, Berlin, 1936.

praise in anti-Semitic Germany, it never deviates from scientific objectivity and fairness. Jesus, according to these views, was formed by later Judaism, which had been greatly influenced by the Cynic and Stoic doctrines. The Palestine of Jesus was really a Greek country. Paneas, Tiberias, Sepphoris were centres of Hellenistic civilization. The conversations of Jesus with the ruler of Capernaum, the Syro-Phœnician woman and Pilate imply that he must have known Greek. Such names of disciples as Andreas, Philippos, Thaddaios are significant. The brotherhood of the disciples reminds us of a Greek *thiasos*, while the relation of the Master to his beloved disciple has something essentially Hellenic. Jesus went among the Gentiles in Decapolis, Tyre and Sidon, Cæsarea Philippi, Transjordania ; the " great multitude " which followed him from Decapolis must have been Gentiles. He certainly met in those parts Hellenistic Sophists, and he himself adopted the wandering type of life of a Cynic or Stoic philosopher.

If they do nothing else, these fascinating and unwarranted speculations help us to realize the universality of the appeal made to men by the person of Jesus. We consider as very unlikely the Hellenized Jesus pictured by Wechssler ; but this picture is useful in reminding us that the chasm created between Judaism and Hellenism by later developments did not exist in the first century. Without speaking of Jesus Himself, or of Paul, or of some Greek-reading Pharisees, let us remember the great part that Alexandrian Judaism played in the history of religious thought. Let us especially remember the person and work of Philo.

At the end of the last century, it was considered an axiom that the Judaism of Diaspora had diverged further and further from the Palestinian tradition. As regards Philo, it was then a matter for wonder how he believed himself to be, and was accepted by his contemporaries as being, an orthodox Jew. There is nowadays a reaction against such views. Leopold Cohn and Israel Abrahams earnestly exhorted students of Greek literature to occupy themselves with Philo more than has hitherto been done, for a closer investigation will reveal more and more points of contact between Philonean and rabbinic thought, and it is with justice that Abrahams has placed Philo's theology among the " permanent values in Judaism." Montefiore speaks of Philo with a kind of enthusiasm : "To any previous Greek philosopher was God so personal, so near, so gracious, as to Philo ? "[1] Again Montefiore : " Jews must be

[1] *The Old Testament and After*, p. 487.

profoundly grateful to the Christian Church for having preserved him to us. For it is only by the work of Christian
copyists and by reason of Christian interest that his writings
have come down to us. Through Christian hands has this
ardent Jew been given back to Judaism."[1]

Have we something to learn from Philo to-day ? He was—
and he remains—a figure of unique interest in the relationship
of Judaism and Christianity. "He has become almost one of
the Fathers of the Church," writes Deissmann.[2] Why ?
Because his Logos-doctrine was so near to Christian ideas.
Whether Paul and the author of the fourth Gospel read Philo
remains an undecided question. But the Logos-doctrine of
Justyn Martyr is closely dependent on Philo's. Clement and
Origen were well acquainted with him. Ambrose quoted him
to such an extent that a Jewish commentator called Ambrose
Philo Christianus. Now the terminology of Philo, his use of
the word *Logos* would perhaps savour too much of Hellenism
to be acceptable to the modern Jewish theologian. But would
this last sweepingly reject the experience and the message which
Philo covered under these Greek garments ? Would he find
them without any link with genuine Judaism ? An endeavour
to think along Philonean lines might contribute strongly to
the recovery of certain values which have been lost, and thus
enable Jews and Christians to go further together.

The combination of Judaism with Hellenism is, both for
Jews and Christians, not merely a story of the past, but a living
problem ; each generation of Jews and Christians must face it
in its turn. Will the challenge which once came from Alexandria
be lost to us ?

CHRISTIANITY AND JEWISH MONOTHEISM

Judaism is not as devoid of dogmatic formulas as one often
supposes. It is true that Jewish scholasticism and its elabora-
tions have to do with Law and conduct rather than with
dogmas and creeds. Nevertheless Judaism has had also its own
creeds and articles of faith.[3] The *Shema Israel* is not only a
liturgical formula and a commandment ; it is also a confession
of faith, and considered as more important than the historical
Jewish creeds. As a confession of faith, the *Shema* is the
affirmation of the unity and uniqueness of God. It constitutes

---

[1] *Ibidem.*
[2] *St. Paul*, transl. Strachan, p. 109.
[3] See special note I.

the highest expression of the "Jewish monotheism" : "Adonai is our God, Adonai is one. . . . ."

The Christian symbols of faith—the Apostles' Creed, the Nicæan-Constantinopolitan Creed, the Athanasian Creed, to quote only the main ones—are considered by the Jews as being in flat contradiction to this fundamental assertion of Jewish monotheism. Claude Montefiore has put it in the clearest way : " As to the nature of God, all Jews maintain that the doctrines of the divinity of Christ, of the Trinity, of the Eternal Son, of the personality of the Holy Spirit, are infractions of the divine Unity and false."[1]

Some other passages of Montefiore on the same subject are also very significant. This one, for instance : " When we are told that the Jewish God is distant, we smile with astonishment at the strange accusation. So near is He that He needs no Son to bring Him nearer to us, no intercessor to reconcile Him with us or us with Him."[2] And this one : " I would not for a moment aver that the most orthodox Trinitarian cannot love God as keenly and profoundly as the most convinced Jewish Unitarian. I would not for a moment deny that many such Trinitarians may love him a great deal better than any such Unitarians. But I believe that it is true to say that the full resources of the Father are only known to those for whom all that the Son and the Spirit may be to others are for them concentrated in Him."[3]

We meet here not so much a theoretical opposition to the Christian dogma as rather a pious fear less the direct access to the Father should be endangered. Montefiore does seem to have closely considered the Christian claim that " the full resources of the Father " are best known to those who become sons in the Son.

Moreover, Montefiore is not always so radical. Several passages in his books qualify his previous assertion that the Christian doctrines on the Son and the Holy Spirit " are infractions of the divine Unity and false." He admits that the way remains open to a reconsideration and a better understanding of both the Jewish and Christian positions. He writes : " We have to re-examine and set forth afresh the

---

[1] *In Spirit and Truth*, p. 316. See also L. Baeck, *The Essence of Judaism*, translated from the German by V. Grubwieser and L. Pearl, London, 1936 ; A. Marmorstein, *The Old Rabbinic Doctrine of God*, Oxford, 1937; A. Lukyn Williams, *The Doctrines of Modern Judaism Considered*, London, 1939.
[2] *Liberal Judaism*, p. 56.
[3] *The Place of Judaism among the Religions of the World*, London, 1918, pp. 51–52.

doctrine of the divine unity. It will be needful for Liberal Jewish theologians to consider the new modern interpretations of the doctrine of the Trinity, and to discuss how far these are, and how far they are not, in accordance with Jewish views of the unity."[1]

He says elsewhere : " The same . . . would apply to the doctrine of the Holy Spirit. Here, too, there is work for Jewish theologians to accomplish within the limits of Judaism."[2]

Here is a positive starting-point. But none of the contemporary Jewish theologians, as far as we know, has undertaken the task thus described by Montefiore.

The most important aspects of this task would be to ascertain what Christians exactly mean by God's unity, and how they may reconcile this unity with their christology and pneumatology. Another aspect of the task, next in importance, would be the consideration of the " trinitarian " tendencies in Jewish tradition. The fact that these tendencies have often been the subject of a superficial and mistaken Christian exegesis must not preclude us from examining them carefully. It was not a Church Father, but Philo himself, who began to give a trinitarian interpretation of the visit of the three Strangers to Abraham at Mamre, and wrote : " The One in the midst, attended by His two Powers, presents to the mind's vision the appearance of One and sometimes the appearance of Three. . . ."[3] We have already seen how the trinitarian idea permeates the Zohar. To what has been said of the triads of Sefirot we can add these words which have, outwardly, the exact appearance of a Christian formula : " The Ancient of Days has three heads. He reveals Himself in three archetypes, all three forming but one. He is thus symbolized by the number Three. They are revealed in one another."[4] The notions of Logos, Memra, Wisdom, Shekinah, Holy Spirit cannot be explained away from historical Judaism. Of course, when we speak of " trinitarian tendencies," we must avoid the pitfall from which so many Christian apologists could not escape. It would be a complete mistake to look in rabbinic literature for the Christian conception of the Trinity as it was elaborated by the councils of the fourth century. But we may find something that could be called *adumbratio* or *praefiguratio* of a trinitarian, though strictly monotheistic,

---

[1] *The Old Testament and After*, p. 561.
[2] *Ibid.*, p. 562.
[3] *On Abraham*, §122.
[4] *Zohar*, iii, 288b.

conception of God. There are strong and unmistakable glimpses of such " trinitarian " views. They will be detailed and dwelt upon in their proper place. In this quest we cannot be helped by a better guide than the Jewish scholar J. Abelson, who wrote a classical work on *The Immanence of God in Rabbinical Literature.*[1]

The following questions should be considered one by one :—

(a) The Jewish idea of the Word and its divine Sonship ;

(b) The Jewish idea of the divine manifested Presence on earth, or Shekinah, and its relation to the Christian idea of Incarnation ;

(c) The Jewish doctrine of the Holy Spirit ;

(d) The Jewish idea of mediation and atonement.

When we have considered these questions it will become easier to see whether the view of God taught by Jewish tradition is so irremediably antagonistic to the Christian view as is generally imagined.

THE WORD AND THE SON

One of the most important features of the Targum literature is the use of the term *Memra,* " word " (in Hebrew *Dibbur* or *Maamar*). The term " Word of God " had been previously used in the Bible, but its use in the Targums has a somewhat different connotation. In the Bible, the Word is connected with three ideas. It creates (Ps. xxxiii. 6) and renews the face of the earth. It cares for the chosen people and protects its development. It inspires prophecy and imparts the Law. There is already, in the Bible, a tendency to personify the Word (Ps. cxlvii. 15; Is. lv. 11, ii. 1; Ps. xxxiii. 4; Jer. xxiii. 29). But this personification is poetical rather than metaphysical. On the other hand, in post-biblical literature, the Word seems to become more and more an intermediary between God and the world.

The Memra must be clearly distinguished from the Hokmah or Wisdom of God. When Jewish thought moved in the direction of Greek philosophy, the doctrine of the Wisdom became coloured by foreign ideas : the Wisdom was thought of as a quasi-independent essence. The latest researches indicate that personal Wisdom is an obvious interpolation in post-exilic Judaism. It shows a startling affinity to a Syrian Astarte with features of Isis ; this personal figure was later on replaced by an Alexandrine cosmic immanent divinity.[2]

[1] London, 1912.
[2] W. Knox, *The Divine Wisdom* in *Journal of Theological Studies,* July, 1937.

Neither must the Memra be identified with Metatron, the Angel of the Presence. As T. Herford says :[1] " Metatron is so far from being identical with the Logos of the Jewish Alexandrine philosophy, or with the Horos of Gnosticism, that he may be regarded as the expression of the rabbinical rejection of those conceptions. . . . No doubt there is common to all three conceptions an idea of the delegation of a divine power; but, in the case of Metatron, the line is sharply drawn between servant and Master, creature and creator."

Philo's Logos, tinged with Platonic and Stoic ideas, is the first-born Son of God, the prototypal Man in whose image all other men are created, the Idea of ideas, the Intercessor, Paraclete and High Priest—a kind of " second Deity." It is true that, in several (and important) respects, this Logos of Philo differs from the rabbinic conceptions. " There are, however," says Abelson, " a few allusions . . . in talmudic literature, which run very near to the Paraclete idea of Philo, similarly in the case of Memra, particularly in the Jerusalem Talmud."[2]

An important passage in the *Song of Songs Rabba* (i. 3) strongly personifies the Word : it is shown coming to and returning from Israel and speaking with a resounding voice. In the same commentary (vi. 3), the Word intercedes before God on behalf of Israel.

Is the Memra merely an expedient for avoiding the ascription of anthropomorphism to God ? Abelson thinks that this " is only half the truth " and that the notion of Memra " has a deep and real theological import."[3] This was also the idea of Nahmanides, whose ideas on the point, in his *Commentary on the Bible* (Genesis xlvi. 4), are of great interest. Nahmanides quotes striking passages from the Bible and Talmud whose anthropomorphisms are not avoided. The Talmud speaks freely of the arm, hand, finger, eyes of God. If the Memra is a term of convenience coined for the purpose of stripping God of corporality, why such crude anthropomorphisms in other places ? Moreover, why does the Targum insert the word Memra when there is no danger whatever of anthropomorphism ? Nahmanides considers that the expressions concerning the Memra are not a mere artifice, but cover a deep mystery : " Their secret," he says, " is known to students." The Memra idea is an essential part of the ancient rabbinic thought on the relationship between

[1] *Christianity in Talmud*, p. 287.
[2] *The Immanence of God in Rabbinic Literature*, p. 147.
[3] *Ibid*, p. 151.

79

God and the world. It is the straight-lined development of
the simple and great utterance of Psalm xxxiii. 9: "For He
spake, and it was."

The Memra is personally prayed to : " Hear, O Memra of
God, the voice of Judah's prayer."[1]

A revival of the Memra idea would not detract one iota from
the absolute unity of God. And it would certainly prepare Jews
and Christians alike to understand better the Prologue of the
Fourth Gospel.[2]

The idea of sonship in relation to God is developed in the
Old Testament and in rabbinical literature. Not only every
Israelite, but every member of the human race enjoys God's
fatherhood. It would be easy but of little use to quote here all
the Old Testament references to the Fatherhood of God. Let
us remember some of the most striking : " Like as a Father
pitieth his children, so the Lord (Ps. ciii. 13). . . . O Lord,
Thou art our Father (Is. lxiv. 7.). . . . I am a Father to Israel
(Jer. xxxi. 9). . . . Israel is my first-born Son (Ex. iv. 22). . . .
Is Ephraim my dear son ? (Jer. xxxi. 19). . . ." The expression
Abinu Malkinu, " our Father and our King," recurs often in
the Synagogue liturgy.

Now, in this universal sonship, there is one exceptional and
unique case. Certain passages in rabbinic literature single out
the Messiah for special sonship. God says to the Messiah :
" Thou art my Son."[3] And the " Son " of Psalm lxxx. 17
becomes, in the Targum, the equivalent of " King Messiah."
Although we can only speak of the Messiah's sonship in
a stammering way, it results from such passages that the
Messiah is the Father's Son in a sense which is peculiar to
him and could not be applied to other men. And it is quite
certain that the rabbis who thus spoke had in mind a personal
Messiah.

Let us, for the time being, leave aside the person of the
Messiah and return to the Word. The Zohar establishes a most
interesting connexion between the notions of Word, Son and
Trinity. The term *omer*, " speech," indicates the mysteries of
the divine diversity in unity. In this word, we find the letter
aleph, first of all letters and symbol of the Father ; the letter
mem, symbol of the Mother (because of the word *em*=mother) ;

---

[1] *Targum* on Dt. 23, 7.

[2] See A. Hall, *Der Logos : Gesch. seiner Entwickelung in der griech. Philo-
sophie und der christl. Litteratur*, 2 vols., Leipzig, 1896–99; J. Réville, *La
Doctrine du Logos dans le Quatrième Évangile et dans les Œuvres de Philon*,
Paris, 1881 ; T. Simon, *Der Logos*, Leipzig, 1902.

[3] *Talmud Babyl.*, 52a.

the letter *resch*, symbol of the Head or Son (*rosh*=head). The union of these three forms the Word or Speech. " Thus the Father, the Mother and the first-born Son radiate one within the other in one union. . . . Thus all are united as to become one . . . they hasten . . . that Speech as a supernatural reign so that all should be one."[1]

Shall we conclude from all this that the Christian doctrine of the Second Person of the Trinity, as Word and Son of the Father, is to be found in rabbinical literature ? Certainly not. But we are justified in saying that there has been, in the Jewish tradition, a movement along the lines which led Christian thought to its historical formulas concerning the Word and the Son. Such a movement could not have taken place if it had been inconsistent with the Jewish faith as a whole, and if it had not answered to certain intellectual and spiritual needs.

The rabbinic use of the term " Son " applied to the Word or to the Messiah—therefore an exceptional usage, with an exceptional meaning—did not scandalize the Jews, because it did not imply a physical descent. Neither is a physical descent implied in the Christian application of the term " Son " to the Messiah and Word. There is nothing in this which could offend Jewish belief. Why should Judaism be afraid of a language which has been its own ?

THE SHEKINAH

From the idea that God has descended " to dwell " among men, the word and the conception of *Shekinah* originated. This conception brings us into the very centre of this theological " translation of meanings," which we indicated as the task of the modern dialogue between Jews and Christians. We definitely think that no conception is more important for a Christian approach to Jewish religious thought.

The word *Shekinah* is a noun derived from the verb *sheken* " to dwell." It means the indwelling, or abiding, or presence of God in a certain place. The term appeared after the close of the Hebrew canon and was first used in the Targum. We frequently find it in the Talmud, Midrash and Zohar and may consider it as characteristic of ancient Jewish theology.

The Shekinah has been the object of many historical

[1] *Zohar, Terumah* 136b.

COMMUNION IN THE MESSIAH

philological and exegetical researches,[1] which we cannot even summarize here. We shall simply try to emphasize a few points.

(a) *Personification of the Shekinah.* We shall quote, among many, some of the most significant passages. The Shekinah was inside the burning bush and spoke with Moses.[2] The cloud of the Tabernacle, spoken of in Exodus xl. 34–38, was, according to the rabbinic tradition, the cloud of the Shekinah. The " left hand under my head " and the " his right hand doth embrace me " in the Song of Songs ought to be interpreted as the " clouds of the Shekinah " which " surround Israel above and below."[3] The rabbinic literature develops in various forms the idea that a man, when he is at the point of death, may see the Shekinah. We often find the expression " to receive the Face of the Shekinah," which is the privilege of the pious man. The " wings of the Shekinah " meant the protective aspect of God's immanence ; to introduce a non-Israelite into the fold was to bring him " under the wings of the Shekinah." Moses died in these wings. " When a man is ill, the Shekinah says : I feel a weariness in my head, I feel a weariness in my arm."[4] Any one coming to visit a sick person should not sit either on the couch or on a chair, but wrapped up on the ground, because the Shekinah rests about the couch.[5] Two men, whose names are given, were once sitting in a synagogue of Nehardea, when they heard the sound of a movement. It was the Shekinah coming. They immediately rose and, in awe, left the synagogue.[6] In the same synagogue of Nehardea, Rabbi Sheshet prayed personally to the Shekinah, and the Shekinah granted his prayer.[7] Rabbi Yannai said that the Shekinah, after the Temple was no more,

---

[1] The book (already quoted) of Abelson, *The Immanence of God in Rabbinical Literature*, especially Chaps. IV–XII., contains the most complete references and inquiries concerning the Shekinah. See also : A. Grörer, *Geschichte des Urchristenthums*, Petersburg, 1838 ; Maybaum, *Anthropomorphien . . . mit besonderer Berücksichtigung der . . . Schechinta*, Breslau, 1870 : F. Weber, *Jüdische Theologie*, Leipzig, 1898; S. Schechter, *Some Aspects of Rabbinic Theology*, London, 1909; the articles *Shekinah* in the *Jewish Encycl.*, Hastings' *Dictionary of the Bible*, Herzog-Hauck's *Prot. Realencycl.*, Schaff-Herzog's *The New Encycl.*, Hastings' *Encycl. of Rel. and Ethics*, and the lexicons of Buxtorf, Levy, Kohut, Jastrow ; and our own essay *Questions Concernant la Chékinah*, in *Judaism and Christianity. Essays presented to the Rev. Paul P. Levertoff*, London, 1939.
[2] *Ex. Rabba* 2, 5.
[3] Treatise *Yalkut* on Song.
[4] T.B. *Sanhedrin*, 46a.
[5] *Nedarim* 40a.
[6] T.B. *Megillah* 29a.
[7] *Ibid.*

disseminated itself and became the possession of the whole world.[1] Before this, it was through the concentration of the Shekinah in the Temple that the immanent God reached the universe. According to some other ancient Rabbis, the Shekinah still abides in the Western Wall of the Temple. According to Rabbi Aha, the Shekinah, having departed from the Temple, returns there at intervals, kisses its walls and pillars and weeps.[2]

(b) *Nature of the Shekinah.* " They saw God, that is to say : the Shekinah manifested herself unto them."[3] How are we to understand this ? Is the Shekinah a mere periphrasis, a synonym of God ? There is certainly more in the idea of the Shekinah than in the idea of God, for the word Shekinah expresses a definite aspect of God : God as present. But what kind of divine presence is implied in the Shekinah ? The general presence of God, His "omnipresence"? or a "special presence," if we may use such an expression ? Taking into account the sayings of the Rabbis who associate the Shekinah with the Tabernacle, Sinai, the burning bush, the pillar of light, etc., we may safely say that the Shekinah means a special presence of God. This presence has the three following characteristics :—

i. It is localized in a definite point of space, it " dwells " in a place.

ii. It is determined in time, it manifests itself at a certain moment.

iii. It is not necessarily given with or bound to the omnipresence of God as infinite essence, but it depends on the free grace and condescension of God.

Such a special Presence once admitted, another question may be raised. Is this special Presence direct and immediate ? That is to say : is it an objectification of the divine essence itself ? Or is this special Presence indirect and mediate ? Does this Presence have, as a support, a kind of intermediary, something which is not of divine essence, like the created light or the angels ? Both opinions have found defenders. In the last century Gfrörer saw in the Shekinah an intermediary of the same kind as Philo's Logos, while Maybaum and Hamburger considered the Shekinah as the presence of the very essence of God. The same question had already been discussed in the Middle Ages. Maimonides, in the *Guide for the Perplexed*, held that the Shekinah is a created light, intermediary between God

[1] Abelson, *The Immanence of God in Rabbinic Literature*, p. 121.
[2] *Ibid.*, p. 107.
[3] *Zohar, Mishpatim* 126a.

and the world. Nahmanides, on the contrary, believed that the Shekinah is the direct manifestation of the divine essence.

A third question remains. If we admit that the Shekinah is the divine essence itself, does it constitute an entity distinct from the Father ? Is the Shekinah identified with the Father in such a way that an " I and Thou " relation between them is impossible ? Or is a personal distinction between the Father and His Shekinah compatible with their essential identity ? It seems highly probable that the Hebrew genius did not enter into such metaphysical precisions. But such frequent expressions as " God sent His Shekinah " or " God caused His Shekinah to dwell " might be legitimately interpreted in their obvious and literal sense, *i.e.*, in the sense of a personal distinction which, however, does not exclude an identity of essence.

(*c*) *Shekinah and Glory*. The Shekinah has often been considered as synonymous with the " glory of Yaweh," mentioned in the Bible and in rabbinical literature. But this is a mistake. The Glory (*Kabod* or *Yekarah*) was a particular physical appearance indicating the divine presence : *e.g.*, the fire or cloud in the theophanies ; but the relation of this physical phenomenon to the Presence itself was the relation of a sign to the thing signified. The Glory constituted an external manifestation or radiance of the Shekinah. Close to the use of the term " glory " is the use of the expression *ziv-ha-shekinah*, " the shining of the Shekinah."

(*d*) *The idea of the Shekinah and Christian thought*. We touch here a complex and most important set of problems, and we do not claim to do anything more than to introduce and formulate them as clearly as possible ; but every one of them could be the object of a whole treatise.[1]

The first problem is a historical one : what is the connexion, if any, between the development of the Shekinah literature and the Christian beliefs of the first centuries ? The Shekinah literature (beginning with the Onkelos Targum) was evolved in Jewish Babylonian circles, during a period in which Christian thought had already taken very definite lines. Now the Jewish and Christian doctrines of immanence present so many points of similitude that they can hardly have co-existed

---

[1] Through the Charles Boys Lectures, which he delivered for a number of years in succession, and also by means of the Boyle Lectureship, which he has twice been deputed by the Bishop of London to undertake, Dr. Paul Levertoff has orally developed a Jewish-Christian theology, of which the notion of the Shekinah is the centre. Levertoff has also written a great work still unpublished on *Christ and the Shekinah*.

without coming into contact. Two possibilities must be considered. Either the early Christian literature, in its immanentist aspects (especially the Fourth Gospel), has borrowed certain ideas already circulating among Jewish circles, or the Jewish immanentist literature, since the end of the first century, has borrowed certain Christian notions. This last hypothesis itself admits of two interpretations. A natural and irenic penetration of Jewish thought by Christian currents may have taken place. Or the contact between Christian and Jewish thought may have provoked in rabbinic circles a polemical reaction. If such is the case, the development of the Shekinah idea would tend to show that Jewish belief admits of a God as near to men and as present among them as the Christian God and, at the same time, that this Presence is a purer and more spiritual notion than the Christian Incarnation. Ludwig Blau writes : " The polemic attitude which the conception of the Shekinah betrays towards the founder and ideal of Christianity is unmistakable."[1] It may be so, although no proofs are available. But, even if the development of the Shekinah idea has been achieved under Christian influences and perhaps as a reaction against them, the genesis of this notion ought to be explained. Neither the Jewish nor the Christian writers of the end of the first century created it wholesale. Was it formed during the period of the Apocrypha ? What was the exact part of Alexandrian Judaism in this formation ? These questions have still to be solved.

Another problem raised by the Shekinah idea falls within the scope of New Testament exegesis. Did the New Testament writers know of this doctrine ? We find at least two New Testament texts where an allusion to the Shekinah seems very likely : these texts are John i. 14, and Revelation xxi. 3, in which the Greek words *eskenosen* and *skene*, both pointing to the indwelling of God among men, and seldom used in Greek, appear to be a play on words with reference to the Hebrew *sheken shekinah*. The Jewish idea of the divine indwelling may also have influenced John xiv. 23, II Corinthians vi. 16, Colossians ii. 9. Moreover the *doxa* of the New Testament corresponds exactly to the *kabod* or *yekarah* (glory) of the Jewish tradition.

The notion of the Shekinah raises still more difficult problems, not of a historical or philological, but of a purely theological character. Could this notion become a bridge between Jewish monotheism and Christianity ? Could a " Hebraic Christology " be built on it ? Could Jews and

[1] *Jewish Encycl.*, vol. XI, p. 260.

Christians unite in considering Jesus as the living Shekinah of the Father—the full manifestation of the Presence, the perfect indwelling of God among men ? It could be, perhaps, very easy for a Liberal or Modernist Christianity to think along these lines, and perhaps not too difficult for Liberal Judaism to come near enough to them (" I would not deny that the dogma of the incarnation of God in Jesus has had its effects for good as well as for evil," says Montefiore[1])—providing that the terminology is not pressed too much into a precise meaning. But could the Shekinah idea become a link between orthodox Judaism and orthodox Christianity ? Would a Shekinah Christology be consistent with the Nicæan faith ? Without giving a direct answer to these questions, we should like to draw attention to the following points :—

i. Christ may be interpreted in terms of the Shekinah only if we give to this term the meaning of a " special " Presence of God—prefigured by the special Presence in the burning bush or the pillar of fire—and not of the divine " omnipresence."

ii. If we believe that Christ is the supreme fulfilment of the Shekinah, we must adopt the interpretation of Nahmanides against the views of Maimonides, *i.e.* we must conceive the Shekinah not as an intermediary, but as the presence of the divine essence itself. To accept the views of Maimonides would mean to give up the consubstantiality of Jesus and His Father. The thesis of Nahmanides, applied to Jesus, would safeguard the doctrine of the *homo-ousios*.

iii. We should understand the Shekinah in such a way that an " I and Thou " relation would always be possible between Jesus and the Father. While asserting the identity of their divine essence, we should maintain a real distinction between their persons.

iv. We should insist on the human reality of Jesus, on His character as complete man, so that He could not be mistaken for a pure appearance, *doxa* or glory of God, devoid of any human reality. And we should also be careful to indicate that while thinking of Jesus in terms of Shekinah, we mean a union of God with man, but not a confusion of divine and human natures. Montefiore has misunderstood the Christian creed when he writes that the dogma of the incarnation of God in Jesus " rests on a confusion, the confusion of God with man."[2]

We do not pretend that these ideas exhaust all the problems raised by a " Shekinah Christology." This should be worked

[1] *Outlines of Liberal Judaism*, p. 304.
[2] *Ibid.*

86

out in detail. We only suggest the possibility of elaborating, on Shekinah lines, a Christology compatible with the historical definitions, which must not be despised. We think this Hebraic way more accessible to the Jews—even perhaps to certain Gentile Christians—than the Greek way. At first sight a Shekinah Christology will appear to be simpler than the Nicæan Creed. And it may remain so, if one does not want to go further than a general conception of things. But, as soon as there is any attempt to clarify meanings and implications, one falls back on the ever-recurrent problems concerning nature, essence, person, etc.—problems to which the Greek councils have given answers of (as we think) permanent value. It would be possible to re-think and re-formulate the same problems along Hebrew lines, along the Shekinah lines. The completion of such a task is still far off. Nevertheless the Shekinah idea can be, even now, an excellent, and perhaps the best, basis of a presentation of Christianity in continuity with Jewish thought. We hope we have given at least a glimpse of the importance of this theme for Christian theology.

THE HOLY SPIRIT

The Old Testament often speaks of the " Spirit of Yaweh " and " Spirit of Elohim." Two views are taken of the Spirit in the Old Testament. On the one hand it is through the Spirit that all living things were created. On the other hand the Spirit is poured out on the men whom God chooses ; by means of the Spirit the prophet hears and sees. One remembers the text of Joel ii. 28–29, quoted by Peter (Acts ii. 16 *sq.*). The expression " Holy Spirit " (Hebr. *Ruah-ha-Kodesh*, in Greek *pneuma to agion*) occurs only in Psalm li. 11 and Isaiah lxiii. 10.

In rabbinical literature, the term Holy Spirit occurs frequently and possesses a somewhat more definite meaning than in the Old Testament. Here are some of the chief features of the rabbinical *Ruah-ha-Kodesh*.

The Holy Spirit is associated with certain physical phenomena : light, fire, wind, sound, water. It can be " drawn up " like water from a well. (The words of the Gospel about the baptism with the Holy Ghost, or the baptism with water and fire, seem to reflect these Jewish ideas.) As in the Gospel again, the Spirit takes a dove-like form. The phrase of Canticles ii. 12, " the voice of the dove " becomes in the Targum " the voice of the Holy Spirit." Rabbi Ben Zoma thus interprets the passage of Genesis i. 2, about the Spirit

87

that moved on the face of the waters : " The Throne of Glory was standing in the air and brooding over the face of the water . . . as a dove that broods over its nest."[1] A teacher of the law heard in a ruin the voice of the Spirit cooing like a dove and complaining of the sins of men.[2] The Spirit is often associated with the *bat Kol* (literally " daughter voice "), heavenly sound which proclaims God's will to individuals and communities.[3]

The Spirit rests not only on the prophets, but also on ordinary children of Israel and even on Gentiles. To have announced the universality of the gift of the Spirit is a great achievement of rabbinical literature. Let us listen to this solemn declaration : " I witness before heaven and earth that the Holy Spirit rests on a non-Jew as well as upon a Jew, upon a woman as well as upon a man, upon maidservants as well as upon a manservant."[4]

The Holy Spirit stands in a particular relation to the Word of God (Memra, Dibbur, Logos). When the Spirit was " brooding over the face of the water," it was " by means of the mouth of God and by His Word."[5] The Zohar clarifies this relation and suggests that the *Ruah-ha-Kodesh* is the organ or voice of the Word : the sentence of the Old Testament " and the Lord appeared to Abraham " contains a secret allusion to the audible Voice which is united to the speech.[6] The conception of the Spirit as a Voice makes it distinct not only from the Word, but from the Shekinah and the Glory.

The Spirit is also associated with the Messiah and has a part in his work. The Spirit of God Who moves upon the face of the waters (Gen. i. 2) is the Spirit of the Messiah.[7] The term " voice of the dove " is paraphrased not merely as " the voice of the Holy Spirit," but, more precisely, as " the voice of the Holy Spirit concerning redemption."[8]

The Spirit is strongly personified. It " cries," " weeps " and " speaks." As the word *ruah* is both masculine and feminine, the Holy Spirit is sometimes conceived as being a man and sometimes as being a woman. To try to formulate the nature of the Holy Spirit in rabbinical thought appears extremely difficult. The phrase may sometimes be a mere

[1] T.B. *Haggigah* 12a.
[2] *Ber.* 3a.
[3] See special note J.
[4] *Yalkut on Judges*, IV, 4.
[5] T.B. *Haggigah* 12a, on Genesis i. 2.
[6] *Zohar, Voyera* 98a.
[7] *Genesis Rabba*, VIII, 1.
[8] *Targum on Cant.* 2, 12.

circumlocution for God, but, usually it has a deeper connotation. " In the Old Testament, there is certainly this element of the inexplicable about it," writes Abelson,[1] and this is still truer of rabbinical literature. Very often we can say with certainty that *Ruah-ha-Kodesh* means neither the Father Himself nor one of His properties. Abelson conceives the Spirit, in the Jewish tradition, as " an emanation of God, a visible, or rather a perceptible, trace of His workings in the world and in the heart of man."[2]

These words are perhaps too weak. They remind us of Philo's pneumatology. According to the great Alexandrian, the Spirit of God is a divine *afflatus* coming to all men, an indivisible wisdom of which every wise man has a share and which can be communicated like fire from torch to torch ; this notion is not far from the Platonic *enthousiasmos*. But the Old Testament and rabbinical conception of the Holy Spirit is far more precise. It sees in the Spirit a quasi-personal or personal energy of God. Could we not say that this traditional Jewish view of the Spirit was a preparation for the Christian conception of the Holy Ghost ? Between the first chapter of Genesis, which represents the Spirit of God as co-operating with the Word in the ordering of the creation, and the last chapter of the Apocalypse, which represents the Spirit as speaking in the Church universal, we do not see a gap or some gigantic hyperbola, but a continuous and organic development. The rabbinic pneumatology is far from the positions reached by Christian thought. It nevertheless offers a common ground equally precious (or able to become such) to Jews and Christians.

THE ATONEMENT

Modern rabbinical Judaism repudiates in the strongest possible language any Mediator, any intervening personality between God and man. Its most authoritative representatives would declare that Judaism has no place and no need for the Christian doctrine of redemption and reconciliation. " After death, we may, indeed, be punished, but the punishment will be remedial. . . . To whom have we to render an account ? To a living and loving Father, Who longs to pardon the repentant sinner. What, then, have we to fear ? *Wozu der Lärm?* That is the modern Jewish position in a nutshell. That is the teaching of the modern Rabbis."[3]

---

[1] *The Immanence of God in Rabbinic Literature*, p. 208.
[2] *Ibid.*, p. 206.
[3] Montefiore, *In Spirit and in Truth*, p. 318.

This may be—and actually is—the teaching of modern Rabbis, orthodox as well as Liberal. But does it exactly express the Jewish tradition ? Let us consider more closely some aspects of Judaism.

(a) *Original Sin.* Most Jews, while admitting that man is responsible for the sins committed out of his free will, do not believe in any original sin. But the rabbinical tradition admits that the tendency of the mind is to evil.[1] The majority of Jewish theologians do not hold Adam responsible for the sins of mankind. Some of them, however, teach that "this so-called ' original sin ' " (the expression is used by J. Eisenstein[2]) is due to Adam's yielding to temptation and has been inherited by his descendants. Some of the Rabbis disclaimed the influence of Adam's sin, but made the sin of the golden calf a hereditary one, affecting twenty-four generations.[3] The famous mystic and cabbalist Isaac Luria taught that, since Adam, all souls have been more or less " confused," so that all are inevitably tainted with sin ; Abelson considers that Luria's theory " might appear . . . an approach to Christian teaching about the truth of original sin."[4]

(b) *Atonement.* The ideas of expiation, purification from sin, propitiation and reconciliation are expressed by the closely connected Hebrew words *kipper, kopher, kapparah,* which belong to the history of the Old Testament. In his work of immense learning and thoroughness on this subject,[5] A. Büchler has shown that, if sacrifices did not purge from sin apart from repentance, the chief part in sacrificial atonement was contributed by an objective rite, the sprinkling of the blood. Has the notion of objective atonement survived in post-Temple, synagogal Judaism? Since the cessation of sacrifices, the Day of Atonement has become the outstanding feature in the rabbinic scheme of repentance. It is true that the Day of Atonement (*Yom Kippur*) avails nothing unless repentance be coupled with it,[6] but *Yom Kippur* has an objective atoning value. "Though no sacrifices be offered, the day in itself effects atonement."[7]

(c) *Intercessors and Expiators.* History shows that Judaism has not rejected the notion of intervening personalities between God and man. The Logos of Philo is an intercessor, described

---

[1] *Yoma*, 20a ; *Sanh.*, 105a.
[2] *Jewish Encycl.*, vol. XI, p. 377.
[3] *Sanh.*, 102a ; *Sotah*, 14a.
[4] *Jewish Mysticism*, p. 171.
[5] *Studies in Sin and Atonement in the Rabbinic Literature of the First Century,* Oxford, 1929.
[6] *Yoma*, VIII, 8.
[7] *Sifra*, Emor XIV.

as the High Priest, because, like him, he expiates sin. He is called *iketes*, " suppliant " on behalf of men, and *parakletos* : " It was indispensable that man, who was consecrated to the Father of the world, should have as a Paraclete His Son, the Being most perfect in virtue, to procure forgiveness of sins and a supply of unlimited blessings."[1]

The *aqedah*, or binding of Isaac, had the most important consequences for the forgiveness of the sins of Isaac's descendants. The Rabbis insist on the willingness of Isaac to be bound as a sacrifice ; they even enlarge on the biblical narrative and say that Isaac asked his father to bind him firmly, so that he might not tremble.[2] If God, in the Passover, spared the first-born of His people, it is because He saw the blood of Isaac, which, however, had not been shed.[3] When mention is made of the binding of Isaac, God gets up from the throne of judgment and sits down on the throne of compassion.[4] Every *Selihah* service (or service of penitential prayers) contains an *aqedah*. One of the reasons for the blowing of the ram's horn, on the Day of Atonement, is that God may recall the *aqedah* and grant forgiveness to the seed of Isaac.

Another intercessor is Phineas. His zeal stayed the plague which had broken out among the Israelites as a punishment for their sin, and God rewarded him with the promise that the priesthood should forever remain in his family (Num. xxv. 7–15). This grandson of Aaron is highly extolled in rabbinical literature. "Even till now he does not cease, but he stands and makes atonement until the dead revive."[5]

Every righteous man is a mediator and intercessor. " As the Day of Atonement atones, so the death of the righteous atones."[6] "The death of the righteous weighs as heavily as the burning of the Temple."[7] "Even for the sake of *one* righteous man, the world would have been created, and for the sake of *one* righteous man it will continue."[8]

In numerous instances, the "Attribute of Mercy " (mentioned in the Talmud and Midrashim) is hypostasized and represented as a personality who speaks and pleads before God for the sins of an individual or of the nation.[9]

---

[1] *Life of Moses*, XIV.
[2] *Gen. R.* 56 (119b) ; *Pirke R. Eliezer*, 31.
[3] *Mekilpa* 8a.
[4] Montefiore and Loewe, *A Rabbinic Anthology*, p. 228.
[5] *Ibid.*, p. 227.
[6] *Ibid.*, p. 225.
[7] *Ibid.*, p. 231.
[8] *Ibid.*, p. 231.
[9] Abelson, *The Immanence of God in Rabbinic Literature*, p. 71.

91

(d) *The Suffering Messiah.* It is usually taken for granted :
(i) that the Jews were not expecting a suffering Messiah ;
(ii) that there is only, in apocalyptic literature, a vague allusion,
and of doubtful import, to this idea. What do we find about
it in rabbinical literature ? Here are some significant texts :

" Sufferings are divided into three portions . . . and one
part to the Messiah, as it is written : He was wounded for our
transgressions."[1]

" Our teachers have said : His name shall be the Leprous
One of the house of Rabbi, even as it says : Surely he bore
our sickness and carried our pains : yet we esteemed him as
one stricken with leprosy, and smitten of God."[2]

" When will the Messiah come ? . . . And what is his
mark ? He sits among the wretched who are laden with
sickness."[3]

" God said to the Messiah . . . They will make thee as
a calf whose eyes have become dim and they will strangle
thy breath under the yoke . . . Wilt thou accept this ? . . .
The Messiah replied : With rejoicing of heart and soul I accept
all this, but under the condition that not one soul from Israel
is lost . . ."[4]

" Our teachers have said : There is no end to the sufferings
with which the Messiah is afflicted in every generation
according to the sins of each generation."[5]

" All the good which I will do unto you I do through the
merit of the Messiah. . . . He is righteous and filled with
salvation. . . . Afflicted and riding on an ass : that is the
Messiah."[6]

" When the son of David appears, they will bring beams of
iron and put them on his neck. . . . And he will weep and
cry. . . . Then God will say : Ephraim, my righteous Messiah,
thou didst accept all this since the time of the creation. Now
let they pain be as my pain."[7]

" The Patriarchs will say : Ephraim, my righteous Messiah
. . . thou art greater than we, for thou hast borne the sins of
all our children and heavy punishments . . . and all this has
fallen on thee because of the sins of our children."[8]

---

[1] *Midrash Samuel*, XIX, 29b.
[2] *Sanh.*, 98b.
[3] *Ibid.*, 98a.
[4] *Pesikta R.*, 161a, b.
[5] *Ibid.*, 146b.
[6] *Ibid.*, 159b.
[7] *Ibid.*, 162a.
[8] *Pesikta R.*, 163a.

The atoning pains of the suffering Messiah are so clearly emphasized in these passages of *Pesikta Rabbathi* that Moore sees there a late appropriation of Christian doctrine.[1] But he does not prove it, and the fact remains that mediæval Judaism accepted the passages in question as the product of genuine Jewish thought. In view of the strength of these texts, the following words of Montefiore about the Messiah : " To his sufferings—and even to his sufferings for the sake of his people—there are occasional allusions "[2] will appear as an understatement. But, even as they are, these words constitute an important admission.

That the idea of a covenant of atonement was a living force in Israel is proved by the existence of a " Damascus sect," the members of which called themselves " the men who entered into the new covenant in the land of Damascus." This covenant was a *berith* of penitence. The believers relied on an atonement to be made by God Himself, and they looked for the advent of a Messiah " from Aaron and Israel," for the coming " in the end of the days " of a Teacher of Righteousness who will be received by " the poor of the flock "—" And, through His Messiah, God shall make them know His Holy Spirit."[3]

We ought to indicate here the five volumes written in French since 1933 by J. Brierre-Narbonne on the references to the Messiah in post-biblical literature.[4] They contain the fullest collection of such texts, with good translations and excellent introductions.

(e) *The Suffering Servant.* The question asked of Philip by the Ethiopian chamberlain about the meaning of Isaiah liii. 8 : " Of whom speaketh the prophet thus ? Of himself or of some other man ? " (Acts viii. 34) remains a matter of dialogue between the Church and the synagogue.

The majority of modern critics hold that the so-called Servant passages refer to a national personage or to the personified collectivity of Israel and are devoid of Messianic significance. The question with which we are here concerned is not whether this or that interpretation is right, but how the

[1] *Judaism*, I, p. 551.
[2] *Rabbinic Literature and Gospel Teachings*, London, 1930, p. 305.
[3] See *Fragments of a Zadokite Work*, IX, 28, in Charles' *Apocrypha and Pseudepigrapha*, 1913, II, 785–834.
[4] *Les Prophéties messianiques de l'Ancien Testament dans la littérature juive*, Paris, 1933 ; *Exégèse talmudique des prophéties messianiques*, Paris, 1934 ; *Exégèse midrašique des prophéties messianiques*, Paris, 1937 ; *Exégèse apocryphe des prophéties messianiques*, Paris, 1937.

Jewish tradition understood these texts.[1] It is true that many Jewish expositors, down the centuries, abandoned the Messianic theory. Saadiah saw in Jeremiah the original of the Servant. Rashi, Ibn Ezra, Qimhi, Abarbanel interpreted the prophecy as applying to Israel. Nahmanides allowed readers to choose freely between Israel or the Messiah. But the classical Jewish exegesis, in Targum and Talmud, interpreted Isaiah liii as referring to the Messiah himself. Rabbi Ibn Danon protested against Rabbi Joseph ben Kaspi, who said that those expounding this chapter of the Messiah " gave occasion to the heretics to interpret it of Jesus " ; Ibn Danon writes : " May God forgive him for not having spoken the truth ! . . . The principle which every expositor ought to rest upon is never to shrink from declaring the truth in order that such as are foolish may not err." Israel Abrahams, speaking of the Jewish exegesis of Isaiah liii declares : " The Messianic interpretation persisted and persists."[2]

Some rabbis united a historical and Messianic interpretation. Ibn Danon himself had received a private revelation as to the Suffering Servant : it had been communicated to him from heaven that the section was originally uttered with reference to King Hezekiah, but nevertheless, as " a word deftly spoken," alluded covertly to the Messiah. Salomon de Marini thought that Israel *and* the Messiah were both intended. Such views gain a hearing to-day. The three interpretations of the Suffering Servant—the Personal, the Communal, the Messianic —do not exclude each other, but may be harmonized as three different perspectives or stages of the same reality. Much of the Servant songs evidently deals with what has taken place in the past and refers to a well-known person, such as Zerubbabel, according to Friedmann (1890) and Sellin (1898), or Jehoiachim, according to Levertoff (1905) and Sellin (1909)— this Jehoiachim who, after being in prison for thirty-six years, was freed and re-established as prince by the King of Babylon. But the national hero could easily become a symbol of Israel, and Israel a symbol of the Messiah. Thus Eduard König, for whom the Suffering Servant is Israel, writes at the close of his *Exile's Book of Consolation* : " . . . The better portion of Yahweh's people which in faith and patience bore the sufferings of the Exile, came to be viewed as a type of Him who, although

---

[1] See Neubauer and Driver, *The Fifty-Third Chapter of Isaiah according to the Jewish Interpreters*, 2 vols., Oxford, 1877.
[2] *Jewish Interpretation of the Old Testament*, in *The People and the Book*, p. 408.

absolutely innocent, yet took upon Himself the heaviest sufferings, in order that He might redeem mankind from that real exile which consists in separation from God."[1]

As a most erudite and remarkable instance of the blending of the personal, national and Messianic interpretations, attention should be paid to Aubrey Johnson's recent reconstruction of the ceremonial of the Feast of Tabernacles.[2] We can only outline the main idea. From certain psalms Johnson infers that the Feast of Tabernacles conformed to some ritual pattern current in the Near East and culminating in the symbolical re-enactment of the death and resurrection (" new life through death ") of the god, whose place was taken by the king. The Israelite king, representative of Yahweh on earth and his adoptive son, and also the focussing point of the psychic life of the people, was symbolically made to suffer humiliation and then delivered and restored, so that the people forming a psychic whole with their king could also be saved from death and proved " righteous." The poet had witnessed or known the ceremonial which took place annually in the Temple at Jerusalem ; he interpreted in the light of this ceremonial the sufferings which the fall of Jerusalem and the captivity brought upon Israel ; hoping that the final outcome would be the same, he established the following correspondences or equations : the nation=the king=the Servant=the Son. And the Son, in the Psalms, is identified with the Davidic king or Messiah. In the defence of this subtle interpretation, Johnson does not confine himself to generalities, but extends his inquiry to minute details.

Rudolf Otto, in his last great contribution to theology, has tried to establish that Jesus interpreted His own death in the light of the second Isaiah's conception of the Suffering Servant.[3] R. Newton Flew, commenting on the views of Otto, writes : " The proof that Jesus transformed the contemporary conception of Messiahship in the light of Isaiah liii. is cumulative, and, I think, convincing."[4] A Roman Catholic scholar, J. S. van der Ploeg, has written[5] an elaborate and well documented defence of the traditional interpretation of the Songs of the Servant, in which he sees a literal prophecy of the

[1] Quoted by I. Abrahams, *ibid.*, p. 410.
[2] *The Rôle of the King in the Jerusalem Cultus*, in the symposium *The Labyrinth*, edited by S. Hook, London, 1935.
[3] *The Kingdom of God and the Son of Man*, translated from the German by F. V. Filson and B. Lee Woolf, London, 1938, chiefly pp. 289–295.
[4] *Jesus and His Church. A Study of the Idea of the Ecclesia in the New Testament*, London, 1938, p. 103.
[5] *Les Chants du Serviteur de Jahvé dans la seconde partie du livre d'Isaïe*, Paris, 1936.

Christian Messiah, due to a direct divine revelation. Thus, notwithstanding the present modern tendency, the Jewish Messianic interpretation of Isaiah liii. has survived, as an unbroken line, till our day.

(f) *The Cross.* The theme of the cross recurs in rabbinical literature, where it does not receive any systematic or explicit treatment, but is rather alluded to in some mysterious undertone. According to a rabbinic interpretation, the words of Deuteronomy xxviii. 66 : " Thy life shall hang before thee " are meant of " him who goes out in order to be crucified."[1] Rabbi Ammi writes : " Thou thinkest that the phrase ' either a Jew or a crucified ' is an offence ; it is not an offence but, on the contrary, a praise,"[2] thus establishing a veiled link between Israel and the cross. In a parable, a king sees how a beam is put on his son, who is led to death, and exclaims : " Put on me as much as you will : I will carry it."[3] (Here we find the two important ideas of the punishment of the king's son and of the voluntary carrying of the cross.) The following moving dialogue goes on between Rabbi Nathan and the community of Israel : " What has happened that thou goest out to be crucified ?—It is because I ate unleavened bread.—Why have they lashed Thee ?—Because I carried palm branches ; these chastisements have won me favour with my Father in heaven."[4] Without forcing such passages into clear and definite interpretations, it is hardly necessary to say what interest they offer to a Christian.

Closing this inquiry about the conceptions of expiation and atonement in the Jewish tradition, we must emphatically say that the ideas of original sin, objective atonement, intercession, vicarious suffering, Messianic suffering—which seem absent from modern Judaism (though we may discover them even there, if we rightly understand the meaning of the Day of Atonement)—have a place in the most ancient and authentic teaching of Judaism.

ELEMENTS COMMON TO JUDAISM AND CHRISTIANITY

We have tried to compare Jewish and Christian beliefs on the very points on which they are said radically to differ. We have inquired whether the Christian doctrines of the Word and Son of God, of the Holy Ghost, of the Incarnation and

---

[1] *Esther R.*, i. I (1a).
[2] *Exod. R.*, 42 (100b).
[3] *Midrash on Psalms*, XXII, 9.
[4] *Lev. R.*, 32 (86b). See Dalman's *Jesus-Jeshua*, p. 190.

Redemption are so entirely foreign and antagonistic to Jewish monotheism as they are commonly supposed to be. We have considered how far the Jewish traditions of the Memra, the Sonship, the Shekinah, the Spirit, the Atonement can help us to solve this problem. What general conclusions are we able to reach ?

One must categorically repudiate the naïve endeavours to find in Jewish tradition the present Christian dogmas of the Trinity, Incarnation and Redemption. Such definite teachings cannot be found in, or deduced from, or proved by the Targums, the Talmud and the Zohar. The question whether they could be established by the Scripture alone will be left on one side, as we do not intend to consider Judaism apart from its historical theology.

But we shall be bold in saying that some fundamental elements are common to the rabbinical tradition and to the Christian christology, soteriology and pneumatology. These elements, in Judaism, are to be found among the various teachings which tried to express the intercommunication between God and man. The Jewish notions concerning the Memra, the divine Sonship of the Memra and of the Messiah, the Shekinah, the *Ruah-ha-Kodesh*, the *kapparah*, the intercessors, and the Zoharic speculations on the triadic aspect of the Godhead contain a theological *nucleus* which is also present at the centre of the Christian doctrines of the Trinity, Incarnation and Redemption. As Abelson said, speaking of the Zohar : " Some of the cardinal doctrines of Christianity are embedded in these ideas."[1]

It seems that the starting point of such ideas was a spiritual experience, a deep need of a " coming down " of God to man and of the expiation of sin by a perfect Mediator. These inner experiences, which agreed with several passages of the Scripture, gave birth to certain thought-tendencies, still vague. At a further stage of development these thought-tendencies became crystallized in definite conceptions : the conception of the Word and of the Spirit, distinct from the Father ; the conception of the unique Sonship of the Word and of the Messiah ; the conception of the Presence of God in this earthly world and of its visible manifestation ; the conception of the mediation of the Word and of the atoning suffering of the Messiah and of the righteous. The sense conveyed by this development of thought is—we should not hesitate to say it—

---

[1] *Jewish Mysticism*, p. 67.

the same sense which the Christian doctrines of the Trinity, Incarnation and Atonement express.

Once more these " prefigurations " and correspondences are no " dogmas " of Judaism. Rabbinical theology presents these truths by quite other and less highly technical terms than the Christian Greek theology. Judaism keeps free from elaborate systems. " No one," says Abelson,[1] " really wanted to know what God was, or what the Shekinah or Holy Spirit were, in their absolute or essential nature. The reality of their existence was experienced in the practical life. This was all, and this was enough."

Nevertheless we find already in the Jewish tradition the embryo of a consistent theology capable of translating into purely Hebraic words and Hebraic meanings the beliefs until now clothed with Greek garments. Let us take, for instance, the prologue of the Fourth Gospel, so often represented as a Hellenistic product : " And the Word (*Logos*) became flesh, and dwelt (*eskenosen*) among us . . . and we beheld His Glory (*doxa*) " (Jn. i. 14). Let us translate these Greek terms into Hebrew thoughts and words. We obtain something like this : " And the *Dibbur* (or *Memra*) became flesh, and was the *Shekinah* among us . . . and we beheld his *kabod* (or *yekarah*)." We recognize these three Jewish conceptions already often mentioned—the Word, the Presence or indwelling, the glory or shining of the Presence—and thus the very heart of the Christian faith is expressed in terms and ideas familiar to traditional Judaism. Of course, the " became flesh " would have to be explained, as distinct from a simple descent or dwelling.

But have these conceptions any interest other than an historical one ? Do they still belong to the living Judaism of our days ? How many contemporary Jews have ever heard of the Memra ? How many of them (save the mystical Hassidim) care for the Shekinah ? Has Christianity any hope of entering into a new relationship with Judaism on a so-called " common ground " which may have been important many centuries ago, but remains entirely alien to the 20th century Jewry ? We must admit that this is a real and difficult problem.

In a practical religious approach to the Jews, the Christian will usually have to choose a ground other than the notions which we have expounded. Even in the golden centuries of Jewish theology these notions, writes Abelson, " were ever for

[1] *The Immanence of God in Rabbinic Literature*, p. 366.

the few rather than for the many."[1] They have been, in later Judaism, largely eliminated from popular religion. Oesterley and Box are right in saying[2] that " they largely belong to the wider and richer Judaism of the earlier period, which has given place to the narrower and more restricted Judaism of subsequent times." Nevertheless, we persist in considering these thought-tendencies as most important. Christianity must have in view not only the Jews of such and such a period, but Judaism itself, as an historical whole. Neither from the Jewish nor from the Christian standpoint is it to be wished that these precious gems of the Jewish tradition should be thrown overboard. A revival of the " wider and richer Judaism of the earlier period " or, at least, a widening and deepening of present Judaism, is not excluded from the possibilities of to-morrow. A Christian can but sympathize with the recommendation of Montefiore : " Let us not persist in keeping to a poorer Judaism than we need."[3]

There are some signs of such widening and deepening. The most intimate friend and disciple of Buber, Franz Rosenzweig, who died, young and much respected, in 1928, published a great work, *The Star of Redemption* (1921), which interprets life by three elements : creation, revelation, redemption. This triadic theology is based on the Old Testament, but contains Zoharic elements and—somewhat " transposed "—much of the Jewish trend of thought which we have expounded.

Apart from the dialogue with Judaism, we are convinced that such conceptions as the Shekinah or the Glory could help and enrich Christian theological thinking, were they fully assimilated by it.

Finally we should not forget that such facts as the mediation of Christ, the sacrificial and atoning value of His death on the cross, His victorious resurrection are approachable only through faith.

The questions concerning the Word, His presence on earth, His mediation, and the Spirit had to be considered first, as they are supposed to be the " chief offences " against Jewish monotheism. The question of Messianism has been left aside, because it is on another plane. We shall turn to it now.

[1] *The Immanence of God in Rabbinic Literature.* p. 366.
[2] *Synagogue Religion and Worship*, p. 220.
[3] *The Old Testament and After*, p. 291.

PART FOUR

THE MESSIANIC HOPE

JEWISH AND CHRISTIAN MESSIANISM

" We all await a Messiah " said the Jew Trypho to Justin Martyr[1]. " Jewish religion " writes Berdyaev (who has seen perhaps more deeply than any other Christian into the essence of Jewish Messianism) " is permeated with the Messianic idea which is, indeed, its pivot. . . . The Messianic idea is the determining factor in the historical drama of the Jewish people."[2] On the other hand, Christians, too, believe in a Messiah, who, according to them, is Jesus of Nazareth. What are the common elements between Jewish and Christian Messianism ? Will these two Messianic beliefs be necessarily conflicting, or can Messianism become a common ground for Jews and Christians ? Before attempting to answer this question, we must consider the respective doctrines of the Messianic idea in Judaism and Christianity.

" The late-Jewish Messianic world-view is the crater from which bursts forth the flame of the eternal religion of love." Thus speaks Schweitzer[3], truly and impressively. But it is not easy to clarify this late-Jewish world-view. The danger is to over-systematize and to make too definite statements. In the time of Jesus, the Messianic belief was far from being fixed. Different writers upheld different theories ; the treatment then given to the whole subject reflected a kind of vagueness and hesitancy, not to say confusion. One of the greatest mistakes of Christian apologetics (especially in the controversies with Jews) has been to assume that the lines of Messianic belief which prevailed later—in Christianity—were already predominant at the time of Jesus. Between the Messianic conceptions of the pious Essenes and those of the patriotic Zealots, there was a gulf. "The angle of vision differed with each observer, for on this subject there was no authoritative teaching."[4]

---

[1] *Dialogue* 49, 1.
[2] *The Meaning of History*, translated from the Russian by G. Reavey, London, 1936, p. 88.
[3] *My Life and Thought. An Autobiography*, translated from the German by G. Campion, London, 1933 ; see pp. 18, 26, 50f, 248.
[4] C. Guigncbert, *The Jewish World in the Time of Jesus*, translated from the French by S. Hooke, London, 1939, p. 138.

In agreement with modern research on Messiahship,[1] it seems that we might summarize the Jewish Messianic belief along the following lines: A Messiah or a Lord's Anointed would be first preceded by Elijah; then he would come himself, heralded by troubles and calamities of every kind: wars, famines, etc. It would be a real upheaval of nature. The wicked would form a coalition under the command of a leader, whose identity remained rather vague. These hosts of evil would be defeated, but the identity of the victor was also undefined; the greater number believed that this conqueror would be the Messiah himself. The Messianic Kingdom would be established in Jerusalem. After a long period of years, perhaps a thousand, this period of peace and unparalleled happiness would come to a climax: all corruptible elements would be destroyed in a purifying fire; the dead would arise; the righteous and the wicked would receive their reward; the sentence would be pronounced by the " Son of Man," giving judgment in God's name. In the Pharisaic circles it was held that the Messiah would belong to the tribe of Judah and house of David, as the prophets had foretold. The idea of the advent of a Messiah of the tribe of Levi had also gained adherents. According to a very widely held view, another Messiah, a son of Joseph or a son of Ephraim, would come, whose relation to the Messiah son of David is hard to define. The Talmud speaks of him. He was to die in battle, and it is in connexion with him that the question of a suffering Messiah might be raised.[2] There is an intimate connexion between the idea of the Suffering Messiah and the words of Isaiah liii. about the Suffering Servant. Hugo Gressmann has pointed out that the Servant " undergoes sufferings and trials with his people, but cannot be identified with them."[3] Guignebert, who is himself very far from Christianity, remarks: " If Gressmann is right, Christians had some justifications for seeing in the passage in question a reference to their own Messiah, Jesus."[4]

The double motive of the Messiah's love for His Own and of Israel's love for the Messiah is never absent from the Messianic expectation. The Messiah is not only the

[1] W. Oesterley, *The Evolution of the Messianic Idea, a Study in Comparative Religion*, London, 1908; M. J. Lagrange, *Le Messianisme chez les Juifs*, Paris, 1909; H. Gressmann, *Der Messias*, Göttingen, 1929.
[2] G. Dalman, *Der leidende und der sterbende Messias der Synagoge im ersten nachchristlichen Jahrtausend*, Berlin, 1888.
[3] *Der Messias*, p. 317.
[4] *The Jewish World in the Time of Jesus*, p 147.

formidable Anointed King or the heavenly Son of Man ; he is also the winning and gracious figure of the Shepherd, with his individual care, his tender love, and his long journey after the lost sheep.

One must admit that the description remains somewhat confused and cloudy. Messianic teaching was sometimes concerned with a Person, sometimes with an era As early as the first century, Jewish imagination was concentrated rather on the coming Kingdom than on the figure of the Messiah. The Messiahship was attributed to various historical personages. Zerubbabel, Cyrus, Alexander, were suspected of being the Messiah, " and Josephus has the incredible effrontery to claim that the Promises found their fulfilment in Vespasian."[1] The Messianic impulse was certainly behind the constant state of. unrest and rebellion in Palestine. The risings of Menahem, Theudas, Bar Kochba, gave a concrete expression to nationalist Messianism.[2]

The Messiahship of Jesus did not win general recognition among the Jews. That does not mean that the personal Messianic hope in Israel vanished after the second century. From the abortive insurrection of Bar Kochba until the 18th century, many self-styled Messiahs arose, their appearance being often accompanied by revolts, uprisings, creation of new sects. More than twenty of those pseudo-Messiahs awoke in the Jewish Diaspora the hope of the Return to the land from which the people were exiled. The most influential of the pseudo-Messiahs was Shabbatai Sebi (=1676), whose name and claims spread from the Mediterranean shores to the North Sea.[3] The lamentable failure of this self-appointed leader, the adoption of Mohammedanism by his adepts, the conversion to Christianity of his most prominent successor, Frank, and the Frankists, deeply discouraged the expectation of a personal Messiah. No other pseudo-Messiah afterwards was seriously accepted by any considerable section of Jewry. The need for finding new outlets for the Jewish religious enthusiasm, so

[1] Guignebert, op. cit., p. 151.
[2] We must mention here the famous work of R. Eisler, Jesous Basileus ou Basileusas. Die messianische Unabhängigkeitsbewegung vom Auftreten Johannes des Täufers bis zum Untergang Jakobs des Gerechten nach der neuerschlossen Eroberung von Jerusalem des Flavius Josephus und den christlichen Quellen, 2 vols., Heidelberg, 1929. Eisler links the " Jesus movement " with those " messianic independence movements." In common with the almost universal opinion, we deplore the fact that Eisler's treasure of erudition should be wasted in the service of a scientifically lost cause.
[3] See special note K.

painfully deceived, partly explains the growth of the mysticism of the Hasidim in the 18th century.

What is the present state of the Messianic belief among the Jews ? The twelfth article of the Jewish creed proclaims : " I believe with perfect faith in the coming of the Messiah, and, though He tarry, I will wait for his coming." This confession of faith says nothing about the nature, the personality and the duties of the Messiah. The Talmud gives a much fuller expression of the orthodox Messianic belief, but modern Jews are little acquainted with the Talmud. Even in Jewish orthodox communities, not much is said about the Messiah, and a very great part of the faithful do not think of Messianism in personal terms. Liberal Judaism is quite explicit on this subject : " The whole doctrine of the Messiah no longer concerns our religious life and aspirations," says C. Montefiore ; he says again : " We do, indeed, believe in the conception of the Messianic age. . . . But we do no longer believe in a *personal* Messiah. . . ."[1]

On one point the orthodox and liberal Messianic beliefs agree still more perfectly : it is on the rejection of the Messiahship of Jesus. Buber writes : " He who acknowledges Jesus to be the Messiah already come cannot belong to us ; he who tries to weaken or divert our belief in a redemption still to come, there is no agreement with him."[2]

Shall we say that Messianism has almost disappeared from modern Judaism ? Certainly not. The Messianic element remains the very special peculiarity of Judaism. The Jews remain what they always have been—a Messianic people. What is this Messianism without (in the majority of cases) a personal Messiah ? Modern Jewish Messianism essentially consists in a Messianic attitude ; the Jews of to-day, like their ancestors, are messianically-minded. Jewish piety, in its most distinctive feature, is the experience of " expectation." Speaking of the Messianic expectation in the time of Jesus, Guignebert rightly says : " I use the term *expectation*, a hope which became increasingly impatient. . . ."[3] This is exactly modern Jewish Messianism : an increasingly impatient hope, the expectation of a future all-illuminating world era, a passionate longing for its coming. Is it only the obsession of justice and its terrestrial fulfilment ? It may be so among

[1] *Liberal Judaism*, p. 176.
[2] Quoted by H. Cosmala in *International Review of Missions*, vol. 26, 1937, p. 110.
[3] *The Jewish World in the Time of Jesus*, p. 139.

the more rationalistically minded Jews, but, for the majority of them, it is the expectation of something wider and less precise, the aspiration towards a divine future, the marvels of which are still veiled. It is the unquenchable thirst for the advent of the Kingdom of God · then the promises made to the beloved People will be fulfilled and all tears will be wiped away. Most of the Jews may have abandoned the faith in a " coming One," but they ardently believe in what Buber designates by the indefinite and complex German term *das Kommende*, " that which is coming."[1]

The Jewish book *Kuzair* (12th century) said that Judaism, Christianity and Islam, are like three rings having such a close resemblance that one can hardly distinguish one from the other. In a recent comment on this saying, the French Arabic scholar Louis Massignon wrote that on each ring one could inscribe a name—on the ring of Islam, faith ; on the ring of Christianity, love ; on the ring of Judaism, hope. Judaism is certainly more than a mere religion of hope ; nevertheless, the Messianic hope remains the centre of Israel's religion.

Let us now turn to Christianity. Can we discern in it an equally intense Messianic consciousness ?

The Christian attitude in relation to Messianism is rather strange. Christians believe in a personal Messiah. Notwithstanding this belief, they are far less messianically-minded than the Jews. Their lack of Messianic consciousness takes two forms. They have largely lost the sense of Jesus' Messiahship. And they have, largely also, lost the Messianic vision.

The Greek name *Christos* means " anointed" and is the literal translation of the Hebrew *Meschiah*. Now the idea of the Anointed is a specifically Jewish idea. It fell decidedly into the background when Christianity left its Palestinian home and became a Gentile religion. In the world-wide Christianity, outside Judæa, the conception of " Messiah " gave way to the Greek conception of *Kyrios*, " lord." As to the name *Christos*, its original meaning was forgotten and it gradually became a proper name. The same thing happens when the name " the Buddha," away from its original Indian home, is understood as a proper name. Christians who think or speak of Christ almost always forget the Semetic word and

---

[1] M. Buber, *Das Kommende, Untersuchungen zur Entstehungsgeschichte des Messianischen Glaubens*, 1936. On the Messianist theses of W. Cohen, see special note. See also Wasserzug, *The Messianic Idea and its Influence on Jewish Ethics*, London, 1913.

ideas which this name translates ; in fact, they forget that Jesus is primarily the Messiah. The very idea of Jesus' Messiahship has passed away from their minds. Deissmann, speaking of this process of transformation, says that he does not believe that the substitution of meanings thus effected has a decisive importance " for the present-day Christian piety."[1] But it certainly has. The whole Christian outlook has been altered by it.

Having lost the original sense of the word " Christ," Christians (or, to be exact, most of them) have also lost the Messianic vision, i.e., the expectation of the divine future, the orientation towards " what is coming." Messiahship, for them, belongs to the past and refers to an historical event which once happened. The Messiah has come in the person of Jesus: no more remains to be said about Messiahship. The dynamic aspect of spiritual life, the gift of grace or of the Holy Spirit, is not connected by them with any Messianic coming. It is true that an important revival of eschatology has recently taken place in theological thinking, but this revival has hardly affected the Christian masses and their practical piety. The " Come, O Lord Jesus ! " of the first centuries, the passionate expectation of the Second Coming are seldom to be found in the Christian Churches of to-day.

There are, of course, exceptions. Some denominations (Irvingites, Adventists, Elim Four Square Gospel, etc.), show an undeniable Messianic and apocalyptic trend. And, for the Orthodox Church, the things that are to come have always been more important than the things that now are. This has given to the Orthodox Church that other-worldly atmosphere and orientation which the secularized West should perhaps learn from the East. The main importance of the Eastern Church lies perhaps in the fact that it became the religion of the Russian people, and that, until our own days and in spite of the Soviet fight against religion, it has maintained a form of Christian consciousness antithetical to Western Christianity— an eschatologic and often apocalyptic consciousness—and has now confronted this consciousness with the apocalyptic and messianic consciousness of the Soviet regime and thus begun a new chapter in the history of Christianity.

But, on the whole, Christian Messianic consciousness looks backward, while Jewish Messianic consciousness looks forward. Thus the situation could be summarized as follows :

[1] *The Religion of Jesus and the Faith of Paul*, translated from the German by W. Wilson, London, 1923, p. 136.

The majority of Jews do not believe in a personal Messiah, but keep a decided Messianic attitude. The majority of the Christians believe in a personal Messiah, but have no longer any Messianic attitude. Now could Jewish Messianism and Christian Messianism be brought together? Could the Christians receive something from Jewish Messianism?

The question of Jesus (this stumbling-block!) cannot be omitted. The Christians will not hide or understate the fact that, according to their belief, Jesus of Nazareth is the Messiah foretold by the Scripture. But it will probably not be found very useful, at least as a starting-point, to concentrate on the " arguments " or biblical texts which lead to the identification of Jesus with the Messiah. The Christians should, first of all, help the Jews to discover and appreciate the Christian Messianic line of thought in its entirety. Now Christian Messianism is not exhausted by the historical life of Jesus. Even a Christian believes that the Messianic kingdom is still to come. It comes every day and it will come in its fulness " at the end of the times." Therefore it remains, to-day as yesterday, an object of expectation. In this expectation of the coming Kingdom a Christian and a Jew can feel themselves at one. When the Jews have understood the Christian expectation of the Messianic kingdom, and sympathized with it, and recognized it as a " looking forward " like their own expectation, the Christians may explain why they consider Jesus as a personal Messiah and the inaugurator of the Messianic times. (The ancient prophecies, if rightly understood, have lost nothing of their strength.) But the Christians will remember that Jesus has only founded the Kingdom of God on earth and not achieved it : the Kingdom is daily growing. The Christians must long for its completion, and in this longing the Jews must be able to appreciate a genuine Messianic attitude.

Will they go further? There is nothing in the spirit and letter of Judaism (if not in Jewish traditional practice and mental habit) that would hinder the recognition of Jesus as the Anointed One and the bearer of the present and future as well as of past Messiahship. But, in most cases, traditional practice and mental habit will have more weight than the theoretical possibility. Nevertheless, a real " Messianic communion " would be possible between Jews and Christians if both were inspired by a common Messianic hope and expectation. Such an authentic Messianic attitude requires a deep change of life in Jews and Christians alike. The former would have to disentangle themselves more and more from these material interests which are always for them the greatest temptation and hindrance and to concentrate on the approaching Kingdom. The latter would have to take more seriously than they ever did the Second Coming of their personal Messiah. If these changes were effected a " Messianic communion " could exist between Christianity and Judaism, although the person of Jesus would not be viewed in the same way by Christians and Jews. And, perhaps more easily than through the medium of thought, this " Messianic communion " could express itself through the way of practical co-operation, of " life and work." Much could be achieved by Christians and Jews messianically-minded and acting together.

Yes, much could be achieved on the empirical plane, but what would be the spiritual value of these achievements ? Speaking from the strict Christian standpoint, what could be a " Messianic communion " that was not, from both sides, a " communion in the Messiah " ? Would it not be a vain attempt to escape the ultimate challenge of Him Whom we hold to be the Messiah Himself ?

Speaking again from the strict Christian standpoint, we may answer that there is no action whatever, sincerely made for the sake of the Messianic Kingdom, which is not made for and in the Messiah. There is no Messianic communion which is not a communion in the Messiah. The Jews who work for the Kingdom may perhaps not know with Whom they have to do. When the Messianic Kingdom appears, they will learn the truth and the Messiah will manifest Himself. Let us quote some beautiful words of Schweitzer, although they do not refer especially to the Jews : " In doing God's will of love, they experience communion with the Messiah, without being conscious of it. On that basis they will, on the day of Judgment, enter into the Kingdom of God by the Messiah's decree."[1] The Messiah will even perhaps reveal His secret and His Name while they are still toiling for the Kingdom. Let us quote again, from Schweitzer, the well-known words which conclude his most important book and have been an inspiration to many souls : " He comes to us as One unknown, without a name, as of old, by the lakeside, He came to those men who knew Him not. . . . And to those who obey Him, whether they be wise or simple, He will reveal Himself in the toils, the conflicts, the sufferings which they shall pass through

[1] *Christianity and Religions of the World*, translated from the German by J. Powers, London, 1923, p. 28.

in His fellowship, and, as an ineffable mystery, they shall learn in their own experience Who He is."[1]

Judaism at its best—*i.e.*, messianically-minded Judaism—may be compared with the " certain Jew named Apollos . . . a learned man . . . mighty in the scriptures " who " being fervent in spirit," taught along the same lines as Jesus, but knew " only the baptism of John," and " began to speak boldly in the synagogue." When Priscilla and Aquila heard him, they expounded unto him the way of God more carefully ; and then he began to preach that Jesus was the Messiah.[2] The main addition of the early Christians to Jewish Apocalyptic was that they knew the name of the coming Messiah. Such are still the position and task of Christian Messianism in relation to Jewish Messianism.[3]

MESSIANISM AND EXISTENTIAL THINKING

We have already alluded to the fact that, while Messianic consciousness seems to have more or less faded away from the practical life of the Christian masses, the Messianic attitude has recently revived, to a considerable extent, in theological and philosophical thought. This fact has a very great importance for the dialogue between Christianity and Judaism and, as such, requires closer consideration.

On the Christian side an unmistakable Messianic orientation may be traced in the works of widely diverse theologians as Schweitzer, Barth, Brunner, or such philosophers as Berdyaev. On the Jewish side we find a corresponding tendency in the philosophy of Martin Buber. All these writers have a common feature ; their thought is, according to recent terminology, " existential." McConnachie will furnish us with a definition of this term : " What is existential thinking ? We shall understand it if we begin by asking what is non-existential thinking. The mathematician or the scientist thinks non-existentially. He is a spectator, registering facts or forces in a cold, objective, disinterested manner. His work demands no personal decision. So also with the philosopher dealing with the totality of things. But when it comes to personal life, in which a man's very existence is involved, he can no longer be a spectator, he becomes an actor. A question is addressed to

---

[1] *The Quest of the Historical Jesus*, translated from the German by W. Montgomery, London, 1910, p. 401.
[2] Acts xviii. 24ff.
[3] See J. Hart, *The Hope of Catholic Judaism. An Essay towards Orientation.* Oxford and London, 1910 ; P. Levertoff, *The Messianic Hope.*

him which a man answers as with his life. If he does not think passionately and personally, as with the passion of a drowning man, he does not think at all. This is existential thinking."[1]

The main trend of existential thinking, in theology proper (as distinguished from philosophy), is the line which goes from Schweitzer's eschatology to Barth's " dialectic " and further on. A Swedish author, Folke Holmström, has recently described the evolution of eschatological theology during the last forty years.[2] He observes that eschatological thought has developed by a dialectical process during three periods. The first period is the eschatology of Johannes Weiss and Albert Schweitzer ; eschatology is here conceived as happening in the time-process ; this period is the *zeitgeschichtliche Epoche* of eschatology. The second period is represented by the reaction of Karl Barth and Paul Athaus ; their eschatology is supra-historical ; it is the *ungeschichtliche Epoche*. The third and present period tries to conciliate history and supra-historical Revelation ; this period, where the names of Karl Heim, Ernst Lohmeyer, Walter Künneth, are prominent, is an *Offenbarungs-geschichtliche Synthese*.

The " thoroughgoing eschatology " of Schweitzer (developing the thought of Bousset, Haupt, Jülicher, Weiss, etc.) was a violent reaction against the figure of Jesus as painted by Ritschl and Harnack—" a figure designed by rationalism, endowed with life by liberalism, and clothed by modern theology in an historical garb," a figure which " never had any existence."[3] Instead of this Master of ethics and religion, Schweitzer painted in striking colours the figure of the Lord and Judge on whose Second Coming the hope of the first Christian generations was concentrated. Schweitzer associated this eschatological vision with the Messianic idea. " All religious mysticism must, indeed, take up into itself some kind of Messianic belief, if it is to receive the breath of life."[4] The weakness of Schweitzer's position was that he himself could not share the simple and ardent expectation of the first Christians in the Second Coming. " It is not given to history to disengage that which is abiding and eternal in the being of Jesus from the historical forms in which it worked itself out

---

[1] J. McConnachie, *The Significance of Karl Barth*, London, 1931, p. 75.
[2] *Das eschatologische Denken der Gegenwart*. Translated into German by H. Kruska, Gütersloh, 1936.
[3] Schweitzer, *The Quest for the Historical Jesus*, p. 396.
[4] Schweitzer, *The Mysticism of St. Paul*, translated from the German by W. Montgomery, London, 1931, p. 379.

and to introduce it into our world as a living influence."[1]
" The names in which men expressed their recognition of Him
as such, Messiah, Son of Man, Son of God, have become for us
historical parables."[2] Schweitzer has felt deeply the tension
between the general affirmation of the world required by life
and society and the personal rejection of the world preached
in the sayings of Jesus. " It is only by means of the tension
thus set up that religious energy can be communicated to our
time."[3] His departure for Africa, his medical and missionary
work in Lambarene, are the admirable personal solution of the
problem. But he has failed (as his recent ethics of " reverence
for life " shows) to work out a consequent eschatological or
Messianic theology applied to contemporary needs. From
this standpoint the Barthian school marks a real progress.
Besides the insistence of Barthianism on the otherness and
absolute transcendence of God (views to which Judaism would
give only a qualified assent), we find in this theology and in
some kindred existential systems of thought several features
in common with Jewish Messianism. We shall dwell at some
length on four of these features : the motive of the " Coming " ;
the motive of " obedience " ; the motive of the " instant " ;
and the motive of the " beyond."

The Messianic Parousia is not an event of the past. Jesus
is the Messiah ; He came ; and nevertheless the coming of the
Messiah is far from complete ; it is a long-drawn-out historical
process. The historical event of Jesus and the Fact of the
Messiah are not synonymous. The decisive and unique event
of the Messiah cannot be part of history, but is its eternal
background and fulfilment ; it is not a matter of perception
like all other historical events, but a matter of faith ; it breaks
continuously through history. It would be insufficient to know
the Messiah only " according to the flesh." We must expect
His definite coming at the end ; we must recognize His constant
invisible coming. It is not the coming of a grace or of a new
life, but the coming of a Person. The Messianic expectation
differs from all other expectations in that it is not primarily
expectation of something—full justice, resurrection, eternal
life, etc.—but expectation of the Lord Messiah. The Word
comes to us. One knows the central importance of the Word
in Barthian theology. Man, created in the Word and having
in it the principle of his life, but fallen away from this Word

---

[1] Schweitzer, *The Quest for the Historical Jesus*, p. 399.
[2] *op cit.*, p. 401.
[3] *op. cit.*, p. 400.

by sin, can be saved only if the Word comes to him again. Now the Hebrew Memra is much nearer to the Word in the Barthian sense than the Greek Logos. The difference between the Logos and the Memra is that the Memra is a concrete event, a personal communication. The Logos speculations of the Greek are the postulate of a Christ, the Memra is this real Word of God for which men long, not only the eternal Thought and the principle of ultimate truth, but the Word of grace bringing salvation and light. The Coming of the Word is the meaning of history. Let us listen to Berdyaev : " History moves towards a central event of absolute importance, namely, the Coming of Christ. And from this point it moves further towards the climax which is to end world history, namely, the Second Coming of the Saviour. . . . Christianity is messianical and eschatological . . . it is a movement towards a goal in which all things are resolved."[1] A beautiful non-Christian rendering of this Jewish and Christian truth of the Coming may be found in the well-known poem of Rabindranath Tagore : " Have you not heard his silent steps ? He comes, comes, ever comes. Every moment and every age, every day and every night, he comes, comes, ever comes."[2]

The idea of the Coming is associated with the idea of the " decision," *i.e.*, the crisis in which man either accepts or refuses the will of God. The Messiah's coming is not completely fulfilled as long as decision remains possible. The Barthian school has laid great emphasis on these ideas of crisis and decision, and consequently on the idea of obedience. There is no sentimentality about the Messianic message. Revelation is neither a mystical feeling nor an intellectual conception, but the Word of God and its absolute demand. As Emil Brunner excellently said : " To believe means to have a Lord, a King, who really, that is unconditionally, without restriction, is King, an absolute Lord with no democracy. The meaning of the revelation is the dethronement of the self, of the rebel, by the rightful monarch. The whole of the revelation is simply the reconquest of the rebellious province, *Regem habemus!* The days of anarchy are past."[3] This is pure Jewish Messianism. For the Messiah is King, and the King Messiah requires from us " radical obedience."

The idea of radical obedience has been impressively

---

[1] N. Berdyaev, *Freedom and the Spirit*, London, 1935, p. 304.
[2] From *Gitanjali*, London, 1929.
[3] Brunner, *The Mediator*, translated from the German by Olive Wyon, London, 1934.

expounded by Bultmann : " Radical obedience exists only when a man inwardly assents to what is required of him, when the thing commanded is seen as intrinsically God's command ; when the whole man stands behind what he does ; or, better, when the whole man is *in* what he does, when he is not *doing something obediently*, but *is* essentially obedient. . . . With Jesus as in Judaism, obedience is bound up with the crisis of decision in which man stands ; obedience is actual only in the moment of action. . . . Jesus sees the act as expressing the *whole* man, that is, he sees his action from the viewpoint of decision : Either-Or. Every half-way is an abomination. . . . He sees the concrete man in the crisis of the decision, and the decision is not relative but absolute. . . . The eschatological message and the preaching of the will of God are to be comprehended as a unity."[1] Notice the " as in Judaism " by which Bultmann characterizes Jesus' claim to radical obedience. Jesus blends the viewpoint of the rabbi and of the prophet ; in his doctrine, interpretation of the Law and eschatological preaching belong together, because the coming Kingdom is so conceived that there is no other condition for it except the one, radical obedience. While Jewish apocalyptic indulges in wishful pictures of the future, in economic and political hopes, in fantasies about revenge, hell and glory, Jesus associates eschatology with the call to repentance and the submission to the will of God. All repentance is Messianic and eschatological, for repentance or atonement and future mean in essence the same : the certainty of the new and the nearness of the far. Karl Barth rightly says that the way into salvation is to enter on a life of obedience, the " obedience of sanctification " (*Heiligungsgehorsam*), a response that must ever again be repeated.

The same emphasis on obedience may be found in the notions of several Christian movements—in the " concerns " of the Friends and in the " divinely girded and guided life " of the Oxford Group. What is the relation of radical obedience to brotherly love ? The Messianic ethic is strictly opposed to every humanistic ethic or value ethic ; it is a pure ethic of obedience. Philanthropy loses the relation to God and substitutes for it a relation to men. Love men, in them you will love God. On the contrary, Messianism, either Jewish or Christian, says : Bow first your own will in obedience to God's. The first command is : Love God. The attitude which I take

[1] R. Bultmann, *Jesus and the Word*, translated from the German by L. Pettibone Smith and Erminie Hunters, London, 1935, pp. 77, 86, 92, 93, 129.

before God defines the attitude which I take towards men. I stand before my neighbour in unselfish renunciation only when I stand before God in sacrificial obedience. Messianic love for men does not mean emotion, sympathy, kindness, but a free attitude of the will answering the call of God when He places us under the necessity of decision.

"Existential thinking links obedience and " moment."[1] The emphasis on the moment is a protest against a kind of timeless mysticism. Many Christians conceive the saving activity of God in an unhistorical way. They have the static idea of a God who is always there and to whom we only need to open our souls—of a grace imparted in a constant manner. Such Revelation is no real happening. Messianism implies that heaven is actually " moved " ; it presupposes a unique and decisive event, a certain once-for-all-ness (the *Einmäligkeit* of the " dialectic " theologians). This uniqueness is not so much linked with a certain point of space and a certain instant of time as with the absolutely decisive character of the continuous " movement " and " coming " of the Messiah towards us. The Coming of the Messiah is no mere event of the past ; it will never come to an end. " In all this whatever becomes historically visible is only the echo of this happening. It is super-history, eschatological history, hence it is no longer historical at all. Again, it is a *perfectum futurum*. . . . We cannot understand the 'Perfectum' without the 'Futurum' nor the ' Futurum ' without the ' Perfectum.' . . . By faith we live now in the city which is to come, which Christ *then* founded."[2] Two periods or rather ages stand over against each other : the passing age (*aiōn houtos*) and the coming age (*aiōn meltōn*). We live between these two ages (*zwischen den Zeiten*), in a state of strain and tension. The coming age, or eternity, is not an endlessly prolonged time, which would still be time, but the Quite Other. In Christ, this new age has broken into our world and is pressing in. The point in which time and eternity touch is defined as the " moment." It is eternity breaking in, it is the Parousia. The Parousia is not a chronological event. It is the arrival, the presence and the victory of the hidden Messiah. I have to decide here and now.

---

[1] In his Jewish drama *Le Père Humilié*, the Catholic, Paul Claudel, has grasped well the link between Judaism and the notion of the moment or instant : " Eternity and Resurrection are ceaselessly renewed in the Instant . . ." The Instant is like " the bank of the whole time which explode and annihilates itself." The Instant is the sign of the death and total sacrifice asked from Israel by its divine Spouse.

[2] Brunner, *The Mediator*, p. 583.

It is my immediate concrete situation that God constrains me to the decision. My " now " must be always for me like the last hour, in which I have to choose either for God, or for the world and my own claims. The present moment is for me the final hour, because it is the hour of decision, the hour of the coming of the Kingdom, the hour of the will of God. As Vischer says : " Now ! and I ! To-day is becoming " the last." . . . The hour of Jesus is the Present Time of God for all time and therefore is ' the last hour '."[1]

All this has an authentic Jewish ring. Common also to Judaism and Christianity is the idea that we can, to a certain extent, hasten the time and the Coming. In II Peter iii. 12, the Greek words *speudontas ten parousian tes ton theou hemeras* may be rendered by " hastening the coming of the day of God " (R.V. margin) as well as by " hastening unto the coming of the day of God." Now a distinguished Rabbi of old said : " The period of the redemption depends solely upon repentance and good works." We read elsewhere : " The Messiah will come at his appointed day, whether the Israelites repent or no, but, if they made complete repentance, God would send Him even before His time." Another Rabbi declares : " It depends upon yourselves. . . . In that very hour, I will bring the Redeemer."[2]

Levertoff gives the following expression to the inner desire of the Jewish mystics : " Everything is longing for that Messianic redemption, through which God's immanence will be fully realized. We must enter deeply into this groaning of Creation, and listen with the ears of the spirit to the plaint of the imprisoned soul of Nature and its longing for redemption. For in the days of the Messiah the inner nature of God will be revealed, and His light will permeate Man. And, if Israel would only pray in the true spirit, the Messiah would reveal Himself in all His glory now."[3]

The true Messianic relationship, the true coming of the Messiah, is to be taken possession of by Him. But this being taken possession of will be perfect only in the " beyond." We believe in the end of the present world and in a new world.

[1] " *Jetz aber ! Ich aber ! Es wird zum ' letzten ! heute* [1] . . . *Die Stunde Jesu ist die Gegenwart Gottes für alle Zeit und eben damit ' letzte Stunde'.*" W. Vischer, *Das Christuszengniss des Alten Testaments*, I Band : Das Gesetz, Munich, 1935.

[2] These passages and other similar ones from Yoma, 86a and 86b ; Sanhedrin, 97b ; Exodus R. xxv. 12 ; Pesikta K. 163b ; Canticles Rabba V. 1 ; Mdr. Psalm xlv. are quoted by H. Loewe in Appendix III to C. Montefiore's *Rabbinic Literature and Gospel Teachings*, London, 1930, p. 408.

[3] P. Levertoff, *Love and the Messianic Age*, London, 1933, p. 45.

The world renewal, linked with the Messianic Parousia, must not remain in the background. We must not be shy of the last things. We should already throw our hearts on the other side, where sin and death will not be. Brunner writes : " Death is the visible aspect of sin. . . . Death and sin merge into one another. . . . A redemption which does not remove death is by that very fact stamped as illusion. . . . Redemption, if it is to be regarded seriously, cannot therefore mean anything less than the cessation of death."[1] Our theology must not be afraid of being realistically eschatological. " The theology of Religious Radicalism will be eschatological ; it will picture God as judging the world and taking sides. . . . Religious Radicalism will have the hope of eschatology as well as its judgment. It will give men a heaven to dream of through dramatising the life of a man as it will be. . . ." Thus speak some Christian Reformers of to-day.[2] The return of the Lord in glory is as unmistakably taught by the synoptic gospels as by the creed. If the apocalyptic " stage scenery " ought to be received in the poetic spirit of its utterance, the essential vision remains unaltered. Whether we use the Hellenistic formula of *Kyrios* or the Jewish eschatological formula of Messiah, we speak in both cases of the One who is the Lord and Judge of the final Judgment, on the side of God and over against mankind as a whole.

The cataclysmic transformation of the world is far from being a hope and inspiration to the Western Church. Berdyaev often repeats that the West behaves with regard to the return of Christ and His establishment of the Kingdom as if it would never happen. The Eastern Orthodox Church has kept more vividly the belief in the Second Coming of the Lord. This belief always exercised a special fascination over the Russians ; it belongs to the core of their apocalyptic thinking. We find it deeply rooted in Khomiakov, Soloviev, Fedorov, Berdyaev, Bulgakov. The Messiah is still for us a rising sun above the horizon. He is not yet the sun at midday, the white brilliance which will pervade all. We should wait for the midday brightness with all the eschatological expectation of the primitive Church. Such an attitude has its immediate practical implications. We ought " to rise from being as the world to being other than the world."[3] There is an antagonism between the Divine and this world. As Barth says : " The Divine is

---

[1] *The Mediator*, p. 568.
[2] In the symposium *Towards the Christian Revolution*, p. 63.
[3] Schweitzer, *My Life and Thought*, p. 71.

something whole, complete in itself, a kind of new and different something in contrast to the world. It does not permit of being applied, stuck on, and fitted in."[1] Therefore an attitude of insurrection will be natural to the Christian eschatologist as it is to the Jew. Barth says further : " Why must we, at the crucial point, in spite of all our resistance, *give in* to the protest which Kierkegaard made against marriage and the family, Tolstoy against the State, civilization and art, Ibsen against the approved bourgeois morality, Kutter against the church, Nietzsche against Christianity as such, and socialism, with concentrated weight, against the whole structure of society, intellectual and material ? "[2] Barth goes on to say that we understand all this without understanding it, affirm it without affirming it, and must take part, without wishing so, in the attack directed against the deepest foundations of society. We are drawn into taking sides with the Attacker as well as into refusing to take sides. We cannot be satisfied with a conception that sees in transitory things only a likeness of Something Else. If there is a likeness, there is a promise ; if there is a promise, there must be a fulfilment. Our hopes cannot be relegated to a Beyond ; the here-and-now must open its gates to the Beyond itself. In the words of Troeltsch : " The energy of the life here is the energy of the life beyond."[3]

We have seen how much this contemporary radical theology or philosophy has in common with Jewish Messianism. The likeness becomes still clearer if we consider the thought of Martin Buber. It is significant that the direct influence of Buber is strongly felt in the works of the Christian eschatologists, Karl Heim and F. Gogarten. Buber is very far from the *desperatio fiducialis* of Barth. He would reject Barth's one-sided emphasis on the transcendence and otherness of God, his doctrine of total depravity, his depreciation of history, his neglect of Revelation in nature. For Buber, faith is a " meeting " ; it is not, as with Barth, a mere reliance on the " wholly other " God. Unless we accept an impassable gulf between God and man, the stressing of God's distance and otherness must be at the same time the stressing of His Presence ; and such is the position of Buber. He is, however, quite close to Barth in his ideas on the Coming, the instant and the decision, and the relation of obedience. A contemporary

---

1 *The Word of God and the Word of Man*, translated from the German by D. Horton, London, 1931, p. 277.
2 *op. cit.*, p. 315.
3 Quoted by Barth, *op. cit.*, p. 322.

dialogue between Christianity and Judaism would perhaps be chiefly a dialogue between Buber and Barth. The book " I and Thou " is the culmination of Buber's study of Jewish mystical writings.[1] A short survey of it will show us how the deepest modern Jewish thought coincides with the Messianic and eschatological trends of present Christian speculation.

To man the world is twofold, in accordance with his twofold attitude and the twofold nature of the primary words which he speaks. The one primary word is the combination *I* and *thou* ; the other primary word is the combination *I* and *it*, wherein the words *he* and *she* can replace *it*. The relation *I-Thou* can only be spoken with the whole being, while *I-it* cannot. In each we are aware of a breath from the eternal *Thou*, we are addressed and we answer. In each *Thou* we address the eternal Thou. If I have both, will and grace, the tree on which I gaze is now no longer *it*. I have been seized by the power of exclusiveness. I encounter no " soul " of the tree, but the tree itself. " So long as the heaven of *Thou* is spread out over me, the winds of causality cower at my heels." Causality has an unlimited reign in the world of *it*. The *Thou* meets me through grace ; it is not found by seeking. In a wonderful way, from time to time, exclusiveness arises and can be perceived and saving. Love is the responsibility of an *I* for a *Thou*. The blessedly protected man, whose life is rounded in that of a loved being, knows the *Thou*. He knows also the *Thou*, and a greater *Thou*, he who is all his life nailed to the cross of the world and who ventures to bring himself to this dreadful point—to love all men. (Would Buber have written this, had he not known Christianity as well as he does ?) *It* is the eternal chrysalis, and *thou* the eternal butterfly. God is the real *Thou*. He who speaks the word of God and really has *Thou* in mind addresses the true *Thou* of his life, which cannot be limited by another *Thou*, and to which he stands in a relation that gathers up and includes all others. Of course, God is the " wholly Other," but He is also the " wholly Present." The approach of God is the *mysterium tremendum*, but, at the same time, God is nearer to me than my *I*. I stand " before the Face." It is not a mysticism of absorption, it is not as if we were taking our refuge in One thinking Essence. Truly God surrounds us and dwells in us, but we never " have " Him in us. And we speak with Him only when speech dies within us. Man receives, and he receives

[1] Translated from the German by R. G. Smith, London, 1937.

not a specific " content," but a Presence—a Presence as a power. (Let us remember the Shekinah.) The *Thou* steps forth and confronts us. He who enters on this " absolute relation " is no more concerned with anything isolated, but everything is gathered up in the new relation and lives only in its light. To step into the messianic relation is not to disregard the things of the world, but to see everything in this relation.

Buber touches—with a great delicacy—the mystery of *I* and *Thou* in the consciousness of Jesus. What he says will, at the same time, find a deep echo in the hearts of Christians—and sorely disappoint them. The *I* of Jesus, writes Buber, was the *I* of unconditional relation in which the man calls his *Thou* Father in such a way that he himself is simply the Son, and nothing else but Son. The Son is perpetually begotten by God in the human soul. The Father and the Son, like in being—we may even say, God and Man, like in being—are the indissoluble real pair.

We have had to expound doctrines which are involved and difficult, and the necessity of being concise has perhaps made them still more obscure. We hope, nevertheless, to have shown, if only dimly, the common inspiration underlying Jewish Messianism and Christian " existential thinking." In both cases, we find a reaction against rationalism, humanism and psychologism, and an attitude of obedience and expectation towards an objective and ineffable Divine reality. We ought to deplore the fact that the Christian approach to Judaism so often has neglected and still neglects to confront the best of modern Jewish thought with the main trends of contemporary Christian theology and philosophy. Neither Maimonides nor Thomas Aquinas, were they alive to-day, would have committed that mistake.

MESSIANISM AND SOCIETY

We ought to distinguish between this world and the next, between inner and outward life ; but it is clear that in both realms we are to do the Will of God. Therefore Messianism does not simply move in the realm of ideology ; it must be a concrete approach to men. A new Community : that is the reality which modern men everywhere are seeking. So we must now consider the relevance of Messianism to the world. What contribution have Jewish and Christian Messianism to make to this quest of a new human fellowship ?

The messianically-minded Christians are generally opposed to the " right wing " totalitarianisms ; most of them are inclined towards the " left." It would be useless to enumerate here the number of movements, societies, periodicals, etc., which try to build a bridge between Christianity and a left-wing revolution. The volume of essays entitled *Towards a Christian Revolution*[1] affords an excellent survey of that ideology.

The same tendencies appear in Judaism. Left-wing religious Judaism is probably less known than revolutionary Christianity. The names and works of Rabbi Morris S. Lazaron[2], A. Bick[3], John Cournos[4] ought to be mentioned in this respect. Lazaron advocates a common front in order to defend " the American tradition of freedom and the democratic organization of society." He thinks that we all should go on being Catholics, Protestants and Jews—but better ones. All this is reassuring, comforting, and rather superficial. Bick is a real religious socialist. Cournos considers from the religious viewpoint " three of the most powerful religious movements of the day— Communism, Nazism and Fascism " ; he says that " we— Jews and Christians alike—must answer the challenge of Hitler's *Mein Kampf* with the counter-challenge of that other struggle, the struggle of Jesus to establish a free spiritual kingdom on earth founded on mercy and love." This is not new, and offers some interest only because Cournos, although he is not a Christian, accepts the leadership of Jesus. M. Levene[5] has tried to introduce Marxism and Judaism ; his book goes deeper than those which we have mentioned, for it raises the whole question of the relation of Messianism to Communism.

This question is extremely complex, because we reach here a cross-road of Christian, Jewish and Materialist influences. Marx and Engels read Feuerbach's *Essence of Christianity*, and this reading was crucial in their development. Is Marxism a sheer Materialism ? It is characteristic of the Jewish attitude to accept all that Materialism claims, even to indulge in an orgy of materialist frenzy, and yet unconsciously introduce into this Materialism something that gives men a sense of life, a working faith, a practical guidance in the problems of conduct, in short, some crude outline of a new religion. This strange

[1] Edited by Scott, R. B., and Vlastos, London, 1937.
[2] *Common Ground*, Baltimore, 1938.
[3] *Fundamental Principles of Religious Socialism*, Lodz and New York, 1938.
[4] *Hear, O Israel! An Open Letter to Jews and Christians*, New York, 1938.
[5] *Realistic Socialism in the Mosaic Law*, London, 1938.

blending of Materialism and religious fervour is peculiar to the Jewish mind. It is interesting to hear this from a Jew, J. Levine :[1] " Marxism as the world has hitherto seen it proclaims loudly its materialism, its fatalism, its religious scepticism. But, paradoxical as it sounds, it has a soul underneath, and in that soul there is latent something we can only call a religious faith. Its outward aspect is repellent enough, brutal enough, ruthless, at times terrifying. But is there not somewhere behind all this an intense zeal for social reform, for a better ordering of human life, for a fairer distribution of economic satisfaction ? Is there not about the whole movement the atmosphere of a crusade, of missionary enterprise, of fanatical earnestness ? Marx is admittedly a rebel, a sceptic, perhaps, as his opponents feel, something of a devil. But in his significance for European life and thought he reveals, not only to His disciples, something of the old Hebrew prophetic zeal, a burning' passion for moral reform, a new and startling faith in humanity."

Berdyaev has expressed the same ideas, but from a Christian standpoint. He says of the Jews :

" Their spirit, although based upon that of the Ancient Testament, evolves in the 19th and 20th centuries a distorted and perverted form of Messianism, that which expects the coming of another Messiah following the repudiation of the true one. It is still animated by the aspiration towards the future, by the stubborn and persistent demand that the future should bring with it an all-resolving principle, an all-resolving truth and justice on earth, in the name of which the Jewish people is prepared to declare war on all historical traditions, sacraments and associations. . . . Marxian Socialism, emerging from an entirely new historical background, reiterates the demand for earthly bliss. It is true that, superficially, the Marxist doctrine breaks away from the Jewish religious traditions and rebels against every sacred principle ; but in reality the Messianic idea of the Jews as God's chosen people is transferred to a class, namely, the proletariat. The working class now becomes the new Israel, God's chosen people, destined to emancipate and save the world. All the characteristics of Jewish Messianism are applied to this class. The same drama, passion and impatience which had characterized Israel, the people of God, are here manifest."[2]

---

[1] *Faithful Rebels. A Study in Jewish Speculative Thought*, London, 1936, p. 97.

[2] *The Meaning of History*, p. 89.

This Messianic character is one of the great attractions of Communism. " Communism is the one living religion in the Western world to-day " wrote Middleton Murry.[1] Many Christians have been drawn to it by these two Messianic features : radical obedience and expectation. Let us hear the pregnant words of Middleton Murry[2] :

" Repentance—*metanoein*—to have one's mind turned upside down. We begin to learn what repentance is when we collide with Communism. Then we are up against the grim reality of repentance. ' What ! give up everything ? ' Yes, give up everything. ' All I possess ? ' Yes, all you possess. ' But my freedom—surely not that ? ' Yes, your freedom—that above all else. . . . You are the slave of interest and self. Freedom is to be free for ever from that bondage, that slavery. . . That bondage to the self, Communism will take away. . . . ' But you want me to destroy myself.' That is required. That you should annihilate yourself. Destroy yourself or be destroyed ! Choose ! This is the reality of repentance. . . . Communism demands all we have, and all we are."

It is true that if we set our hearts on values that are perishing and let ourselves be dragged forward unto the future by forces which we do not even attempt to understand, we deserve to disappear with the old world to which we remain emotionally attached. It is true also that real religion finds its worst enemy not in the irreligion of Communism, but in the sham religion which worships gold and the Devil under the name of God. It is true, finally, that Communism identifies religion with idealism, with an imaginary consolation for the frustrations of actual life, in short, with illusion. This explains and even partly justifies the hostility of Communism to the historical forms of Christianity. It remains, nevertheless, impossible for the Messianism of Israel and of the Christians to come to terms with the Messianism of Communists. The reasons for this impossibility have often been expounded by Christians, but, in view of our special purpose, it is particularly interesting to hear them expounded by a Jewish writer. Ivan Levisky enumerates[3] the following reasons for disagreement :

(a) Against the Marxian economic interpretation of history, Christianity opposes the moral interpretation of history ;

---

[1] *Necessity of Communism*, London, 1932, p. 111.
[2] *op. cit.*, p. 118.
[3] In *Christianity and the Social Revolution*, London, 1935.

(b) Against the Marxist hope in social Apocalyptic, Christianity holds that the sinfulness of man makes a human Utopia impossible ;

(c) Against the Marxian view that coercion is legitimate, Christianity believes in peaceful persuasion and the victory won by love alone ;

(d) Against the Marxist view that social change is economically and historically determined, Christianity believes that individuals are the creative principle in history.

" The only answer to the atheism of the Communist is the revelation, as a creative force in material human life, of the religion of reality " says John Macmurray.[1] But under what form will this answer be given ? Would it be possible to oppose a Christian and Jewish Messianic mass movement to the Communist mass movement ? Could a Messianic revival, heralding the hope of the Kingdom and individual self-sacrifice, be started and succeed ? This is theoretically possible. It is, indeed, to be wished that in synagogues and churches alike the expectation of the Messianic Coming should be preached with burning accents now seldom heard. But we do not think that any spiritual or moral reform has ever resulted from mass movement. We find in the Scripture a clear doctrine of the relation of Messianism to Society, and this doctrine is the very opposite of the mass movement idea. This scriptural doctrine, is the doctrine of the Remnant.

The " Remnant of Israel " (Hebr. *sheerit Yisrael*) is a concept of frequent occurrence in the writings of the Prophets and closely interwoven in the construction of Israel's destiny. The greater part of Israel will fall or be carried away, but a remnant will return and be saved (Is. x. 5, 20, 22). The Remnant will be gathered (Micah ii. 12 : v. 6–7). It will be visited by God and will despoil its discomfited enemies (Zeph. ii. 9). Jeremiah makes the most elaborate use of the theory. To the " Remnant of the flock " is promised restoration and increase (Jer. xxiii. 3). Ezekiel asks whether the Remnant will not be spared (Ezek. ix. 8 : xi. 13). The poor and the meek, so often referred to in the Psalms and the martyrs of the Maccabean times, belong to the Remnant. But the Remnant is not only a factor of Jewish history ; it is also a factor of the history of Christianity.

T. W. Manson has examined the notion of the Remnant in connexion with Christian Messianism. He identifies the Remnant with the Son of Man : the " Son of Man " in the

---

[1] *Creative Society. A Study of the Relation of Christianity to Communism*, London, 1935, p. 57.

Gospel is the final term of a series of Old Testament conceptions, which are : the Remnant in Isaiah, the Suffering Servant in Deutero-Isaiah, the Son of Man in Daniel. The mission of Jesus is to create the Son of Man., *i.e.*, the Remnant. And the mission of the Remnant—in our days as of old—is to prepare the Messianic reign. " The final consummation " writes Manson[1] " is not a compensation for the sufferings of the faithful in the present, but the result of them. The Remnant is committed to a present role of service and sacrifice, not as something to be endured until better times come, but as something to be embraced in order that better times may come." The seed growing in silence and secrecy is an interim state towards the full corn. The leaven in the dough is an interim state towards the loaf. The final consummation will not be a reversal, but a fulfilment of the present Messianic elements.

Rufus Jones has attempted to interpret the idea of the Remnant and of its function and mission in the light of modern history.[2] According to him, the Remnant means small groups of persons who have vision of the true life of action for their age and travel on to the goal, ahead of the rest. They are necessarily a rare and chosen few, willing to pay the costly price involved in spiritual advances. They are an intense and devoted band inside of the larger community, an *ecclesiola in ecclesia*, resolved to keep the revelation pure and uncontaminated. They are tiny islands in a vast sea. Let us remember some of the "remnant" experiments in history. Without speaking of Montanism (the history and interpretation of which are still to be written), we may consider the hermits and monks who attempted to create a spiritual remnant within the Church. They wanted to attain the climax of renunciation and, although they could not keep continually to the height of the ideal, they offered very often beautiful patterns of holiness ; moreover they turned waste stretches of country into arable soil and were the purveyors of culture for centuries. Francis of Assisi created a new type of remnant, whose dedication and radiance came quite close to primitive apostolic Christianity. The " Spirituals," doomed to outward defeat, tried to maintain the original Franciscan ideal. The Waldensian remnant inaugurated a new era of apostolic life. The " Friends of God " of the Rhine valley prepared the Reformation. The Anabaptist, Jacob Huter, who was

[1] *The Teaching of Jesus. Studies of its Form and Content*, Cambridge, 1931.
[2] *The Remnant*, London, 1920.

martyred, worked out a type of communistic society. The Quaker "seed" sown by George Fox was a seventeenth-century Remnant. The Moravians, the Brotherhood movements, etc., were other instances of Remnant fellowships. We must notice that a certain social and economic ideal was always part of the religious message of these groups. Who applied the Gospel to the circumstances of human society more powerfully than the Franciscans or the Society of Friends? The Remnant idea has not only an historical significance, but an extraordinary value as a method of achieving social and spiritual gains. The formation of a Remnant brings a vigorous challenge and, in most cases, there is no way forward except the way of the Remnant.

We think that Rufus Jones commits a mistake when he identifies the Remnant with some minority groups. Those minority groups—which it would be wrong to treat as "sects" with a kind of contempt—had a useful task to achieve. We do not ignore their dangers and shortcomings. The judgment of a Remnant group runs the risk of being partial and one-sided. A minority aware of following the truth or striving towards it may become self-willed, stubborn and narrow. Nevertheless, there may be occasions when a Remnant can serve the Church best, not by yielding to its historic conventions, but by the championship of some vision, of some ideal which ought to prevail against the existing reality. We all know cases of divided loyalties : loyalty to the personal vision and loyalty to the Church or State. Here lies the hardest choice, here begins a path which goes over Golgatha. Such a way should never be one of violence and boasting, but one of meekness and humility. It is a pioneer work : one must resolutely go forward, make the experimental trial, and take the consequences. The world and its commonsense, the State and the Church will fiercely turn upon the Remnant. Therefore we can only speak with the utmost respect of the minority groups who suffered for the sake of a genuine Christian vision. But to identify the Remnant with any organized minority group is to alter the very nature of the Remnant. The Remnant is to be found in such groups, without being these groups ; it is to be found, and no less, in majority groups, without being the majority. The Remnant is everywhere to be found in the Church universal—it is present in every man on whom God's grace has descended.

The idea of the Remnant has been developed here at some length, because it is the most authentic Jewish doctrine on the application of Messianism to society. Although most Christians are not accustomed to think in Remnant terms, they may easily adapt this notion (which belongs to them also, since it is biblical) to their faith in Jesus the Messiah and in His Church. John Oman writes : " The early doctrine of the Church is only a continuation of the doctrine of the Remnant. It consists of those who are wholly consecrated to knowing God's mind and obeying it ; and the essential point is that they are not only redeemed but redeeming."[1]

The Remnant idea is particularly apt to correct the wide-spread illusion of a spiritual revolution through mass move-ments. There are in England some Christian groups truly messianically-minded, like the Catholic Crusade, the Socialist Christian League, the League of the Kingdom of God, the Christian Social Council, etc. ; they reflect the fervour associated with the early days of Christianity and the apocalyptic expectation of the Kingdom. Perhaps they are not quite free from the mass-movement illusion ; and they have no contact with Judaism. A small and little known group is receiving more directly its inspiration from Jewish Messianism. The Jewish Christian historian, Hugh Joseph Schonfield, has started a movement for the constitution of a " Holy Nation," a nation of unique character and purpose whose builder will be God, a " Christ-nation " that will " take away the curse of disobedience " and show a pattern of " national godliness full of grace and truth." It seems that some small but thoughtful groups have received this message and that, in some cases, lives have been completely transformed in response to this call.

It is greatly to be wished that Christian movements for social reform should grasp every opportunity to co-operate with similar Jewish movements. This would be a real approach to Messianic communion. Moreover, in the application of eternal principles to concrete and pressing problems, the Jewish example and thought has something of value to offer to the Christian world, which often needs to discover the authentic guidance of God in the sharply defined problems, either personal or social, of our day.

One last word about Messianism and society. We must never lose sight of what Oman calls " the abiding significance of the Apocalyptic." Jews and Christians can offer to the world the very thing which Communism cannot offer : the hope of eternal life. They must not be ashamed of or minimize this supra-earthly character of their message. As Principal

Micklem said in a sermon preached at King's Weigh House Church, London : " Much has been lost because our religious teachers confine their ideas to the present life alone. Our business in this world is not to establish a new order, or to aid in the progress of civilization, but to prepare ourselves for the higher experiences which will be ours when this life's schooling is ended."

PART FIVE

THE JEWISH LIFE OF GRACE AND ITS RELATION TO CHRISTIANITY

JEWISH WORSHIP

Judaism is not only a belief : it is a method of sanctification, a way to holiness ; and an intelligent and deep contact with the present forms of Jewish piety appears as a necessary condition of any real approach to Israel. Jewish religion lays a special emphasis on its communal and national character ; it is therefore natural to consider first the collective aspects of Jewish worship, *i.e.*, liturgical prayer.

The history and detailed description of modern synagogue worship (as distinct from Temple worship and the ancient Hebrew synagogue service, which belong to Old Testament study) have been already excellently written[1] and lie outside our field. Our purpose is rather to examine what could and should be the Christian attitude towards the prayer of the Synagogue.

First of all, the Christian should acknowledge the debt of Christian worship to the Jewish liturgy. The influence, both in

[1] The earliest *Seder Tephilloth* (order of prayers) or simply *siddur* (order) dates from the ninth century. The first printed Jewish Prayer-book was issued in 1486. There are considerable differences between the *minhag* (custom) of the *Ashkenazim* (Jews from German and North Slavonic countries) and of the *Sephardim* (Spanish, Portuguese and Oriental Jews) ; the German Prayer-book seems to have been derived from Galilee and that of the Sephardim from Babylonia. The Jewish Liberal congregations have shortened the service by the elimination of obsolete prayers and the curtailment of the *piyyutim* or mediaeval hymns.*

* See *The Authorized Daily Prayer-Book of the United Hebrew Congregations of the British Empire, with a new translation by the Rev. S. Singer* (1 vol.) and *Service of the Synagogue : a new edition of the Festival Prayers with an English translation in prose and verse* (6 vols.) ; and *The Annotated Edition of the Authorized Daily Prayer-Book*, with historical and explanatory notes and additional matter, compiled in accordance with the plans of the Rev. S. Singer, by Israel Abrahams, 1914. The Sephardic rite uses *Forms of Prayer* edited, with an English translation, by D. A. De Sola, and revised by Dr. Moses Gaster, 1901-1906. As characteristic of the Reformed Ritual, one could consult *The Union Prayer-Book for Jewish Worship*, edited in 1895 by the Central Conference of American Rabbis. There are modern editions of the liturgies of the Yemenite Jews, of the Falasha Jews of Abyssinia, of the Samaritans and of the Karaites, but it does not seem necessary to deal here with their pecularities. On the history of Jewish ritual, see Ismar Elbogen, *Der jüdische Gottesdienst in seiner geschichtlichen Entwicklung*, 1913. As an introduction to the whole subject, see W. Oesterley and G. H. Box, *The Religion and Worship of the Synagogue*, London, 1911.

thought and word, of certain elements of Jewish ritual on early forms of Christian worship is recognized by all liturgiologists; but the feeling of this parenthood is still far from being part and parcel of the consciousness of the average educated Christian. Of course, great care is needed in order to determine what portions of the Jewish liturgy are pre-Christian and have left marks of their influence on the Christian ritual, and the views of authoritative liturgiologists differ widely. But, in a general way, the Jewish ancestry of many of our Christian forms of worship cannot be contested.[1] The difficulty is to make the bulk of Christians more alive to this truth.

The reading of Scripture and the exposition (homily), the singing of Psalms, the responsorial *amen*, the Decalogue, the congregational confession of sins are, all of them, pre-Christian elements of the synagogue worship which have been incorporated into the Christian ritual. Without insisting on these elements, let us turn to the two central sacraments of the Christian Church : baptism and eucharist.

Next to circumcision and sacrifice, baptism was an obligatory condition for a proselyte to Judaism.[2] The complete immersion or *tebilah* had to be performed as an initiatory rite bringing the proselyte " under the wings of the Shekinah." Moreover, baptism was practised as a means of penitence and purification by Essene Judaism and by John the Precursor. Christianity read a new significance and a new purpose into the word and the act of baptism ; the Christian rite has nevertheless kept the initiatory and cleansing character of Jewish baptism, while establishing a more precise link between the purifying water and the person of the Messiah. As Gavin says : " Christian baptism, indebted to this prototype, was invested with a new meaning and, in part, refashioned it, yet it has ever preserved the tokens of its origin."[3]

The question of the Jewish antecedents of the eucharist is one of the most debated among liturgiologists. Was the Lord's supper a Passover meal ? Was it a *kiddush*, one of these religious meals which small gatherings of friends (*chaburoth*) used to arrange on the eve of festivals ? Much has been written in advocacy of both opinions, and it is perhaps as well to leave the question open. But one thing remains quite certain : it

[1] See W. Oesterley, *The Jewish Background of the Christian Liturgy*, Oxford, 1925; F. Gavin, *The Jewish Antecedents of the Christian Sacraments*, London, 1928.

[2] W. Brandt, *Die jüdische Baptismen oder das religiöse Waschen und Baden im Judentum mit Einschluss des Judenchristentums*, Giessen, 1910.

[3] *The Jewish Antecedents of the Christian Sacraments*, p. 114.

is that the breaking of the bread and the sanctification of the cup by Jesus had a character derived from the Jewish table ritual, while at the same time a new meaning was infused into it.[1]

On the sacraments generally, let us quote Gavin again : " Christianity has transformed its inheritance—yet heritage it is nevertheless . . . again and again emerge the sure tokens of an indebtedness to Judaism, immeasurably transmuted in meaning by His Power, who was Jesus the Jew. . . ."[2]

This historical feeling of continuity with and an indebtedness to Judaism, should be the first reaction of the Christian when confronted with the thought or the actuality of Jewish worship. But a mere genetic and more or less antiquarian consciousness is not sufficient. The prayer of Israel must be approached by us with a true spiritual insight. We ought not only to understand it, but to open our hearts to it and to try to share in it. Sympathy is our second task in relation to Jewish worship.[3]

Let us take, for instance, the Sabbath. The false view taken of the Sabbath by most Christians has helped to widen the gulf between the Jews and ourselves. This false view is largely responsible for the popular misconception of Judaism as a mere legalistic religion. It is a deep error to consider the Jewish Sabbath as a time of rigorous and exacting observance. The Sabbath is essentially a festal day, a day of joy and loveliness. A most beautiful expression of the Sabbath feeling may be found in the hymn *Lekah dodi*, sung on the Friday evening, which compares the Sabbath to a bride and God to her husband : " Come, my Friend, to meet the bride. Come, O my Friend, to greet the Sabbath. . . . We greet the Sabbath at our door, source of everlasting blessing. . . . Crown of the Husband, come in peace." In the Jewish home, candles or a special lamp are lit. The father celebrates the *Kiddush*, sharing the cup of wine and the loaf of bread with the members of the family, as a Holy memorial of the work of creation. At the end of the Sabbath, another cup of wine is drunk ; the wine, symbol of joy, is allowed to flow over the cup ; a lighted wax candle is put out ; spices or scented herbs are distributed : the Sabbath will perfume the whole following week. This closing ceremony

[1] On this point, besides the books, already quoted, by Oesterley and Gavin, see Paladini, *De primitiva liturgia christiana ejusque necessitudine ad liturgiam judaicam*, in *Ephemerides liturgicae*, vol. 36, Rome, 1922, and Dom Moreau : *Les liturgies eucharistiques*, Bruxelles, 1924.

[2] *The Jewish Antecedents of the Christian Sacraments*, p. 114.

[3] G. Box, *The Spiritual Teaching and Value of the Jewish Prayer-Book*, London, 1906.

is the *habdalah* or " separation." Will these ancient and beautiful rites not speak to the heart of the Christian ? Will this Christian, if he lives in some Jewish quarter—let us say, Whitechapel or Bethnal Green—not feel the coming and peace of the Lord's day, when, on Friday evening, life seems to stop and concentrate on its innermost recesses? Will he not recognize behind the forbidding exterior of the Rabbinical enactments, " the heart of passionate feeling and emotional tenderness that pulsates behind ?"[1] A Christian unable to feel the warm, the radiant Sabbath atmosphere of the Friday evening and Saturday morning, will never acquire the right approach to Judaism.[2]

Or let us take the feast of the Atonement. The day of Atonement (*Yom Kippur*)—or simply " The Day "—has a unique place in the life of the Jewish people. Many Jews who do not keep Jewish customs still attend Synagogue and fast on this day (the " Yom Kippur Jews " !) A Christian attending the Synagogue on the day of Kippur will receive there an overpowering impression of the existence and aspirations of Israel. A minute description of the Temple service of the day of Atonement is read. The rabbi reminds the modern congregation how, in the days of old, the High Priest laid his hand on the head of a young bullock offered as his sin-offering. Certain features of the Kippur, as the singing of the *Kol Nidre*— which the wireless and the gramophones have made popular all over the world—and the sounding of the *shofar* or ram's horn at the end of the *neilah* (concluding service of Kippur about sundown) are strangely impressive. But the Christian present in the Synagogue will not be moved only by the apparent emotional beauty of the service. He will see in all this a hidden meaning. He will think of the Lamb of God that takes away the sins of the world. And here we reach the deepest and supreme value of the Jewish liturgy : the Christian can accept the whole of it with its immediate meaning, and at the same time he can link it with this personal Messiah whose name he is able to utter.

The same applies to the Passover. How beautiful, how rich in meaning is the Passover to the Christian who witnesses it in Jewish surroundings ! He will see every particle of leaven (*biur-chamets*) carefully removed from the house, and he will remember the words of Paul about the unleavened bread of sincerity and newness of life (I Cor. v. 7–8). At the *seder*, or

[1] Oesterley and Box, *Synagogue Religion*, p. 373.
[2] See special note Y.

Passover home-service and meal, he will perceive the symbolical significance of each of the dishes placed on the table. The *matsoth*, unleavened cakes, mean absolute purity. The *haroseth*, mixture of nuts, raisins, cinnamon, and scraped apples, signifies, on account of its reddish colour, the clay out of which bricks were made by the Jews. The *moror*, bitter herbs with salt water, represents the hard slaving of Israel in Egypt. The hard-boiled egg symbolizes the freewill offering brought to the Temple. The roasted shank-bone is a relic of the Paschal lamb. During the meal the Christian will listen to the *haggadah*, or telling forth, with comments interspersed, of the history of Israel's captivity and deliverance ; he will realize that this ancient victory of the Jews was his own victory and liberation, since every Christian spiritually belongs to Israel, and he will think of another saving blood, staining, no more the wood of the door lintels, but the wood of a cross. The other Passover rites—the washing of the hands, the recitation of Hallel, the blessing and drinking of the cups of wine—will remind him of another Supper celebrated in a Jerusalem Upper Room. The ritual words : " Let all who are hungry come and eat : let all who require come in and celebrate the Passover. . . . This year here, next year in the land of Israel. This year as slaves, next year free " will pierce his heart with their passionate tenderness and hope.

And so it will be with every Jewish festival. *Shabuoth*, the " feast of weeks," or Pentecost a harvest-festival, but also the feast of Revelation, the memorial of the Law-giving on Sinai will bring to the Christian the memory of that Pentecost described in the second chapter of Acts. The booths and garlands of *Sukkoth* (Tabernacles), the procession with the palm-branch (*lulab*), the lights of *hanukah* (festival of lights), the *enkainia* or feast of the dedication referred to in John x. 22, will be associated, in the Christian mind, not only with episodes of the Jewish Bible, but also with episodes of the Gospel. Shall we dare to say that only a Christian will be able to give to the Jewish liturgy its fullest sense ?

Even if he is not a Hebrew scholar, the Christian will perceive something of the deep verbal beauty and suggestiveness of the Jewish prayers. Is it possible, for instance, not to be moved by the exquisite melody of this line of the Psalm xxiii : *Alme menuhoth yenahaleni* (By the waters of restfulness he leadeth me) or the tenderness of the opening verse of the fortieth chapter of Isaiah : *Nahumu, nahumu ammi* (Comfort ye, comfort ye my people) ? As G. A. Smith says : " It would be hard to find in any language words that more gently woo the broken heart of a people."[1]

A third aspect of the relationship of the Christian with Jewish liturgy has to be considered. This aspect is well expressed by Oesterley and Box who, speaking of Christian interest in Jewish worship, say : " . . . That interest must be greatly enhanced when it is realized that in the Jewish liturgy are embedded the prayers, praises and thanksgivings offered by Our Lord Himself. . . ."[2] It is nowhere directly asserted in the Gospels that Jesus pronounced a Jewish prayer (apart from the Psalms). Nevertheless, the silence of the Gospel in itself offers some justification for the belief that Jesus worshipped in the traditional way, and attention should be drawn to some prayers which he almost certainly used. We shall here restrict ourselves to the consideration of four ritual formulas :

(a) *Shema.* The most important element in Jewish prayer is the recitation of the *Shema Ysrael.* The *Shema* consists of some paragraphs from the Law : " Hear, O Israel : the Lord our God is one Lord. And thou shalt love the Lord thy God with all thine heart, and with all thy soul, and with all thy might, and these words which I command thee this day shall be upon thine heart. . . ." Originally the *Shema* consisted only of Deuteronomy vi. 4 and xi. 13–21, and Numbers xv. 37–41. That the *Shema* was of pre-Christian origin is shown by references to it in Josephus and by the discussions of the schools of Hillel and Shammai on various points connected with its recitation. The *Shema* was to be said—and still should be said—morning and evening ; it is also the last utterance to be proffered by an Israelite on his death-bed. This solemn assertion of God's unity was originally directed against the polytheism of heathendom ; later on, the mistaken idea that the Christians worship three Gods lent to the *Shema* an anti-Christian intention ; but the great Rabbi Rashi, in the 11th century, gave to the *Shema* its full meaning when he interpreted it as a hope as well as a confession of faith and saw in it a declaration that the Lord now worshipped by Israel will hereafter be alone worshipped by all mankind. Jesus was familiar with the *Shema.* The Gospels allude to it (Mk. xii. 29, and parallels).

(b) *Shemoneh Esreh.* This is a prayer composed of eighteen benedictions, which occupy the central place in the Synagogue

[1] *Legacy of Israel,* p. 13.
[2] *A Short Survey of the Literature of Rabbinical and Medieval Judaism,* p. 142.

worship. The various benedictions of the *Shemoneh Esreh* belong to different periods, but we may take as established that, with two exceptions, all of them belong substantially to pre-Christian times. The *Shemoneh Esreh*, already in the first century, had to be said three times a day. The familiarity of Jesus with the eighteen blessings is shown by their influence on the Lord's Prayer. The address *Abinu* (Our Father) occurs in the fifth and sixth benedictions. The petition for daily bread is in some sense reminiscent of the ninth benediction. The two last benedictions are parallel to these two benedictions of which it is said that their pre-Christian origin cannot be considered as evident, " while granting the probability that this may be so."[1]

(c) *Kaddish.* This word means sanctification, and the prayer thus named refers to the Name of God. It is clear that the *Kaddish* was anterior to the destruction of the Temple. The opening sentences of the *Kaddish* : " Hallowed be His great Name in the world which He created according to His will. May He establish His Kingdom . . ." suggests, by the identity of thought (name, will, kingdom), that Jesus knew this formula and derived from it the first three petitions of the Lord's Prayer.

(d) *Grace before meals.* There is a strong probability that the blessing over bread now recited : " Blessed art thou, O Lord our God, King of the Universe, who bringest forth bread from the earth " was already in use at the time of Christ.

These prayers which, if not certainly, at least very probably, were used by Jesus Himself, have disappeared from Christian practice. Some Christians will feel this as a loss. Why not give them a place again in Christian life ? It would impress Christians with the sense of following more closely in the earthly steps of their Master. And it would bring them nearer to the Church of Israel, mother of the Christian Church.

Speaking more generally, we dare to advocate here a kind of *communio in sacris* between Christians and Jews. We do not give to the term the technical sense which it assumes in Roman Canon Law, but we mean by it a sincere sharing in the sacred things of prayer and worship. A capital feature of the present movement towards Church unity (" œcumenical movement ") is the understanding participation of members of certain confessions in the worship of other confessions. The deep feeling of unity created by such participation is

[1] Oesterley, *The Jewish Background of the Christian Liturgy*, p. 154.

perhaps a greater " œcumenical " result than the theological agreements so strenuously obtained in discussions and conferences. This way—fellowship in prayer—has seldom been tried between Judaism and Christianity. And yet much of the devotional life of the Christian could help the Jew, as much of the devotional life of the Jew could help the Christian. The Christian has here an advantage. Many Christian prayers, including those most expressive of the Christian attitude, cannot be said by a Jew, while there is not a single Jewish prayer in which the Christian could not whole-heartedly join.[1]

One of the most moving experiences of common worship takes place when a Christian, attending the Atonement service in a synagogue, hears the words of Numbers xv. 26 said three times by the *cantor* and the congregation : " And all the congregation of the children of Israel shall be forgiven, and the stranger that sojourneth among them. . . ." There is more here than a mere psychological feeling. There is, or there ought to be, the consciousness of a sharing in the blessing of Israel (for the gifts of the Father are " without repentance ") —the consciousness of the real and objective value of the means of grace once imparted to Israel and even preserved by it. The Christian should feel at home in a Jewish sanctuary : everything there is also his heritage. Like Jesus and His disciples when they attended the Temple or the synagogues, he should feel that he is " in the House of the Father."

FROM THE INNER LIFE OF THE JEWISH BELIEVER

Congregational worship and synagogue ritual do not exhaust the deep reality of Jewish religious life. They are but the outward garment of an inner life of devotion and grace. The centre of Jewish worship, *i.e.*, the ritual Sabbath, the Sabbath of tradition, is the visible acme of an inward spiritual joy and the counterpart of the essential Sabbath—the Sabbath of the heart (*o quanta qualia sunt illa sabbata* !). If too many Jews are contented with a mere ritual observance and have lost the sense of the inner life, it is still truer that most Christians have not the slightest idea of the treasures hidden in Jewish personal piety. The knowledge and appreciation of this piety form a necessary part of the right relationship between Christianity and Judaism. We would like to give here at least a glimpse of personal religion in modern Israel. The

[1] See special note W.

134

simplest way to do it is perhaps to enumerate and briefly explain some of the most essential terms and notions connected with Jewish spirituality.

Hesed, grace. We put this term first, because it expresses the very foundation of Jewish inner life. Abelson doubts[1] whether " the intensity of intimacy " conveyed by the word *hesed* " is ever done justice to in a translation." *Hesed* means indeed more than grace. It includes all that is suggested by the Greek words *charis, agape, eleos,* and by the English words " goodness," " kindness," " mercy." It is best rendered by the beautiful word " lovingkindness," which we owe to Coverdale. *Hesed* is used of God's love to man rather than of man's love to man or to God. It is a mercy which comes down, a divine condescendance, a pure gratuitous gift.

Mitsvah, commandment. We already know the importance of obedience in Judaism, and we have also seen that this obedience is not a mere legalism. " Commandment," in rabbinical terminology, means every moral and religious duty grounded on God's will. But it expresses also any act of human kindness, any " good action." When a Jewish boy has completed his thirteenth year, he reaches the age of religious responsibility and becomes a *bar mitsvah*, " son of command " ; a special ceremony in the synagogue solemnizes this attainment. The keeping of the commandments means the faithfulness to a continuous guidance. The ancient Rabbis said that an angel goes forth before every *dibbur* or word of God and asks every Israelite whether he accepts such and such particular *dibbur* and all that it implied.[2] God's yoke is not heavy and painful. In close connexion with the idea of *mitsvah* stands the *simkha shel mitsvot*, the " joy in the commandments " ; again and again we meet this characteristic rabbinic phrase. To the same sphere of ideas belongs the term *lishmah*, which expresses the service made for the sake of God Himself, without any ulterior motive of reward.

Emunah, faith. Not until medieval times did *emunah* receive the meaning of dogmatic belief. In ancient rabbinical literature as well as in the Bible, *emunah* denotes either faithfulness and trustworthiness or confidence and trust in God.

Kavanah, intention. Originally the word *kavanah* conveyed a general idea of devotion, a state of religious consecration of mind and heart to the work to be done. In a precise and

[1] Article *Mysticism (Jewish)* in Hasting's *Encyclopædia of Religion and Ethics*, vol. 9.
[2] *Yalkut on Song of Songs*, I.

technical sense, it means the intention to carry out a divine precept. This intention is strictly necessary. The Rabbis discussed whether certain religious acts prescribed by the Law, if performed without thought of the divine command, could be considered as satisfying the Law. A distinct intention and inward preparation before the performance of a "command" is called for. This shows how Judaism is far from being a mechanical and legalistic observance. Rabbi Meir wrote : "All depends upon the *kavanah* of the heart."[1]

Teshubah, repentance. This name occurs only in post-biblical literature, but it is derived from the biblical verb *shub*, "to return." It corresponds, if not adequately, at least very closely to the Greek *metanoia*, the "change of mind" heralded by the Gospels. There are in rabbinical writings many beautiful passages on repentance and forgiveness, such as the following : "God says : My hands are stretched out towards the penitent ; I thrust no one back who gives me his heart in repentance." "God's hand is stretched out under the wings of the heavenly chariot to snatch the penitent from the grasp of justice " ; "Open for me a gateway of repentance as big as a needle's eye, and I will open for you gates wide enough for chariots and horses " ; "He who truly repents " is regarded by God as if he had gone to Jerusalem, rebuilt the altar, and offered all the sacrifices of the Law.[2]

The hasidic writings say : "Like the Messiah, the awakening of the sinner to repentance comes unexpectedly. . . . The sinner, in whose soul the light of the divine fire has been quenched, is greater when he repents than the righteous who have no need of repentance. . . . Since he possesses nothing in himself that could awaken spiritual life, he throws himself entirely into the arms of God."[3] This again is very far from legalism.

Repentance is associated with Messianism : "The King Messiah . . . will lead all men in repentance before God."[4]

Repentance and penitence are very closely allied notions. The consideration of the *teshubah* raises the whole question of asceticism and suffering in Judaism. It has become a commonplace to contrast Jewish joy in life with Christian asceticism and to assert that, for the Jew, this world is not a vale of tears, but a beautiful world. Jewish optimism and passion for life are strikingly evident. A careful scrutiny of the Jewish

---

[1] *Meg.* 20a.
[2] These passages are quoted from an article of C. Montefiore on *Rabbinic Conceptions of Repentance* in the *Jewish Quarterly Review*, January, 1904.
[3] Quoted in P. Levertoff's *Love and the Messianic Age*, London, 1923, p. 45.
[4] *Song of Songs*, Rabba VII, 5.

tradition will, however, show that it by no means excludes asceticism. "Which is the way which brings a man to the life of the world to come ? Sufferings. Rabbi Nehemiah said : Beloved are sufferings, for, even as sacrifices brought acceptance, so sufferings bring acceptance."[1] The world is only a halting place on the journey, "the ante-chamber to the palace,"[2] "a wayside inn."[3] Is this different from the Christian ascetic view ? We entirely agree with Montefiore's words[4] : "Such stories as that one of Chanina, for whom a measure of coarse bread was enough food from week to week, seem to me to show that the Rabbis were not the tiresomely moderate and golden-mean sort of people whom, in opposition to Christian asceticism, some of their modern apologists would wish to make them out. They knew what fervour meant, and they knew something of the passion, the exaggeration, and the paradoxes of true religion."

Something of this ascetic tendency may be found in the marriage-laws and all the prescriptions concerning sexual life.[5]

Tefillah, prayer. Great stress is laid on the outward rites of individual prayer. The fringes and the phylacteries, for instance, have a deep symbolism. To envelop oneself in the fringes and to put the phylacteries on one's head and arm means to invigorate oneself in faith. "God is found in the man who crowns himself with the phylacteries and envelops himself in the fringes."[6] But a still greater emphasis is laid on the inner aspect of prayer. The Talmud says : "What service is heart service ? Prayer."[7] Rabbi Simon recommends that prayer should not be made a fixed task.[8] Rabbi Eliezer thinks that, if a man finds that he does not feel a real heart-devotion, then he should not pray.[9] The medieval theologian, Bahya, says : "The communion of man with God usually follows the lines of stereotyped prayer. But this is not necessary. Prayer can be a thing of the heart, without any words."[10] According to the Zohar,[11] the prayer of the poor man takes precedence of the

[1] Montefiore and Loewe, *A Rabbinic Anthology,* p. 545.
[2] *Aboth* IV, 16.
[3] *Moed Katon,* 9b.
[4] *The Old Testament and After,* p. 399.
[5] *Kedoshim,* 81a.
[6] *Zohar, Tol' doth,* 141a.
[7] *Talmud Babyl.,* Taamith, 2a.
[8] *Aboth* II, 18.
[9] *Talmud Babyl.,* Berachot, 30b.
[10] *Shar Hesbon ha Nephesh* (On Self-examination), ch. 3.
[11] *Balak,* 195a.

137

prayer of Moses or David, for the poor man is the broken of heart and God is near to the broken-hearted. When the poor man prays, God opens all the windows of the firmament ; all other prayers have to make way for that of the poor man. God says : Let all other prayers wait, and let this complaint come before me.

Ahabah, love. The true lover of God and man is he who can " receive offence and resent not ; hear words of contumely and answer not ; act merely in love and rejoice even in trials as tests of pure love."[1] Love is represented as a cosmic principle in the philosophy of Hasdai Cresias and, through him, of Spinoza (*amor intellectualis*), while, for Maimonides, creative intellect is the essence of the Deity. The idea of love as an all-unifying principle was developed especially by Leo Hebræus or Abravanel.[2]

Shekinah, presence of God. We have already spoken at length of the Shekinah and of the importance of this notion in the dialogue between Judaism and Christianity. The Shekinah plays a great part in the personal experience of the pious believer.[3] The Presence is both in heaven and on earth. The upper Shekinah abides on high ; the lower Shekinah rests with the twelve holy tribes ; but the upper Shekinah and the lower Shekinah are " intertwined " and " operate together."[4] " From the first day that God created the universe, He wanted to dwell with His creatures in the nether world."[5] The true Israelite, according to Nahmanides, will, after death, find his manna, his food, the source of his continued vitality in a blessed union with the Shekinah. " He who prays must regard the Shekinah as standing over him."[6] In the Zohar, Rabbi Simeon applies beautifully to the Shekinah the word of the biblical Shulamite to her husband : " Let us make for the man of God a little chamber in the wall, and let us set before him a bed, and a table, and a stool, and a candle-stick." By our evening prayers, says the Rabbi, we provide the Shekinah with a bed ; by reciting the " sacrifice " in the morning, we provide her with a table (the sacrificial altar) ; by the prayers which are said sitting, we provide her with a stool ; by the blessings said

---

[1] *Shab,* 88b ; *Sotah,* 31a.
[2] Leone Ebreo, *The Philosophy of Love* (*Dialoghi d'Amore*), translated from the Italian by F. Friedberg-Seeley and J. H. Barnes, with an introduction by Cecil Roth, London, 1937.
[3] See special note L.
[4] *Zohar, Vayeze,* 159b.
[5] Numbers, *Rabba* xiii. 6.
[6] *Sanhedr,* 22b.

with the lights, we provide her with a candle-stick. " And blessed is the man who thus concentrates daily on giving hospitality to the Holy One! The Shekinah will greet him as her Spouse with delight day by day."

We could note many other important features of Jewish piety, e.g., humility and alms-giving ; but perhaps what has already been said is sufficient to give a true—although very rudimentary—idea of the inner life of a pious Israelite. A few words might be added concerning the Jewish conception of saintliness. Jewish tradition distinguishes saintliness (hasidut) from holiness (kedushah). Holiness is the state of separation of the sacred (persons or things) from the profane and exists in connexion with Mosaic Law. Saintliness is a lofty type of personal piety and implies much more than a mere obedience to the commandments. The Talmud recognizes the " early saints," like Hillel and Elder, Rabbi Simeon the Saint, the martyr Judah ben Baba, the Babylonian Rabbis Huna and Hisda, the great teacher Mar Sutra (who, when discipline made it necessary to put a student under the ban, would, out of humility, first proclaim the anathema against himself and then against the student), Rabbi Jose Kantanta. Among the " later saints," i.e., the saints of the Middle Ages, Rabbi Judah ben Samuel he-Hasid, of Regensburg, is perhaps the most representative type. Rabbi Phineas ben Jair (second century) described nine successive stages by which saintliness can be reached : study of the Torah, energy, cleanliness, separatedness, purity, modesty, fear of sin, inspiration, and power to bring about resurrection.[1]

None of the elements of this Jewish piety is hostile or foreign to the Christian mind. Many of the spiritual ways described above are common to Christianity and Judaism. One can imagine a Christian who would develop his own spiritual life along the traditional Jewish lines, giving, for instance, a prominent place to the experiences associated with the terms *kavanah* and *shekinah*. It is at least necessary that those Christians who have to deal with Jews from a religious standpoint should be familiar with the ascetical and mystical ways of Israel. Ramon Lull favoured and used personally, in his own Christian meditation, the Moslem emphasis on the unity and attributes of God. A good many Christians familiar with Hinduism adopt in their own piety the Indian methods of *bhakti*. The same could be done with regard to Judaism. It is remarkable and regrettable that Christian

[1] *Abod. Zarah*, 20b.

students of mysticism (for instance Evelyn Underhill) have paid little or no attention to the specifically Jewish inner life.

This inner life has perhaps been expressed at its best in the poems of the medieval mystic, Judah Halevy.[1] We shall quote some of his beautiful expressions :

" My heart is in the East, and I am far away in the West. How could I find any savour in food ? . . . My love, by thy life and the life of love which has shot an arrow at me, I have become a slave to love. . . . Let my beloved come into his garden and lay out a table and a seat, to feed in the gardens. Show thyself in my tent, among the beds of my aloe trees, to gather lilies. My beloved is mine and I am my beloved's, when I knock at the gates of his temple, to feed in the gardens. His banner is love, floating over me, and his left hand is under my head, to gather lilies. . . . O Lord, before Thee is my whole desire, and yet I cannot express it with my lips. . . . But why make any longer speech, why ask any more questions ? O Lord, my whole desire is before Thee. . . . My love, hast Thou forgotten Thy resting on my breast ? Hast Thou sold me for ever to them that enslave me ? Is there a redeemer beside Thee, is there a captive of hope beside me ? . . . He is my beloved, how could I sit solitary ? He is my lamp : how could my light be quenched ? . . . As I was going out to meet Thee, I found Thee coming towards me. . . . Who should pity my children, but I, their God ? "

Who, having heard such accents, would still say that the God of Judaism is a distant God ? Listen to another beautiful rabbinical saying : " When a man goes on his road, a troop of Angels proceeds in front of him and proclaims : Make way for the image of the Holy One."[2] And we shall conclude with a sentence which expresses the very heart of Jewish piety. Some disciples of Rabbi Isaac asked him why, in the text of Deuteronony iv. 7 (" What great nation is there that has God so nigh unto them ? ") the term " nigh " was in the plural. The Rabbi could have drawn the attention of his pupils to the plural form of *Elohim*. But he chose to give a deeper explanation. This plural affecting the term " nigh," said he, means that " God is near with every kind of nearness."[3]

---

[1] Though it is not reproduced here, we are glad to mention the English translation of the *Selected Poems of Judah Halevy* by Nina Salaman, from the text edited by G. H. Brody, Philadelpia, 1924.

[2] Montefiore and Loewe, *A Rabbinical Anthology*, p. 86.

[3] *Talmud Jerus, Ber.* ix. 1.

HASIDISM

" Throughout the whole of that field of theological literature which deals with the genesis and course of religious movements, there is probably none whose history, whose name, even, is so little known to English students as that of Chassidim. And yet it would be difficult to point, in comparatively recent times, to a dissenting movement more strikingly complete in its development, more suggestive of analogy, more full of interest in its original purpose, more pregnant of warning in its decay." Thus spoke, almost half a century ago, S. Schechter, the great Cambridge talmudic scholar.[1] Since then the literature of Hasidism[2] has grown considerably and much useful information on this subject has been made available to the English reader.[3] Nevertheless Hasidism is still far from having won in Christian theological circles the recognition which it deserves. Several motives should move these circles to a careful study and a sympathetic appreciation of Hasidism. In the first place, many of the Eastern European Jews with whom we may come into contact are Hasidian or influenced by Hasidism. Secondly, Hasidism is perhaps the most vital form of Jewish religious thought, and inspires the whole of modern Judaism far more than it did in Schechter's time. And thirdly, Hasidism could prove exceedingly valuable as a bridge between the Jewish outlook and the theological concepts of Christianity.

Hasidism has been not only a religious movement, but a momentous spiritual revolution which influenced the Polish and Russian Jews in the eighteenth century and won over nearly half of the Jewish masses. The word *Hasid* means " pious." In ancient Jewish history, during the Maccabean

[1] *Studies in Judaism*, London, 1896, vol. I, p. I.
[2] The forms of *Chassidism* and *Hasidism* are both used.
[3] *Elements of Bibliography on Hasidism* : Löw, *Vergangenheit und Gegenwart der Chasidäer*, 1859 ; S. Dubnow, *Vvedenie v Istoryiu Khasidizma* and *Istorya Khasidskago Raskola* (Russian) ; M. Buber, 100 *Chassidische Geschichten* ; *Die Geschichten des Rabbi Nachman* ; *Die Legende des Baalschem* ; *Der Grosse Maggid und seine Nachfolge* ; *Das verborgene Licht* ; *Mein Weg zum Chassidismus* ; *Die Chassidischen Bücher* (Berlin, 1927, including in one volume the five precedent works) ; *Des Baal-Shem-Tob Unterweisung im Umgang mit Gott* ; *Deutung des Chassidismus*, Berlin, 1935; the chapters on *Hasidism* in the *Histories of the Jewish People* by Grätz and Dubnow. In English, besides the already mentioned *Studies in Judaism* by Schechter (vol. I, Chapter I: *The Chassidim*), and the article *Hasidism* by Dubnow in the *Jewish Encyclopædia*, see S. Horodetzky, *Leaders of Hasidism*, transl. by M. Horodetzky-Magasanik, London, 1928; and M. Buber, *Jewish Mysticism and the Legends of Baalshem*, transl. by L. Cohen, London, 1931. Under the title *Love and the Messianic Age*, P. Levertoff has published (1923) an English adaptation of his German work *Die religiöse Denkweise der Chassidim* (1918).

wars, a religious and political party of Hasidæans—the party of the pious—had played an important role. Hasidism is, etymologically, synonymous with " pietism " ; and modern Hasidism resembles this Protestant tendency in so far as they both assign the first place, not to dogma or ritual, but to " religious experience " and emotion. The birth of Hasidism was an episode of the immemorial struggle for supremacy between formalism and mysticism. In the 18th century the Jewry of Poland and the Ukraine felt discontented with Talmudic as well as cabbalistic rabbinism. Both had become locally transformed into something bookish, dry and formal, stern and gloomy. They could satisfy neither the learned men nor the unlearned people. The Messianic movement of Shabbetai Zebi and the mystical sectarianism of Jacob Frank had given only illusory responses to their needs. Then the burning desire of the common people for a simple and living faith created Hasidism.

The initiator of Hasidism was an obscure Polish Jew, Israel ben Eliezer Baal Shem Tob (1700?–1760), better known under the name of Besht (formed, according to a Jewish use, with the first consonants of the complete name, *i.e.*, *B, Sh, T*) Besht is the nearest Jewish approach to Francis of Assisi. We must deeply regret that this beautiful figure of sainthood is almost unknown among Christians.[1] Fervent in prayer and ecstatic, healer and miracle-worker, extraordinarily simple and sincere, Besht won the confidence of the masses by his insight into their needs. He taught them that prayers coming from the heart are more acceptable to God than scholarship and ritual. Having gathered about Him numerous disciples, He instructed them not by a theological exposition, but by sayings and parables. The disjointed words of Besht, orally trans-mitted and later written down by his followers, became the frame of the Hasidic system.

However artificial and imperfect such classifications may be, we may discern, in Hasidism as taught by Besht and his disciples, seven fundamental conceptions :

(a) *The omnipresence of God.* Some sayings of Besht have a pantheistic flavour. One could think that he really identifies God with the matter everywhere diffused, if Besht himself did not supply the corrective " so to speak." In reality Besht means something quite different from the Indian : " Thou art that " (*tat twam asi*). He considers that material things are the image of God : to look at them is to gaze at this image.

---

[1] See special note O.

God is not everything, but He is in everything. " With this in mind," says Besht, " man will always serve God even in small matters." An unbroken intercourse unites God and the world. Besht has been influenced by the cabbalistic idea of the correspondence between the upper and lower spheres, but his own mysticism remains primarily a thing of the heart : he thus reacts against these conceptions of the Cabbala which Buber calls " the magification of the mystery " (die Magisierung des Mysteriums) i.e., the undue emphasis upon numbers, names and letters, and " the schematization of the mystery " (die Schematiesierung des Mysteriums), i.e., a merely gnostic intellectualism. Buber rightly says that Hasidism is a " pansacramentalism," and that Besht has in some way answered Spinoza. Both Spinoza and Besht see that the world is not " the place of God," but that God is " the place of the world " (der Ort der Welt) ; only Besht, instead of interpreting this truth, like Spinoza, in an intellectual and pantheistic sense, gives it a practical, spiritual and sacramental meaning.

(b) *The communion with God through prayer.* This is the essence of religion. Prayer must achieve two conditions : it must be a concentration of all thoughts on God, and therefore it implies a detachment of the soul, so to speak, from its material dwelling ; it must be constant, and therefore the presence and guidance of God are to be sought even in our worldly affairs.

(c) *Shifluth.* This Hebrew word is best rendered by " humility," but, in Hasidic usage, as Schechter says,[1] " it includes the ideas of modesty, considerateness and sympathy." Conceit and vanity were the faults which Besht conceived as the most seductive of all forms of sin. *Shifluth* has two sides : the negative side, *i.e.*, thinking humbly of oneself ; the positive side, *i.e.*, thinking highly of other men and loving them.

(d) *Shimkhah.* This means " cheerfulness." A glad heart, said Besht, is necessary to the service of God. Sadness, sorrow and gloom darken the soul. Asceticism is injurious when it hinders communion with God. One should also avoid anxious scrupulosity in details. By its free, happy and confident disposition, Hasidism reminds us of Franciscan joy.

(e) *Hithlahabuth.* We can translate this substantive by our word " enthusiasm," but then we miss an essential element of *hithlahabuth :* this term is derived from a verb meaning " to set on fire " or " to kindle." We find here again the Jewish idea

[1] *Studies in Judaism*, I, p. 36.

of the connexion between fire and the mystical life (the fiery Chariot). Communion with God creates enthusiasm. Ecstatic fervour makes prayer complete. Ecstacy will often find expression in bodily motions, such as shouting and singing.

(f) *The power over nature.* A constant communion with God gives greater or less influence in the " higher spheres " and makes possible the gift of mental vision, the gift of prophecy, and the gift of working miracles.

(g) *Zaddikism.* Under this name, we understand the whole system of ideas centred around the hasidic conception of the *zaddik, i.e.,* " just " or " righteous " man. The Zaddik is one who has reached the highest degree of communion with God. He is much more than the Indian *sadhu,* or the Greek *pater pneumatikos,* or the Russian *starets.* He really becomes an intermediary—nay, a mediator—between God and ordinary men. Salvation of souls and earthly blessings are obtained through him. This notion of the Zaddik existed already in the Zohar. The Zaddik is identified with the emanation or *sefirah* called " Foundation " ; he is " the basis of the world," " the gathering of the waters," " the tree bearing fruit."[1] But it is among the Hasidim that Zaddikism received its full development. The ideas about Zaddikism have been expounded, not by Besht himself, but by his disciples, especially by Elimelek of Lizianka in his book *Noam Elimelek.*

Hasidism was spread chiefly by two of the immediate disciples of Besht, Baer of Meseritz and Jacob Cohen of Polonnoye. The Jewish masses of Poland and Russia absorbed Hasidic literature with astonishing rapidity. Everywhere arose Hasidic prayer-houses into which the ritual books of the Palestinian cabbalists were introduced. The Hasidim used to dress in white, on Sabbath, as a symbol of the purification of the soul. Miracle-working Zaddikim appeared in many places. It is difficult to pass an unbiased judgment on Zaddikism. While the presence of a Zaddik often led to the relief of the spiritual needs of the people and to their genuine conversion, one must acknowledge the fact that Zaddikism developed some unpleasant features. Credulous crowds gathered around the Zaddikim and supported the holy men by pecuniary contributions. The vocation of Zaddik became profitable and often hereditary. There were important dynasties of Zaddikim at Chernobyl, Ruzhin-Zadagura, Lyubavich, Lublin. Some of the Zaddikim derived considerable incomes from their adherents and led a lordly life : one of them (18th century) even had a

[1] Zohar, on the first chapter of Genesis.

court jester in his numerous suite. Individual Zaddikim, not associated with these dynasties, became well known in the 19th century : among them Motel of Chernobyl, Nachman of Bratzlav, Israel of Luzhin, Mendel of Lyubavich. Many Zaddikim were real spiritual fathers to their people. Moreover, the excesses of the cult of the Zaddikim must not blind us to the benefits and vitality of Hasidism. This fervent stream brought into the stagnant Judaism of Poland new powers and satisfied the needs of the masses who were tired of formalism.

Rabbi Zalman of Liozna (1747–1812), aware of the dangers of religious exaltation and of a debased Zaddikism, created the so-called rational Hasidism or *Habad* (term formed by the first letters of the words *hokmah,* " wisdom," *binah,* " understanding," *deah,* " knowledge "). He advocated an intelligent faith, a mental preparation for prayer, a lessening of the cult of the Zaddikim, and the pre-eminence of teaching over miracle-working. The *Habad* succeeded with the most advanced minds among the believers.

A crusade against Hasidism was started from two sides. Rabbinical orthodoxy began a bitter struggle to preserve learned and ritualistic Judaism. The rabbis saw in the Zaddikim dangerous competitors. About the end of the 18th century, the Hasidim were expelled from the Jewish communities ; intermarriage and even intercourse with them was forbidden. The antagonists of Hasidism, who called themselves *mitnaggedim* (opponents) and at whose head stood Elijah ben Salomon, denounced the Hasidim to the Russian authorities as dangerous agitators. Hasidism remained under strong suspicion ; some of its leaders were even arrested. The conflict between rabbinism and Hasidism led to the formation of the Hasidim into a separate religious organization which often crowded out established Judaism (the case of the Wesleyans and the Church of England over again). About the middle of the 19th century, orthodoxy discontinued its struggle with Hasidism and intermarriages took place. But opposition against Hasidism had arisen from another quarter. The " enlightened " Mendelssohnian school and the Haskalah movement, advocating the adoption of European culture by the Jews, bitterly attacked Hasidism (in the pamphlets of Joseph Perl in 1819 and of Isaac Bär Levinsohn in 1830). It is true that, in the last part of the 19th century, Hasidism did not produce any prominent personality, that it became darker in intellect, and even showed itself more reactionary than rabbinism : therefore Schechter, in the lines which we have quoted, could speak of a decay of Hasidism. Even then one can ask whether these "obscurantist" Jews were not brighter at heart than their orthodox brethren and whether the apparent stagnation did not hide stored-up reserves of spiritual power.

A revival of Hasidism has taken place since. After having vituperated Hasidism, orthodox and liberal Jews began to take it as an object of scientific investigation, and they found it not only interesting, but inspiring. To many souls who were satisfied neither by traditional orthodoxy nor Reform Judaism, Hasidism gave a pure, simple and strong food. The books of Martin Buber on Hasidism illustrate such a state of mind. At the beginning of the 20th century, Buber was the leader of the "neo-hasidism" of Vienna, to which belonged Hugo Bergmann, Adolf Böhm, Max Brod, Hans Kohn, Robert Weltsch, Arnold Zweig. Hasidism was also revitalized by the important part which it took in the Zionist movement.

Till the fateful month of September, 1939, Hasidism, persecuted in Russia, was flourishing in Palestine and still more in Poland. Some of the Zaddikim still represented a great force and had a large following, e.g., the Zaddikim of Gora Kalvarya, near Warsaw, and Belz, in Galicia.[1] These places were centres of pilgrimage. On the Sabbath and on festivals, the Hasidim take their meals at the table of the Zaddik. They eat in silence, listening to the Zaddik's words. The Zaddik tastes a little of each course and divides the *shirayim* (remains) of the "sacred meal" among his guests. The Hasidim call such meals "sacrifices of God." They term the table the "Altar of God" and compare the Zaddik with the High Priest making the offering to the Lord. One is reminded of a passage from the Zohar[2]: "a man's table can purify him of all his sins," for, from it, blessings and words of the Torah may ascend to the Holy one, and food may go forth to the poor; and when such a table is removed after the meal, angels appear at its right and at its left.

The Hasidim give complete equality to the women in all religious matters. She may even rise to the rank of a Zaddik. The mysterious figure of the "Maid of Ludomir" has been immortalized in Hasidic legends. This Jewish Polish girl, Hanna Rachel Werbemacher, born in 1815, excited astonishment by her inspired and ecstatic prayers. Though she married twice, she remained a virgin. She became a wonder worker,

---

[1] The atmosphere surrounding these "miraculous rabbis" has been described (but very much from the outside) in the "Jewish" novels of the French writers Jerome and Jean Tharaud. See also S. Agnon, *In der Gemeinschaft der Frommen.*

[2] *Terunah* 153b.

and men and women went to her in pilgrimage. Towards the end of her life, Hanna Rachel settled in Palestine.

Schechter says that, among Hasidim, " there is not one in ten thousand who has the faintest conception of those sublime ideas which inspired Baalshem and his immediate disciples." Could not reproaches of the same kind be made to the orthodox Jews and to Christians as well ? But Schechter himself counterbalances this statement when he adds : " Amid much that is bad, the Chassidim have preserved through the whole movement a warm heart and an ardent, sincere faith. There is a certain openness of character and a ready friendliness about even the modern Chassidim which are very attractive. Religion is still to them a matter of life and death."[1] Buber pays a magnificent tribute to Hasidism in these simple lines : " Among all movements of the same kind, certainly none has, as much as Hasidism, heralded the infinite Ethos of the *now*."[2]

This would be quite enough to make Hasidism interesting from a mere psychological or historical view-point. But the Christian student of Judaism has deeper reasons for being interested in Hasidism.

The Christian will acknowledge in Hasidism a genuine mysticism which is very much at one with his own mysticism, and he will appreciate in it perhaps the greatest achievement of modern Jewish piety.

His attention, moreover, will be specially drawn towards one of the aspects of Hasidism. There is, in Hasidism, a full doctrine of " mediation " between God and man. S. Horodetzky writes[3] : " In Hasidism the Zaddik plays a part similar to that of Jesus in Christianity." This is exactly true : a part similar (though not identical). Such a similarity between the Hasidic " Just " and the Christian Savour affords a basis solid enough for a sincere and understanding dialogue between Christianity and Hasidism.

---

[1] *Studies in Judaism*, I, p. 54.
[2] Unter allen bewegungen seiner Art hat wohl keine so wie der Chassidismus das unendliche Ethos des Augenblicks verkundet. (*Deutung des Chassidismus*, p. 9.)
[3] *Leaders of Hasidism*, p. 126.

PART SIX

CHRISTIANITY AND THE EARTHLY
PROBLEMS OF ISRAEL

THE CHRISTIAN ATTITUDE TOWARDS THE
JEWISH DIASPORA

Judaism is inadequately treated if one considers it only from an intellectual or spiritual aspect, as a doctrine or a religious life. Israel is a concrete and present (and shall we say conspicuous ?) reality. As Montefiore said : in Judaism " a universal creed is wedded to a nationalist embodiment." This mixture constitutes the originality of Judaism. When the racial tie is broken and Judaism conceived of as simply a " religion," then the essentially Jewish element in the Jewish belief disappears. As an earthly community, Israel has its acute earthly problems.[1] What should be the Christian attitude towards these earthly problems of Israel ?

To-day, as in biblical times, Israel may be seen in two conditions : dispersed among the Gentiles, and settling in the land of Promise. All Israel's earthly problems refer to one or the other of these two situations, to the Exile or to the re-building of Zion. We shall now consider the first group of problems, *i.e.*, those centred on the Jewish notion of *Galuth* (exile, dispersion, *diaspora*).

Most of the "enlightened" minds of the 18th and 19th centuries, either Jewish or Gentile, thought that the general ideas which triumphed with the French Revolution could afford a simple and reasonable solution of the problems of Israel in exile. This solution, secular and liberal, was expressed in three magical words : emancipation, equality of rights, assimilation. Let the Jews keep in touch with the times ; let them acquire the manners and aspirations of the nations among whom they dwell ; let all avenues of political life and social intercourse with their Gentile neighbours be open to them ; then the distinctions will, little by little, be abolished and the problems of the exile will vanish. Such were the ideals of the German *Haskalah* movement of which Mendelssohn, Hartwig Wesely, Daniel Itzig and the Friendländers became the prototypes and sponsors. The " Edict of Tolerance " of the Emperor Joseph II (*Toleranzpatent*, 1782) constituted the first step in that

[1] See A. Ruppin, *The Jews in the Modern World*, London, 1934 ; J. Parkes, *The Jewish Problem in the Modern World*, London, 1939.

148

direction. The decisions of the French National Assembly (1790) and later of Napoleon (decree of 1806, establishment of the Sanhedrin in 1807, Madrid decree of 1812) effected more for the Jewish emancipation in Europe than had been accomplished during the three preceding centuries. In England the disabilities which affected the Jews were removed by the bills of 1845, 1846, 1870 and 1890. Liberal circles everywhere cherished the hope that Jewry as a distinct social entity having disappeared, there would remain only Englishmen, Frenchmen and Germans " of the Jewish (or still better : Mosaic) persuasion."

Now, while making full allowance for the core of human justice contained in the ideals of emancipation and equal rights, we do not think that this " secular and liberal " view was an adequate approach to the problems of the Jewish *diaspora*. First, this solution did not work in practice as was hoped : in the last decade it has even proved to be a lamentable failure. Moreover, from a Christian standpoint, a purely secular solution of the Jewish problem will always remain deficient. The Jewish problem is a theological problem and ought to be handled by us as such. We can solve it only in the light of the Scripture and under the guidance of the Spirit. We think it a grave defect that so many Christian writers on this question, including bishops and other clergy, take a secular and superficial view of it. The Christian has something to say as a Christian on the practical problems of Jewry. And the Jews have no reason to fear that they will lose by the Christians' repudiation of the humanitarian background. The truly Christian solution of the Jewish *diaspora* problems will be deeper and give much more to the Jews than the humanitarian one.

The first task of a Christian approach to the problems of the *Galuth* will be an exact conception of this term, so rich in temporal and spiritual meaning : The Jewish community.

Hebraism insists on the Hebrew nation as the mediating term between God and the individual. For the Greek, it is enough to find the One in the many, and the nation is not associated with any values higher than language, culture, political institutions. The Jewish tradition, following the Bible, takes an opposite view. According to this tradition, the words " community of Israel " mean not merely the concrete-empirical people of Israel, but the people of Israel in connexion with the Shekinah.[1] The phrase " The community of Israel

[1] See the glossary of the vol. III of the edition of the Zohar by Simon and Sperling and the appendix to vol. V.

came down to earth,"[1] for instance, must be understood of God, as synonymous and associated with His people. One may speak of God *qua* " the Holy King " or *qua* " the community of Israel." Some rabbinic sayings on the subject are very illuminating : " He who helps Israel helps God " ; " He who opposes Israel opposes God " ; " He who blesses Israel blesses God " ; " He who hates Israel hates God."[2] Or : " As long as Israel does His will, God travels far and wide among the nations, and, wherever He alights upon a saintly man among them, He brings him forthwith into Israel's fold."[3] God feigns deep sleep while Israel is sinning. God is with Israel even in his sin, because he has implanted repentance within him.[4] The Christian will be the last to deny that Israel has been chosen by God as a people. Karl Barth goes so far as to say that the existence of the Jewish " chosen people " among all other peoples is the only possible " natural-theological " proof of God's existence.[5]

The community consciousness has been fortified or re-awakened among modern Jews by their trials. It had never disappeared. The Jew has always been the " island within," to use the title of a book by Ludwig Lewisohn ; the Jew, as Zangwill once said, is " everywhere and anywhere, but at home nowhere." The ghetto certainly was a hideous achievement of oppression and hatred ; but through it the Jews did succeed in keeping up their life as a community ; within this gloomy shelter they found room for study, for charity and for social life. The abolition of the ghetto (nowadays being revived) has never and nowhere resulted in a perfect assimilation of Israel to the *Goyim* (Gentiles). The community of Israel is still strongly conscious of its separatedness, of its special mentality and of its God-given mission. The German Jewish novelist, Lion Feuchtwanger, said : " I am convinced that Judaism is not a race, is not a common soil, is not a common way of life, is not a common language. What, then, is Judaism? I think Judaism is a common mentality. . . ."[6] In his book *My Life as German and Jew*, Jacob Wasserman describes his search for the answer to the question : What is Judaism? It is neither a blood nor a confession, then what is it? And

[1] Zohar, *Vayikra*, 4b.
[2] Abelson, *The Immanence of God in Rabbinical Literature*, p. 133.
[3] *Yalkut on Song of Songs*, vi. 2.
[4] Abelson, *The Immanence of God in Rabbinical Literature*, p. 140.
[5] *Kirchliche Dogmatik*, I, 2, pp. 566–7.
[6] Quoted by B. Matthews, *The Jew and the World Ferment*, London, 1934, p. 104.

Wasserman answers that it is the consciousness of an election and a mission. The Jews, he continues, have called themselves the chosen People. A conviction so obstinately proclaimed for thousands of years entails quite extraordinary obligations which the group can never wholly fulfil : hence a state of moral and mental tension whose inevitable discharge results in a catastrophic existence, when appeasement is not obtained in arrogant self-righteousness. We quote these Jewish writers (who, by the way, are not religiously " orthodox ") in order to convince the Christian reader that the naïve liberal dream of perfect " assimilation " will always break itself against the divine fate and destiny of the community of Israel. It is as useless as it is undesirable to try and explain away this community. We must rather help Israel to fulfil its call. As Berdyaev said : " An ultimate solution of the Jewish problem is possible only on the eschatological plane. Such a solution will coincide with that of universal history. And it will represent the last act in the struggle between Christ and Antichrist. Therefore the problem of universal history cannot be solved without the religious self-determination of Judaism."[1] But this eschatological aspect of the Jewish question must not blind us to its immediate requirements.

We should notice, by the way, that the re-awakening of the Jewish community feeling is so strong that, when the Nazi anti-semites began to deny the Jewish origin of Jesus, many of the Liberal Jews of Germany felt all the more drawn to Him.

Thus the first task of the Christian, when he considers the problems of *Galuth*, is to free himself from the " atomistic " conception and to see clearly that he has to face, not individual Jews whose assimilation is devoutly to be wished, but the divine hard fact of the total and irreducible Israel. The second task is to understand the nature and causes of Israel's present sufferings (which are only the latest and acutest forms of a constant pain).

" I know well this people. They have not on their skin a single spot that is not aching . . ." wrote Péguy.[2] This suffering has been singularly intensified during the last ten years.[3] In this time of war (1941), Judaism is persecuted in all countries which have fallen under the domination or

---

[1] *The Meaning of History*, p. 107.
[2] " Je connais bien ce peuple. Il n'a pas sur la peau un point qui ne soit pas douloureux." (*Notre Jeunesse.*)
[3] See A. Sachar, *Sufferance is the Badge, The Jew in the Contemporary World*, New York, 1939 ; B. Matthews, *Supreme Encounter*, London, 1940.

influence of the " Axis Powers." Even France is become the
prey of an undiscriminating anti-Jewish madness. The apex of
horror has been reached in Germany, Poland and Rumania :
burning and closing of synagogues, pogroms, confiscations,
ghettos, concentration camps, torture. . . . The times of
Antiochus Epiphanes are being revived, and in a far worse way.
Jewish refugees, even in friendly countries, have had also to
suffer poverty, strict police restrictions, family separations,
deportation and internment abroad. All this is so well known
that it is useless to dwell on it.

It may, however, be useful to complete our information.
Axis anti-semitism has not been the only blow struck at Israel.
In the Soviet Union is one of the least known, but most acute
problems of modern Judaism. Between 1917 and 1921, the
White armies systematically tried to exterminate the Jews,
whom they identified with bolshevism : over 1,500 pogroms in
more than 900 places resulted in the slaughter of at least
100,000 Jews. In the Soviet dominions, religious education of
children is forbidden ; a kosher meal is no longer obtainable ;
Zionism has been made a crime ; synagogues have been
closed ; the Jewish Republic of Birobidjan has generally
accepted unbelief. If there is almost no Jewish problem in
the Soviet Union, it is because so many Soviet Jews are no
more worrying or talking about Judaism. " Russian Jewry has
bartered its faith for liberty. . . . A whole limb is being
lopped by the Soviet from the Jewish body."[1]

Such is the situation of Israel in exile. Why all these
sufferings and persecutions ? If we go to the root of the matter,
we reach the question of anti-semitism. We have to see the
causes of the opposition which Israel never failed to arouse
among his own neighbours.[2] And here, again, mere historical
or psychological explanations will remain utterly defective if
they are not complemented by a theological, or rather a
specifically Christian, view of things.

Although modern anti-semitism was born only about 1875,
it borrowed most of its arguments from the old Jew hatred.
The well-known and ridiculous story of the forgery called *The
Protocols of the Learned Elders of Zion* shows how the popular
mind may readily accept preconceived ideas. The same power

---

[1] Editorial of the *Jewish Chronicle*, London, 29th June, 1934.
[2] See M. Mieses, *Der Ursprung des Judenhasses*, Vienna, 1923 The German
Weekly *Mittheilungen aus dem Verein zur Abwehr des Antisemitismus* (Berlin,
since 1893) is the best reporting of the history of anti-semitism in the last
quarter of the nineteenth century and the first years of the twentieth century.

of human credulity, when fed by liars and fanatics, is illustrated by the renewal of the " blood accusation " in Julius Streicher's pamphlets.[1] But let us look at some apparently more reasonable accusations.

Greed and money making are often mentioned as Jewish characteristics. Werner Sombart has made the Jews responsible for the worst features of capitalism. R. H. Tawney, J. B. Kraus, A. Fanfani have corrected Sombart's thesis. Max Weber finds the origins of modern capitalism in Puritanical calvinism ; Labriola, in the accumulation of wealth by the monasteries and Italian banks of the Middle Ages. So the responsibilities seem to be pretty well divided. As to the reputation of usurers which clung to the Jews even up to modern times (e.g., " The Merchant of Venice "), there is little evidence of the Jews being especially addicted to it.[2] The legend of Jewish wealth and the Jewish attempt to control world affairs is exploded by statistics ; over against that legend must be set the fact that the majority of the Jews in the world are poor, often very poor, and that one part of the community must save the other from starvation. Now it is true that there exists, between Jews and " business," a special connexion, the nature of which is deeper than one generally perceives. The Jewish sociologist, Ruppin, points out that the Jews find in trade and finance this atmosphere of risk, uncertainty and hope which they need as a mental stimulus. According to Maritain, bargaining and money operations give to the Jews a kind of " spiritual " satisfaction ; money attracts them in an almost mystical way : through this sign, in this sign, by the multiplied signs of this sign, the highly intellectualist and realist Jew sees that he may become all-powerful. Money is the symbol of omnipotence. It may be, for an unbelieving Jew, the most dangerous " religious " temptation and open the way to an " invested theocracy."

It has often been argued that the Jews constitute morally and socially a corruptive force. There are, for instance, many Jews in the film industry, the moral quality of which is often low. This is true, but one should bear in mind some of the worst films have been produced by Gentiles ; that some of the best films have been produced by Jews ; and that, after all, the cinemagoers themselves are the real cause for the sources of immoral films. These Jews are not representative of Judaism ; they have, like many Christians, adopted the standards of modern

[1] On ritual murder, see H. Strack, *The Jews and Human Sacrifice. An Historical and Sociological Inquiry*, Berlin, 1891, English translation, 1909.
[2] Scherer, *Rechtsverhältnisse der Juden*, pp. 185–196.

paganism. The German Protestant theologian, O. Piper (now an exile), makes some very pertinent remarks on this subject.[1] The Jews, as such, are no more immoral than any other race. But, by reason of the specific gifts which have been imparted to the Jewish people and have been developed in their history, a Jew who indulges in immoral actions becomes far more dangerous than a non-Jew under the same circumstances.

Another argument is that the Jews are social revolutionaries and should be blamed for Communism. As far as Communism is a system of thought which excludes or denies God, Judaism rejects and opposes it ; as far as it means a certain social and economic order, Jews may, even on religious grounds, share its tenets. But Marx was a Jew ! It should be pointed out that Marx was baptized at the age of six, that he was brought up as a Christian, and that, during his whole life, he remained entirely alien to Judaism. Nevertheless, the author of *Das Kapital* seems to have inherited the passion for social righteousness which is characteristic of the Hebrew prophets.

The Jews are reproached with obstrusiveness and lack of social tact. It is true that quite a number of them often show arrogance and ostentation, but is it not a result of the conditions under which their forbears have for so long been compelled to live ?

The fundamental objection against the Jews is that they are too successful in everything. This somewhat disproportionate success cannot be denied and may irritate the Gentiles. The Jews undoubtedly take a leading part in modern civilization. One must notice that the special kind of intellect which enables them to do so has been more or less developed, as Piper says, by their constant meditation on the Law. The study of the Torah has created in them a mentality in many respects akin to the rationalism which underlies modern culture. Minds used to fine distinctions and discriminations, and to all the niceties of the Talmud, are bound to excel in science, jurisprudence, trade and organization. Souls filled with the thought of a transcendent God and eschatological expectations will express their lofty visions in philosophy or music. The upright sense of justice inherited from the Bible will make of the Jews the passionate champions of the oppressed and the leaders or auxiliaries of all modern revolutions. With their sense of charity they will contribute lavishly to all kinds of causes and appeals. Insisting on the realization in life of an absolute ideal of justice, they are naturally apt to create difficulties for

[1] *God in History*, New York, 1939.

Governments. As a prophetic people (and they are such with intensity), the Jews are essentially extremist and impracticable, always at war with the existing institutions, always demanding more than can be given, always crying in the wilderness, incapable of acquiescing in half attainments.

John Macmurray rightly emphasizes the fact that this stream of restlessness cannot be isolated or localized. The Jews have, willingly or unwillingly, become a universal community, in the sense that they permeate the whole world. Israel, though self-sufficient and separated, is immanent in all the Christian Churches and nations of the earth. " Hitler's declaration that the Jewish consciousness is poison to the Aryan races is the deepest insight that the Western world has yet achieved into its own nature. . . . It is the hidden penetration of the Jewish spirit into the Gentile mind that is the danger ; and it is a danger because the ' Aryan ' mind cannot resist it, but must succumb."[1] The Jewish spirit is a force able to create universal communism ; to destroy the ideology of blood, race, heroical struggle for power ; to promote equality and brotherhood. The task, from the anti-semitic point of view, is therefore to extirpate from the world Jewish influence, to get the leaven out of the lump. So writes Macmurray. But this Gentile sociologist and philosopher of culture, who gives such an accurate account of the anti-semitic ideology, takes personally a view of Jewish infiltration which directly opposes Hitlerism. Judaism, like the Platonic Good, is *diffusivum sui*, and Macmurray sees in this a progress : " I have learned from the greatest genius of the Jewish race to recognize it (the Jewish consciousness) as the water of Life. . . . The thought of the triumph of Jewish consciousness fills me with joyous exhilaration."[2]

In the present analysis of the causes of anti-semitism and of the persecution of the Jews, we have kept to the natural ground of psychology and history. This is not enough. The factors which we have discerned are undoubtedly there, and very potent. But the hatred of the Jews and sufferings of Israel have deeper causes which belong to the realm of theology and which only a believing Jew or a Christian can discern. Here we reach the heart of the problems of *Galuth*. No modern Christian has better expressed the supernatural aspect of these problems than Jacques Maritain.[3] We shall try to summarize

[1] Macmurray, *The Clue to History*, London, 1938, p. 226.
[2] *The Clue to History*, p. 227.
[3] *Anti-semitism*, translated from the French, London, 1939. See special note P.

his ideas on the subject. The election of Israel was an incursion of God into history for the purpose of using one people as the " means of grace," as a " sacrament," to the whole of mankind. The dispersion of Israel among the nations is and remains a sacred mystery. There is, between Israel and the world, the same superhuman relation as between the world and the Church. Only this analogy with the Church can help us to form some idea of the mystery of Israel. In its own way, Israel is a *corpus mysticum*. The promises of God being " without repentance," Israel continues its sacred mission. Like the Church, Israel is in the world, but not of the world ; the tragedy is that Israel loves the world and becomes its prisoner, though it shall not be and never can be of this world. " Israel, we believe, is assigned, on the plane and within the limits of secular history, a task of *earthly activisation* of the mass of the world. Israel, which is not of the world, is to be found at the very heart of the world's structure, stimulating it, exasperating it, moving it. Like an alien body, like an activating leaven injected into the mass, it gives the world no peace, it bars slumber, it teaches the world to be discontented and restless as long as the world has not God; it stimulates the movement of history."[1] The world hates the Jews because they will always be " outsiders " in a supernatural sense. Their passion for the absolute inflicts on the world an unbearable stimulus.

We should like to supplement the words of Maritain in two ways. In the first place, it is important to discriminate between " pious Jews " and the Jews who are practically foreign to religious Judaism. We all know a certain type of cultivated and agnostic, musical and pleasure-loving refugee from Vienna, which does not breed saints. It sometimes seems difficult to believe in the divine mission of these amiable, but rather estranged, sons of Israel. Neither can we overlook the fact that there are criminal elements among the Jews. And yet they are not cut off from the people of the Covenant. They are the very kind of Jew of whom Maritain says: "Israel loves the world and becomes its prisoner, though it shall not be and never can be of this world." To these Jews is especially imparted the task of " stimulating " and " exasperating " the world by their own impatience, agitation and reckless quest for (ungodly) intensity. In the very evil which they often commit, they unconsciously fulfil the God-given mission of moving history forward. But we must carefully distinguish the " good Jews " from them. These are also stimulating the world, but

[1] *Anti-semitism*, pp. 19–20.

in another way. They irritate it by their very Jewishness, by their fidelity to a transcendent Law and a prophetic vision which Hitler and Mussolini abhor. Maritain is careful to restrict the Jewish task of " activation " of the world to " the plane " and " the limits of secular history." We shall go further and say that these true Israelites belong to sacred history and achieve a redeeming work in the *diaspora*. With Piper, we shall acknowledge in them the Remnant of Israel for whose sake Judaism as a whole is allowed to entertain hope for the future ; and we dare to affirm that, in the modern dispersion as in the first biblical exile, they suffer vicariously for the whole people.

How can we help Israel in his present distress ? Here is a third aspect of the Christian attitude towards the problems of the Jewish *diaspora*. We have seen what a true understanding of the community of Israel means. We have also seen what a true understanding of the hatred and persecution of the Jews means. We must now reach a true understanding of the Christian help to be given to the Jewish people.

This question has become to-day more or less identified with the question of Jewish refugees.[1] Much has been done on their behalf by Christians, and this is certainly right. The Christian protest against anti-semitism and aid extended to its victims have built bridges of close fellowship between many Christians and many Jews. We shall nevertheless maintain that this charitable activity does not necessarily constitute the best form of Christian help to the Jewish people. It is often done from a merely humanitarian motive which deserves all our respect and sympathy, but remains foreign to Christianity. That we ought to help by all means the Jewish refugee is quite clear ; how can we help him as Christians is not so clearly perceived by everybody.

The " goodwill movements " between Jews and Christians are undoubtedly useful and interesting. A Youth Council of Jewish and Christian Relationships, for instance, has been brought into existence in order to promote a true fellowship between the younger members of the Jewish and Christian communities. The programme of the council includes visits of young Christians to synagogues (with attendance at the service), to Jewish restaurants, to lectures by leaders of Jewish youth, to Jewish museums, settlements and centres of social

---

[1] Full information on this subject, up to 1940, may be found in *The Refugee Problem* (Oxford University Press), and *Refugees* (Royal Institute of International Affairs), both edited by Sir John Hope Simpson.

work.[1] Such efforts ought to be encouraged and developed. They evidently do not exhaust the conception of Christian help to the Jewish *diaspora*.

Here again a supernatural light is necessary. Psychologism and humanism may mislead us in forming a view of this service. Even the most practical problems of aid to the Jews require a certain "theology." This is no dogmatic fancy. An eminent (perhaps the most eminent) modern Jewish authority will tell us the same. Buber, while acknowledging the generosity with which Christians have relieved Jewish distress in recent times, remarks (shall we say complains ?) that "Israel is not received by the Christians as Israel " ; Israel is " not accepted as Israel, but as a multiplicity of Jewish individuals " ; and he asks : "Is a genuine reception of Israel possible ? "[2] These words go to the very root of the question. Shall we receive Israel as Israel ? The aid given to a Jew because Christian love enjoins the succouring of any man in need may be a Christian help; but it will not be the Christian help to Israel as Israel, the reception of Israel as such.

What does this " genuine reception of Israel," spoken of by Buber, mean ? We may give to this term a threefold meaning. First, the Christian who assists a Jew in any way ought to be willing to fulfil thus a duty not only towards an individual, but towards the whole people of which the individual is a member. Secondly, the Christian must admit that Israel has a special claim on the goodwill of all Christians ; one can really speak of a privilege and priority of Israel : the Jews have a birth-right ; they are the elder sons of the Fathers and our elder brothers. However radical may have been the parting of the roads, we should always look to the house of Israel with veneration, tenderness—and nostalgia. Thirdly, the Christian ought to be aware that to help a Jew means to help the whole of Israel to fulfil the mysterious destiny to which it is called and which is inseparable from the destiny of the Christian Church itself. All these considerations may be summed up in the idea of the *corpus mysticum* of Israel on which the Gentile Christians are grafted. We shall develop this conception in the last pages of

[1] See William W. Simpson, *Youth and Anti-semitism*, London, 1938. The author, who is general secretary of the Christian Council dealing with refugees in England, has also published two books of the same inspiration, *The Christian and the Jewish Problem*, and *Jews and Christians to-day* (Beckly Social Service Lectures, 1940).

[2] *Israel ist von den Christen nicht als Israel rezipiert . . . nicht als Israel aufgenommen, sondern als eine Vielheit jüdischer Individuen . . . Ist eine echte Rezeption Israels möglich?* In *Die Stunde und die Erkenntniss*, pp. 161–162.

this present book. It will now be sufficient to say that, if we admit the Pauline idea of the grafting of the Gentiles on the tree of Israel, even the earthly problems of Israel will cease to be outside problems for us ; they will become our own.

The Anglican and Protestant worlds have extended to the Jews, in their recent trials, a most hearty welcome. But it is certainly the Roman Church which has emphasized to the utmost the reception of Israel " as Israel." Not only were " racialist " errors condemned in a pontifical document (April 13, 1938), but Pope Pius XI said in a speech : " Notice that Abraham is called our Patriarch, our ancestor . . . Anti-semitism is unacceptable. Spiritually we are Semites." (September 1938.) Perhaps the most thorough-going literature on Jewish problems to-day emanate from Roman circles.[1]

What forms could this Christian aid to Israel assume ? Let us listen to a Jewish suggestion. Israel Zangwill once wrote :[2] " The drastic method of love—which is the only human dissolvent—has never been tried upon the Jew as a whole." We do not want to " dissolve " the Jew among the Gentiles : on the contrary ! But these very words, " the drastic method of love . . . " contain a full programme of action. How can they be concretely expressed ?

The " drastic method of love " could hardly be identified with official organization and assistance. These are difficult to identify even with private group assistance. They are good and necessary, but drastic love always implies a personal concern. It goes out from the individual to the individual. It means a " sharing " in things both spiritual and temporal. It will not be " drastic " unless it includes some real sacrifice. We do not think that this " drastic method " in relation to Jews is required from every Christian. It is rather a special way corresponding to a special call ; it is nothing less than a vocation and ministry. The Christian who has received such a call ought to examine how, in the circumstances of his own life, he can take upon his shoulders at least a part of the burden of an individual Jew or perhaps of a few individual Jews in distress. He will endeavour to create between himself and them a relationship of " give and take " ; he will open to them his home and his soul ; he will help them with his work and money, accepting the hardships which this may involve and which are indeed a necessary condition of the method ; he will mix with them in their everyday life ; he will make of them his

[1] See special note P.
[2] *The Voice of Jerusalem*, p. 254.

" neighbour," in the thorough and most literal sense of the word. Such relationships may be best achieved, either between an individual and another individual, or within very small groups of three, four or five persons who would adopt a communal life. These little cells of brotherly life would be—in a rather unusual, but most real sense—"religious communities." We indicate only a very general line. The " drastic method of love " is essentially plastic and can adjust itself to a thousand different cases.

One last word about the Christian aid given to Israel "as Israel." Do not let us think that our aid may put an end to the trials of the Jews, the explanation of which belongs to a higher plane. Let us by all means everywhere defend the Jews against injustice and oppression—and, at the same time, let us see deeper into their tragedy. If we do ascribe a religious significance and purpose to the existence of the Jews, we must consider their sufferings as part of this purpose. While we certainly must help them in escaping from the conditions responsible for such sufferings, we must interpret Israel's woes in the light of the teaching about the Suffering Servant; the sufferings of Israel emphasize its testimony and reveal its divine power. Therefore, as wrote a Jewish Liberal leader, Rabbi J. Mattuk, "the religious point of view does not seek a complete escape from the difficulties in the Jewish position."[1] By its many sufferings, Israel may help the consummation of the divine purpose in history; this is the holiest way in which the Suffering Servant may "justify many."

Israel has been and still remains the figure of the Coming One. The human demolition of Israel means that Israel arises now as a signpost and a threshold. A door of hope is open to the Jewish soul. Broken and shattered, Israel can more vigorously bear its message and attempt its boundless task. All the nations shall see and hear the Suffering Servant of God, if he understands the Word spoken to him and repeats it in spirit and truth.

THE CHRISTIAN ATTITUDE TOWARDS ZIONISM

Judah ha-Levi said that certain places reveal a more secret meaning of existence and communicate to us a religious interpretation of our destiny. Such is the Land of Israel.

The exile from Zion and the dispersion among Gentiles are the most conspicuous aspects of the Jewish problem. The

[1] *What are the Jews. Their Significance and Position in the Modern World*, London, 1939.

rebuilding of Zion is another aspect—less conspicuous, but perhaps still more important—of the same problem. Both processes are simultaneous and parallel, as were, under Zerubbabel, the exile in Babylonia and the rebuilding of the Temple. As a matter of fact, Zionism dates from Zerubbabel ; far from being a modern creation, it is the continuous historical attachment of the Jews to Zion. The contemporary forms assumed by this attachment, chiefly since the publication of the pamphlet entitled *The Jewish State* by Theodor Herzl (1896), have become a matter of general knowledge. Our present aim is not to retrace the history of Zionism,[1] but to consider the question of the Christian attitude towards this movement.

The Christian attitude towards Zionism has been generally, though not universally (we think of England), an attitude of detachment expressing rather a lack of sympathy. Since the Balfour declaration to Lord Rothschild (November 2, 1917), many Christians of Continental Europe and of the Near East have become openly hostile to Zionism ; it would perhaps not be inexact to say that, during the Palestinian conflicts of these last years, the greater part of Christian opinion has sided with the Arabs (who undoubtedly have a very strong case). Even among the Christians who have no preconceived hostility against the Jews, Zionism seldom receives the attention, the interest and—we do not hesitate to say—the sympathy which it deserves. Zionism no less than the Jewish *diaspora*, is for the Christian a " theological " question ; we should see it in the light of the Scripture and of our faith. This question assumes a growing importance in Judaism ; the Zionists themselves hold that Zionism is neither a part of, nor an addition to, Judaism, but its concentration and fullness. No real Christian approach to the Jews can ignore it.

The Christians should remember that the racial revival of Judaism in the Holy Land was largely fostered by convinced English Christians like Lord Shaftesbury and Laurence

---

[1] See N. Sokolov, *History of Zionism*, 2 vols., London, 1919 ; L. Simon, *Studies in Jewish Nationalism*, London, 1920 ; A. Böhm, *Die Zionistische Bewegung*, Berlin, 1935 ; N. Brentwich, *Fulfilment in the Promised Land*, London, 1938 ; T. Feiwel, *No Ease in Zion*, London, 1938 ; Ben N. Edidin, *Rebuilding Palestine*, New York, 1939 ; Einstein, *About Zionism*, speeches and letters translated by L. Simon. We select these few books as particularly interesting, among the enormous amount of literature on Zionism and Palestine. *Palestine*, by J. Parkes (Oxford Pamphlet on World Affairs, 1940), gives an outline of the subject. Of course, the British White Papers (reports of the High Commissioners and of the Royal Commission) and other official documents (reports of the Zionist Executive) are the most solid basis for an objective study of modern Palestinian questions.

Oliphant. English novels like Disraeli's *Tancred* (1847) and George Eliot's *Daniel Deronda* (1876) show the sympathy with which Jewish aspirations were regarded by cultivated Western minds. Thus, running parallel to the work of Sir Moses Montefiore, of the Rothschild family and of the *Alliance Israelite Universelle,* a Western school of ideas helped in the awakening of modern Zionism. Surely this tradition should not be lost ?

Christians must also realize the nature of the link between Judaism and Palestine. We are often inclined to consider the Jewish origin of Christianity as a mere historical fact, devoid of any special religious significance. That Christianity originated in Palestine does not matter to the majority of Christians : it could as well have originated anywhere else. We tend to imagine that the spiritual aspect of reality is essentially situated out of time and space. For the Jews, this spiritual aspect not only was, but always is related to an actual process of historical development. The spiritual idea is attached to something concrete, to an actual land as the symbol and guarantee of the nationality. Jews do not think merely of "heavenly Jerusalem." Palestine is for them "the land of Israel" (in Hebrew *Erets Ysrael,* or simply *Erets,* the land). This land has not become and can never become an abstraction. It is impossible to establish a real Hebrew life anywhere else than in Palestine ; the Hebrew, outside Palestine, is a Jew ; only in Palestine can he feel himself entirely Hebrew. And yet the attachment to Palestine is less material than spiritual. Palestine's physical features and scenic beauty will always remain unknown to millions of Jews who pray and give money for it. The attachment of the Hebrew to his land is fundamentally different from the usual attachment to a homeland. The Jew is less attached to the actual Palestine, the physical Palestine, than to the idea of Palestine as a memory, a hope, a promised land, a basis for national consciousness. This "interdependence of Israel and Erets Israel" (*Zusammenhang von Israel und Erez Israel*), as Buber says, in some way participates of the nature of a sacrament : it is the visible and efficacious sign of a spiritual reality. The Christian ought to understand the divine element underlying the eternal pilgrimage of the Jewish soul to Zion. For the Christian, the whole of Palestine is not only the shrine of Jesus' life, death and ressurection ; it is also the land of the Presence, the meeting-place of Yaweh and Israel, and the Shekinah may still be felt there.

Then, too, the Christian must disentangle Zionism from its purely national manifestations. We hear so much about Zionism as a political movement that we are tempted to identify it with Herzl's idea of the Jewish State. There is certainly a Zionist nationalism ; there is even a Zionist militarism.[1] Zionism had its Judas Maccabæus in the person of Joseph Trumpeldor, who, with a hundred men, gave his life to defend the colony of Tel Chai against two thousand Arabs and who remains an immortal figure of contemporary Jewish epic. ("Where has more noble Hebrew blood been poured out than on the field of Tel Chai ?") We feel a deep respect for Trumpeldor as we feel a sincere admiration for so many material and cultural achievements of the Jewish Agency in Palestine. But the spiritual essence of Zionism is to be found elsewhere.

The Zionist idea was first clearly expressed by Moses Hess in his book *Rom and Jerusalem* (1862) and Leo Pinsker of Odessa, in his book *Auto-emancipation* (1882). The Russian forerunners of Zionism formed in Odessa, in 1885, the society *Khovere Zion* (Friends of Zion). Individuals and groups inspired by this society found their way to Palestine in order to live a " Hebrew " life. This pre-Herzlian Zionism was not nationalist. For Nathan Birnbaum, one of the orthodox Jews who, already before Herzl, taught the idea of a national home, Judaism was first of all a religious principle ; he formulated thus his interpretation of Zionism : " From and with the Law through holiness to the Messiah." Spiritual Zionism received its classical expression in the essays of the great Jewish writer Achad-Ham (1856–1927). His *Ten Essays on Zionism and Judaism*[2] look forward to a "centre of Judaism to which all Jews will turn with affection, and which will bind all Jews together ; a centre of study and learning, of language and literature, of bodily work and spiritual purification : a true miniature of the people of Israel as it ought to be . . . so that every Hebrew in the *diaspora* will think it a privilege to behold just once the ' centre of Judaism ' and when he returns home will say to his friends : If you wish to see the genuine type of Jew, whether it be a Rabbi or a scholar or a writer, a farmer or an artist or a business man . . . then go to Palestine and you will see it." Achad-Ham used to say : " Zionism is a faith." He also wrote : " The salvation of

---

[1] V. Jabotinsky, *The Jewish War Front*, London 1940.
[2] Translated from the Hebrew by L. Simon, London 1922, p. 154f. (The pseudonym Achad-Ham or Ahad-ha-Am means " one of the people.")

Israel will be achieved by *Prophets*, not by *Diplomatists*."[1] At the first Zionist Congress of Basel (1897), purely spiritual Zionism was swallowed up in nationalist Herzlian scheme. Herzl described it as " trying to raise a heavy load by the steam of a tea-kettle." The motive force of spiritual Zionism is not the striving of the politician or economist, but the vision of Isaiah and Amos. The position of spiritual Zionists is a difficult one : they are not popular leaders or legendary heroes like Herzl (+1904) ; they do not satisfy the call of the mass for glamour and a flag. Thus the ideal of Achad-Ham seemed defeated by the Herzlian ideal of the Jewish State. This does not mean that Herzl himself was not interested in spiritual values. At the third Zionist Congress (1899), he declared that Zionism wished "to open up new means of communication between nations and prepare the way for social justice." Only the conception of " the Jewish State " on a grandiose pattern was more congenial to him then the idea of "a Jewish home " with a quiet educational and colonizing aim. Canon Danby[2] thinks, however, that the " new British policy" in Palestine marks a departure from the Zionist ideals as envisaged by Herzl and the entrance into an " Achad-Ham stage"where quality will be fostered rather than material quality.

Martin Buber has emphasized the spiritual side of Zionism even more than Achad-Ham did.[3] As the title of his main work on this subject indicates, Zion is for him not only an aim, but a task. He condenses this view in a striking formula : " One can only reach Zion if one has passed through Zion."[4] To reach Zion through Zion means that the coming Jewish generations must be freed from " all degeneracy " which has affected Jewry and that Jews must give an opening to" the things which are in them and have not been expressed, to the powers which are in them and still remain, waiting for their day."[5]

Feuchtwanger has impressively proclaimed the universalist aspect of spiritual Zionism. ". . . I am bold enough to dream further than the most ardent Zionist, to dream that Jerusalem would become the centre, not only of Judaism, but of the whole world. . . . The world rule of which I think is very

---

[1] H. Danby, *The Cultural Aims of Zionism* in *The Church Quarterly Review*, January, 1931, p. 339.

[2] *Ibid.*, p. 335.

[3] Buber, *Zion als Ziel und als Aufgabe*, Berlin 1936.

[4] *Nach Zion kann man nur über Zion gelangen.* In *op. cit.*, p. 5.

[5] *Op. cit.*, p. 14 : . . . *die ganze Entartung . . . aus der wir unsere kommen-den Geschlechter befreien müssen . . . Wir fühlen auch, dass noch Dinge in uns sind, die nicht hinausgestellt worden sind, dass noch Gewalten in uns sind, die auf ihren Tag warten.*

different from that of many Zionists. It is a spiritual rule, and only of the spirit. I conceive of Zionism as at the bottom the old Messianic mission of Judaism. . . . The true Jewish nationalism is cosmopolitan, is in its best essence messianic. Yes, Jewish nationalism longs to be dissolved away in a united world, like salt in water, itself dissolved, no longer visible, yet it is omnipresent and existing forever."[1]

As concrete embodiments of spiritual Zionism, we should mention three of the recent cultural achievements of Judaism in Palestine : the formation of the neo-Hebrew language, Hebrew theatre, and the Hebrew University of Jerusalem.

The task of national redemption in Eretz is helped by the language. To transform Hebrew into the language of ordinary life has been the work chiefly of Eliezer ben Yahuda (+1922), who came from Russia to Palestine. The achievement of this " idealist philologist " has been to secularize Hebrew, of which Renan said that " like the Jubilee horn of the sanctuary, it will never be put to profane use." A group of Hebrew poets, also from Russia, has given a new expression to the Hebrew spirit. Outstanding among them was Nachman Bialik.[2]

The theatre now forms a most important part of the life of Eretz. The Palestinian companies, *Habima* and *Ohel*, have become world-famous. This new Hebrew theatre, since its beginning, has assumed a spiritual significance ; it has acquired something of the historical and religious, even ritual, character of the Greek theatre and became, in Jerusalem and Tel Aviv as in the Athens of old, a means of deepening the inner life.

The Hebrew University of Jerusalem is not only the brain of Zionism, but the greatest cultural centre of the whole Jewish world. It was founded in June, 1918. In the only speech delivered on this occasion, the Zionist leader, Chaim Weizmann, said that the ceremony itself proclaimed that the Jewish people rely on knowledge, not on arms. The twelve foundation-stones of the new University were laid on Mount Scopus by representatives not only of Jewish Palestine and of the *diaspora*, but also of the Christian and Moslem communities : does not this fact express a programme and a hope ? The appeal of Zionism has brought to the Hebrew University of Jerusalem a number of spiritual leaders, one of them being Martin Buber, who exercised such an influence over the Jewish community in Germany during recent years. The young University has already made substantial contributions, not only to Jewish

[1] Quoted by B. Mathews, *The Jew and the World Ferment*, p. 105.
[2] See special note Q.

м 2

studies (Klausner, Sholem, Torczyner), but to Arabic studies (critical Arabic editions and Hebrew translations from the Arabic, which aim at building a bridge between Jewish and Arab intellectual circles), and in mathematics and natural sciences (Adler, Kligler, Eig, Reubeni, Fraenkel, Zondek, Halberstaedter). From our point of view, the most important fact is, perhaps, that the New Testament is critically expounded in the University of Jerusalem.[1]

Christians should know and appreciate all these sides of Zionism more than they have done until now. And they should realize their religious significance. Religion is not always apparent or conspicuous in these achievements ; but a warm religious current, like a hidden gulf-stream, runs through the stormy waters of Zionism. A first contact with Zionism may give an impression of materialism and practical, if not theoretical, atheism. The worship of the nation is, for many Zionists, self-sufficient. They would say with Heinrich Graetz : " The Jewish nation is its own Messiah, and should bring about its own rejuvenescence and redemption without waiting for the coming of a single person as a Redeemer."[2] Many of the Jews who have settled in Palestine are non-religious or even anti-religious; if they come from Eastern Europe, they opposed religion because the religion which they knew opposed what they considered as justice and social progress. The boys and girls of the settlements are strong, beautiful and clever ; do they care about Adonai ? They know perhaps little about Him, but God sanctifies them with a spirit of self-sacrifice for Zion. When a deputation of orthodox Jews came to the Ashkenazi Chief Rabbi Kook and complained about the irreligion of many young men, the Rabbi reminded them that, according to tradition, the High Priest could only enter the Holy of Holies after long and elaborate preparation, but the masons and workmen could enter at any time, without any special preparation, for carrying out repairs to the fabric ; so the pioneers of to-day who are repairing the breaches of the House may deal freely with the Sabbath and should not be condemned as sinners. Moreover, several Zionist youth societies, *Zeire Mizrachi*, *Dat Waawoda*, *Poale Mizrachi* bear a distinctly religious character. The conservative *Agudath* and the whole *Mizrachi* group aim at developing the Jewish commonwealth in Palestine within the framework of the Torah and religious Laws.

---

[1] See C. Adler, *The Hebrew University, Jerusalem : Its History and Development*, Jerusalem, 1939.
[2] *Die Verjüngung des judischen Stammes* (1864).

The land itself seems to exercise a divine and mysterious influence and to turn—*suaviter ac fortiter*—the hearts of the children to the God of their fathers and of their ancient prophets. A striking illustration of the influence of Eretz upon the soul is afforded by the poet, Saul Tchernikowsky. While in Russia, Tchernikowsky was considered as a " pagan," overflowing with the joy and freedom of life. But his later work in Eretz was fully affected by the " burden of holiness " that is felt there. Judaism in Eretz is not mere synagogue-going and ritual observance ; it is a way of life—and the Way of the Land. Old religious customs, obsolete in Europe, have been revived in Palestine : observance of the Sabbath, restoration of the ritual religious feasts connected with the agricultural seasons : new strength has been given to ancient symbols and ceremonies. Since 1937, a united religious council, representing all sects, has been established in Jerusalem. The believers inside the community are still awaiting the Ezra of the second Return. will he come ? But Zionism itself, becoming a religious faith, has begun to regenerate the Jewish communities outside Palestine. A mystical feeling touches assimilated and denationalized Jews when they come to Eretz ; yet this little fraction has changed the outlook of the whole of Jewry.

At the same time religious and irreligious, Zionism is truly a symbol of contradiction. What is its attitude towards Christianity ? We can do no better than to quote O. von Harling's words on this subject : " Zionism must be mentioned as a modern form of Jewish ' irreligion ' which yet contains a large element of messianic hope. . . . It is, in fact, among Zionists that are found those unprejudiced minds which, because they would like to reknit the threads of Jewish history where it has been rent, seize on the problem of Christ and are not afraid, in the light of the history of Israel's relations to Christ, to undertake a scrutiny of it."[1]

Another side of Zionism ought to be known and rightly appreciated by Christians : we mean its social side. The colonization of Palestine is the most strange and hopeful social adventure of modern times.[2] There is among Zionists a small Communist wing. But the most important organization of Jewish workers in Palestine is the *Histadrut*. Though affiliated the Second Socialist International, the Histadrut is unlike any other trade-union. In 1938, it united 100,000 Jewish

[1] *Missions to Jews To-day*, in *International Review of Missions*, vol. xxii, 1933, p. 348.
[2] See M. Pearlman, *Collective Adventure*, London, 1938.

workers in one single organization. It is a Zionist colonization, co-operative rather than a mere trade-union; it includes not only workmen, but agricultural small-holders and a middle-class element. There is no dictatorship in the Histadrut ; all its achievements are the product of a smooth teamwork. Berl Knatzelson, who has been called "the spirit of the Histadrut," is an opponent of Maxzism and rejected Bohorov's materialist conception of a struggle for world revolution to be carried by Jewish workers to Eretz. Still more interesting than Jewish party politics are the Communal Settlements of Palestine, unique not only in the modern world, but in history. There were 140 in 1938. They differ widely from each other, but all of them are characterized by the absence of privately owned property and social caste. Let us take, as an instance, the Commune Mishmar Haemek, near Haifa. The whole organization is based on a structure of committees appointed by a general assembly. But the basis of the commune is not democracy : it is unanimity. All property in the commune belongs to the whole group in common, apart from a few little personal amenities. The work, meals, recreation, care and education of the children are regulated by the members of the commune. Agriculture is developed on a scientific and experimental basis. The schools are run by young teachers in continuous touch with the latest educational systems. The standard of sexual morality is very high in the settlements. The whole communal life is not easy ; it requires an unusual self-restraint and subordination. That type of life is " an incessant endeavour to improve, to bring everything up to the highest level a group of intelligent people can achieve, by reading, experiment and ceaseless discussion."[1]

The Zionist social experiment has not received, in the world at large, the recognition which it abundantly deserves. It is a practical application of Jewish Messianism to the transformation of society. The much advertised reforms of Soviet Russia seem to have hypnotized the world. We should greatly surprise and probably shock many people if we told them that, in our eyes, the most interesting social phenomenon since 1918 has been, not the establishment of the Union of Soviet Socialist Republics, but the development of the Jewish centres of communal life in Palestine. Russian Communism has not been. in the " dialectic of history," the final revolutionary movement. Norman Bentwich shows how, in Palestine, the teaching of Karl Marx has been happily modified. The idealistic tradition

[1] Feiwel, *No Ease in Zion*, p. 277.

of the Jews has superseded the materialistic interpretation of history. Zionism has " fostered the development of a Socialist community without either the dictatorship of the proletariat or the capture of the State. The Jew may be the best socialist because he believes in the millennium."[1] Maurice Pearlman writes :[2] " Quite apart from their purely Jewish significance, the communal settlements should be considered in the wider sociological context. . . . The absence of private property in the communal settlements is an innovation in modern society which, if it obtains successfully over an appreciable period, may lead, at the very least, to a serious modification of the popular theory. Nowhere in the world is the principle of collective ownership applied so comprehensively and accepted so willingly as it is in the settlements. In no country are all occupations regarded as of equal importance, both economically and socially. Nowhere is there a complete breakdown of class barriers. Nor is there any place in the world which can boast a political democracy as perfect as that which exists in the settlements. But there is yet a further feature which makes them still more outstanding and enhances the sociological value of the settlements. All these experiments and innovations are being undertaken simultaneously and in the same laboratory. They are all allowed to develop side by side and become component parts of a larger and far more ambitious experiment —an order of society."

Buber views the Zionist experiments from a standpoint which transcends mere sociology. The settlements have recovered and demonstrated the cosmic significance and value of work. In the silence of that small country which so few people know, man and earth, *adam* and *adama* have met again ; and the silence of that small country has already proved that it possesses a power that is working slowly and confidently. The communal settlement, the *kvutsa*, has " for mankind the significance of an advanced post " (*eine Vorpostenbedentung für die Menscheit*) and prepares " a new community of men " (*eine neue Menschengemeinschaft*). " In what is happening to-day in Palestine, Spirit and Reality meet each other."[3]

Palestine, geographically intermediate between East and West, may become the laboratory not only of a new social order, but also of a new international order. The conflict between Jews and Arabs is perhaps the painful preparation of

[1] Bentwich, *Fulfilment in the Promised Land*, p. 49.
[2] *Collective Adventure*, pp. 288–290.
[3] Buber, *Zion als Ziel und Aufgabe*, p. 58 : *In dem was heute in Palästina geschiet begegnen einander Geist und Wirklichkeit.*

new international adjustments and formulas, of which a Palestinian Community, created to meet the need of a unique situation, will be the prototype. The Jewish-Arab problem also requires a " theological " solution, for it is the biblical problem of the relationship between Isaac and Ishmael. Rabbinical literature, in many places,[1] gives beautiful and hopeful hints on this subject : Abraham came to see his son Ishmael who had grown skilful and prosperous ; the first time Ishmael's wife refused Abraham food ; Ishmael drove away his wife and married another woman, who received Abraham kindly ; Ishmael then went to Canaan and settled with his father. The name of Ishmael is an allusion to God's promise to hear the complaints of Israel, whenever Israel suffers at his brother's hands. And he who sees Ishmael in a dream will have his prayers answered by God.

The Zionist upbuilding of Palestine is a unique achievement, in spite of the haste, the rough edges, the brusqueness and even the arrogance which often mar this new creation. When a Christian has acknowledged that (and acknowledged it with sympathy), can he do something more ? Can the words " Christian Zionism " have a meaning ? Some believers in Jesus may feel themselves called to co-operate in a direct and concrete manner with the Jewish rebuilding of Zion. In 1933 the members of the "Association of Christian Hebrews," converted Jews who assert their unity with the Jewish people, acquired land in Southern Palestine with a view to establishing Jewish Christian settlements there. We know that the case of a Gentile Christian who, out of spiritual sympathy with Zionism, contributes to the national Jewish funds *Keren Hayessod* and *Keren Kayemeth* is not merely imaginary. Though Christians living in Palestine could always become friendly and perhaps co-operate with the Zionist efforts, the majority of Palestinian Christians are doing the reverse. We ought to mention, as an example of what Christians can do in Palestine, the noble service of the English " Peace Army." This organization tried to create social and medical centres in Palestine and to promote friendship between Jewish colonies and Arab villages. One of its young workers was killed in the autumn of 1940 by an Arab bullet. This is real Christian Zionism.[2] Few Christians have such opportunities, but we

[1] See Beer, *Leben Abrahams nach Auffassung der Jüdischen Sage*, Leipzig 1859 ; art. *Ishmael* in *Jewish Encycl.*, vol. VI.
[2] Information about the Peace Army in Palestine may be obtained from the President, Dr. Maude Royden, or from Joyce Pollard, The Peace Army, 63, Meadway, London, N.W.11.

believe that even those who are not Israelite by blood or who do not live in Palestine may share in a Zionism of faith and hope. This means first that we should turn our hearts towards Jerusalem. Has Jerusalem a place in our spiritual life ? Does any emotion within us respond to that sacred name ? Are we " lovers of Zion " (*choveve Zion*), as those poor Russian Jews who started Zionism named themselves ? Of course, such feelings are mere dreams and fancies to a Christian who thinks that the great prophetic words of Micah and Isaiah are now abolished. But one can be a Christian and still hope in the future glory of a spiritual Zion, to be revealed when the mysterious design of God shall have raised up the tribes of Jacob and restored the preserved Israel. Without being fundamentalist in a narrow sense, one can pray God for a fully Messianic Jerusalem which would become a light of salvation unto the ends of the earth. Such a Christian Zionism we do ardently accept and proclaim.

We can express the faith of this Christian Zionism in the following way. With the Jews, we believe that out of Zion went forth the Law, and the Word of the Lord from Jerusalem. Without the Jews (to our grief), we believe that out of Zion and Jerusalem went forth One who was the Word Himself. With the Jews again, we believe that the Word of God will still go forth out of Zion and from Jerusalem (these terms may be understood in a wider sense than the topographical one, though they do not exclude it, and they may be co-extensive with Israel itself). In all these three articles of Christian Zionist belief, we feel that a secret God-given unity binds us to the Jews. It is true that they would not subscribe to the second article. But the Word made flesh is identical with the Word Who went forth and the Word Who will go forth out of Zion. The Jews ignore this identity ; nevertheless the identity remains.

Because of this identity, we repeat with confidence the words of the Scripture : " In those days it shall come to pass that ten men shall take hold, out of all languages of the earth, even shall take hold of the skirt of Him that is a Jew, and say : We will go with you, for we have heard that God is with you. . . . Arise, shine ; for Thy light is come, and the glory of the Lord is risen upon Thee. . . . Pray for the peace of Jerusalem : they shall prosper that love Thee. . . . If I forget thee, O Jerusalem, let my right hand forget her cunning. If I do not remember thee, let my tongue cleave to the roof of my mouth ; if I prefer not Jerusalem above my chief joy."[1]

[1] Zech. viii. 23 ; Isaiah lx. 1 ; Ps. cxxii. 6 ; Ps. cxxxvii. 5-6.

PART SEVEN

ISRAEL AND THE MISSION

CHRISTIAN MISSIONS TO JEWS

The relationship between Judaism and Christianity is not only the theoretical relationship between Jewish faith and the Christian faith ; neither is it only the practical relationship between two ecclesiastical communities, the Church and the Synagogue, or, as we might also put it, the Christian Church and the Church of Israel. It is this specifically ecclesiastical aspect of the problem which we have now to consider. And we fully realize that it is the most difficult aspect of the whole question. The relationship between the two ecclesiastical bodies is inseparably linked with the missionary idea. We should speak of: "Israel and the Mission" rather than of "The Mission to Israel" because we think (and in this we differ from most Christian missionaries) that the word "mission," used in connexion with Israel, has a twofold meaning: there is, and there ought to be, a mission of the Christian Church to Israel ; but there is also a Mission of Israel to the Christian Church, and this (as we think) divinely appointed mission must not be overlooked. We shall first consider the origin and development of the Christian missions to the Jews.

A. Christian Missions to the Jews in the past.

We have already seen what the relation of the Church Fathers and mediæval theologians to Judaism has been ; we have underlined the moments of "genuine dialogue" between Judaism and Christianity which can be found in patristic times and in the Middle Ages. But, on the whole, the patristic and mediæval literature concerning the Jews belongs to the history of the polemics rather than to the history of the missions. The homilies of Chrysostom, the "disputations," the books of the type of *Capistrum Judaeorum* and *Pugio fidei*, all the controversies of Raymund Martini, Pablo Christiani, Alphonse and Salomon of Burgos, Petrus Alphonsi and so many others are attacks against Judaism, and do not express a real missionary idea, in so far as the repression of Judaism and the more or less forcible conversion of Jews differ from an apostolical "sending" or "being sent" (*missio*) to them. The case of Ramon Lull is different. The " Illuminated Doctor," the great Mallorcan martyr, had his own original views on the Jewish as well as on the Moslem world and he was always animated by a warm charity. He will remain not only as one of the most splendid mystics of all times, but also as a pattern of authentic missionary mind and life. Notwithstanding his (unsuccessful) missionary experiences with the Jews, he was more concerned with Islam than with Judaism.[1] It is from the Reformation that we can date the beginning of the missions to the Jews, in the modern sense of the word.[2]

Germany and England were the birth-places of these missions. Emmanuel Tremellius, a professor at Cambridge, himself a converted Jew, wrote *A Catechism for Inquiring Jews* in 1554. In the University of Halle, where the pietist movement of Spener and Franke was specially strong, Johannes Heinrich Callenberg taught Yiddish to large classes of Christians ; the Callenberg *Institutum Judaicum* was established in 1728, in connexion with the University, for the training of Jewish missionaries. It was suppressed by the Prussian Government in 1792.

The Quakers and the Moravians were the first bodies to undertake definite mission work among the Jews. Their attitude to this question certainly deserves our attention and sympathy and ought to be contrasted with some of the methods prevalent later on. Fox learned Hebrew, and the title-page of one of his books bears his own initials in Hebrew. At his trials before the Lancaster assizes (1664) Fox, refusing to swear, quoted—strangely enough—in their Hebrew rendering the New Testament words : " Thou shalt not swear by anything."

It is not generally known that George Fox wrote a letter in Hebrew to the Jews of Barbados ;[3] he sent the same letter, in 1684 or 1685, to the Jews in Holland ; the letter met with a rather indifferent reception, and, according to John Becke,

---

[1] On this too little known apostle, see E. Allison Peers, *Ramon Lull*, London, 1929.
[2] On the history of the missions to the Jews, see J. F. A. de le Roi, *Die evangelische Christenheit und die Juden . . . von der Reformation an*, 3 vols., 1884–1892 ; A. Lukyn Williams, *Mission to the Jews : An Historical Retrospect*, S.P.C.K., 1897 ; W. T. Gidney, *History of the London Society for Promoting Christianity among the Jews : from 1809–1908* ; A. Thompson, *A Century of Jewish Missions*, Chicago, 1902.
[3] A copy of this letter is preserved at Friends House. A facsimile of it is given in *Quakers, Jews, and Freedom of Teaching in Barbados*, 1686, by Henry J. Cadbury, *Bulletin of Friends' Historical Association*, Autumn Number, 1940.

" some of the Jews did grieviously Raile at, and abuse G. F."
Besides this correspondence, Fox published *A Visitation to
the Jewes from Them whom the Lord hath visited from on high*
(1656), *A Declaration to the Jews for them to read over in which
they may see that the Messiah is come* (1661), *An Epistle to all
Professors in New England, Germany and other parts of the
called Christian World, also to Jews and Turks throughout the
World* (1673), *A Looking-Glass for the Jews* (1674). The
Quakeress Margaret Fell wrote *A loving Salutation to the Seed
of Abraham*, in a later edition of which (1660) the English text
and a Hebrew translation are printed in parallel columns.
Caton, Stubbs, Fisher were busy with the distribution of
this book. The Quaker William Caton attended the Jews'
Synagogue at Amsterdam and held a service in one of their
houses (1656). About thirty years later, the Quaker Thomas
Wilson had a public discussion in the synagogue of the same
city. Barclay writes that several Dutch Jews were coming
to Friends' Meetings. William Tomlinson advocated the
admission of Jews to England in his pamphlet *A Bosome
opened to the Jews* (1656). Isaac Pennington wrote several
pamphlets to the Jews, among them *Some considerations
propounded to the Jews*. There is no evidence that Jews
embraced Quakerism or were influenced by it. But the
Quakers did not depart from a loving and appreciative
attitude towards them, an attitude which finds its expression
in a letter written by Caton to Margaret Fell (1657) : " As
touching the Jews, it is no marvel if thou . . . be sensible of
something among them, for I believe there is a spark in many
of their bosoms, which in process of time may kindle to
a burning flame."[1]

The Moravian Church, founded by Zinzendorf, has evinced,
from 1738 onwards, a great interest in the Jews. One may say
that the Moravians had a prophetic insight into the connexion
between Israel and the fullness of the Christian Church. " As
long as the Jews remained unconverted, Zinzendorf
conscientiously believed that the only heathen who would
accept the Gospel were a few Candace-Souls specially chosen
by God. The time to convert whole nations had not yet come ;
only a few ' first fruits ' might be expected."[2] " In this idea
we find the key to Zinzendorf's missionary policy."[3] The

---

[1] See the essay *Hebraica and the Jews in Early Quaker Interest* by Henry J.
Cadbury, in *Children of Light*, symposium edited by N. Brinton in honour
of Rufus Jones, New York, 1938.
[2] J. Hutton, *A History of Moravian Missions*, London, 1922, p. 183.
[3] *Op. cit.*, p. 146.

Moravian missionary, Samuel Lieberkühn, adopted this policy in Amsterdam : " He attended the Synagogue every morning and evening, took lessons in Jewish law with a Rabbi, joined one of their benefit societies and subscribed to their charitable funds, and even abstained from eating food which they accounted unclean. He was soon a welcome guest in every home. The Jews nicknamed him ' Rabbi Samuel,' and, a hundred years later, stories of his goodness were still repeated. . . . He avoided dogmatic theology. He never preached that Jesus was the Creator ; never asserted, unless challenged, that Jesus was God ; and never even referred to the Holy Trinity. The more a man preached such dogmas, he said, the more he would be involved in barren discussions. . . . Lieberkühn laid great stress on what he called the ' Inward Witness.' ' We Brethren,' he said, ' are certain that Jesus lives, because we experience His saving power.' "[1]

The 19th century saw an extraordinary development of missions to Jews. It will be sufficient to mention here the names of some missionaries : in Great Britain, Samuel Frey, Joseph Wolff (who spent fifteen years in the East, visiting Palestine, Persia, Turkestan, Afghanistan, India and Arabia), Ridley Haim Herschell, Benjamin Davidson, Salkinson and Ginsburg (translators of the New Testament into Hebrew) ; in Holland, Carl Schwartz, Meyer, van Andel, Isaac da Costa, Abraham Capadose ; in Norway, a remarkable woman, Ragnild Haerm, her relative Peter Lorentzem Haerm, Caspari and Bernhoft ; in Sweden, Lindstrom, Gordon, Gjessing, Waldenstrom ; in Denmark, Kalkar, Moritz ; in Switzerland, Carl Brenner, P. Bernoulli ; in Hungary, Adolf Saphir ; in America, Karl Freshman. Most important in the German missions to Jews have been the Jewish Institutes—a return to the methods of Callenberg—such as the *Institutum Judaicum Delitzschianum*, established in Leipzig in 1880 under the leadership of F. Delitzsch, and the Institutes of Erlangen (W. Faber), Berlin (Strack), Halle, Breslau, Greifswald.[2]

Russia has been the home of half of the Jewish race. Russian Jewish missions were undertaken by the Emperor Alexander I, who employed with success the converted Jew, J. C. Moritz. Under Nicholas I, the Mission was restricted to Poland and placed (1830) under the Lutheran Church.

---

[1] *Op. cit.*, pp. 150, 152.
[2] See *Fünfzig Jahre : Institutum Judaicum Delitzschianum*, 1886–1936, herausgegeben von Hans Kosmala, Vienna, 1937. It is a record of fifty years of Christian work among Jews in Europe. The *Delitzschianum* is to-day continuing its existence in London.

In the Roman Church, Maria-Alphonse Ratisbonne
(1814–1884) is said to have been converted from Judaism by
an apparition of the Virgin Mary; with his brother Teodor he
founded the Sisterhood of Our Lady of Zion and the Congregation of the Fathers of Zion, who labour near Jerusalem for the
conversion of Jews and Mohammedans. Another convert,
Paul Libermann (1804–1862), founded the Congregation of the
Holy Ghost and has been declared Venerable.

We shall not discuss, at this point, the efforts directed
towards the formation of a Jewish Christian Church, for this
movement will be considered separately.

B. Christian Missions to Jews to-day.

According to the estimate of De la Roi, 205,000 Jews adopted
Christianity during the 19th century.[1] A more careful estimate
made in 1932 by Dr. Julius B. Maller, of Columbia University,
established that in the 19th century at least 250,000 European
Jews were converted. It is difficult to form an exact idea of
the sincerity and value of these conversions. Pope St. Gregory
the Great initiated certain well-known missionary methods
when he offered the Jews working on the estates of the Church
a reduction of their rent if they accepted baptism. Economics
and social considerations have played a part in too many
conversions of Jews to Christianity. In Vienna, for instance,
numerous Jewish parents have had their children baptized
from purely secular motives. But one must not generalize
nor forget the painful sacrifices which sincere conversions
almost always imply. If there are " rice-Christians " everywhere, many Jews, on becoming Christians, have had to face
cruel ostracisms. A Jew may become an agnostic or an atheist
and remain a Jew ; but even a Jew who thinks of Judaism only
in terms of race would deny membership of the Jewish race
to a Christian Jew. Under the pressure of the present racial
persecutions, this attitude is beginning to break down. But
it has been almost the general rule, for many years. The
Orthodox Eastern Jews call baptism shmad, which means
both apostasy and persecution of Judaism. The conversion of
Jews to Christianity means sometimes a complete disruption
of their economic and social life ; moreover, racial and social
cleavages within the Church often deprive them of the full
enjoyment of Christian fellowship. In a certain American
Church, Christians converted from Judaism were not even

[1] *Judentaufen in* 19. *Jahrhundert,* in the review *Nathaniel,* Nos. 3 and 4,
Berlin, 1899.

allowed to sit down with their Gentile brethren at the communion table.[1] A contemporary Rabbi speaks of the tragedy of the Jewish convert to Christianity : " Severed from his heritage and from his living spiritual tradition, his soul withers and his character suffers irreparable damage. Hence the innumerable tragedies in the lives of the converts and the moral failures."[2] Einstein's comment on Hans Hertzl, the son of the Zionist leader, who became a Christian, drifted from one communion to another and finally committed suicide, was : " This shows the horrible danger of cutting oneself off from the Community."[3] Another striking case was Otto Weininger, the famous young writer of *Gescheecht und Character,* who, after a tentative conversion to Christianity, took his own life. One must highly respect a Jew who, for conscientious motives, has the courage to become a Christian. At the same time, one must admit that the Christian Church, until now, has failed to create a climate or atmosphere appropriate to the needs of most of the converted Jews. A place for Israel, as Christian Israel, has not yet been found in a Church which boasts of its universalism.

Official Judaism is resolutely fighting against Christian " missionarism " and " conversionism." Claude G. Montefiore declares : " The missionaries and their efforts are a perpetual irritant, a constantly running sore."[4] Rabbi Israel Goldstein, of New York, appeared before the Home Missions council at its annual meeting in Atlantic City, January, 1929, to protest against missionary work among the Jews. To an official declaration that " every group of people has the right to propagate its faith," he issued a reply in the *Jewish Tribune,* saying that Christian missionary effort might be justified among uncivilized races, but not in connexion with a community of a high ethical standard like Judaism. There are, however, Jewish voices which discriminate between a real Christian missionary effort and campaigns fomenting strife and ill-will. Rabbi Cohon, in the article already quoted, opposes to the " way of militant conversion " the " way of holding out a kindly light for those who, for their own accord, wish to follow"; he says : " Missionary work of the second order is not only the prerogative, but the obligation of every

---

[1] *Christians and Jews,* New Jersey, 1931, p. 90.
[2] Samuel Cohon, in a paper contributed to the *International Review of Missions,* October, 1933.
[3] Quoted by Olga Levertoff in *The Wailing Wall,* p. 120.
[4] *The Hibbert Journal,* January, 1930, p. 251.

COMMUNION IN THE MESSIAH

religious fellowship. If Christianity, as embodied in private
and social life, in the home, the market-place, and the Church,
awakens the esteem of Jews and arouses their desire to 'share
its joy and fruitfulness,' it will not meet with the criticism of
thoughtful Jews." Montefiore himself writes: "When Jews
cavil at Christian missions, they should, at all events, remember
that all this ardour and self-sacrifice and enthusiasm are for
the sake of others, and not for the salvation of the missionaries'
own souls."[1]

A good synopsis of Christian missionary work among the
Jews, as it existed before the present war, may be found in
the proceedings of the Conferences of Budapest and Warsaw
(1927) and Atlantic City (1931), in which about fifty societies
or organizations of missions to Jews were represented.[2] The
spirit of these proceedings marks an immense progress upon
the spirit prevalent in the same branch of missions before
1914. The horizon has become definitely wider. The
Conferences emphasize the need for kindness, courtesy and
good understanding. They exhort Christians to repentance
for the wrongs done to the Jews in the past and the present.
They recommend the grateful recognition of the rich religious
heritage of Israel, the duty of receiving into a cordial Christian
fellowship all Jews who accept Christ, the careful training of
workers among Jews so that they may be acquainted with the
best Hebrew scholarship, the prevalence of a spirit of respect
and friendliness towards Jews, the avoidance of harsh
controversy, the fight against racial discrimination, and relief
efforts on behalf of suffering Jews. All this is excellent. And
yet some deficiencies must be acknowledged. The exhortation
to kindness towards the Jews may sometimes be clumsy and
irritating. C. Montefiore said about the report of the Budapest-
Warsaw Conferences: "If we dislike anti-Semitic hostility
and hatred, we perhaps dislike condescending amiability and
soft soap even more."[3] The Budapest Conference, dealing
with medical missions, declared: "All patients should be
invited to attend religious services at which the message of
the Gospel is presented. Under some circumstances it may
be wise to make attendance a condition of admittance to the
hospital. . . ." This provision inspired Rabbi Cohon to make

---

[1] *In Spirit and Truth*, p. 329.
[2] *The Christian Approach to the Jews. Report of Conferences held at
Budapest and Warsaw in April,* 1927, London, 1927; and *Christians and Jews.
A Report of the Conference on the Christian Approach to the Jews*, Atlantic
City, New Jersey, 1931.
[3] *The Hibbert Journal*, January, 1930, p. 251.

the following remarks : " What a commentary upon the parable of the Good Samaritan ! In times of stress and sickness, poor and helpless patients are expected to pay with their souls for the charity which they receive."[1] The Jewish comment does not seem to be unjustified. As to the views of the Conferences about evangelization itself, we are afraid that, in the midst of generous and sometimes vague formulas, they miss the very points which might give to the evangelization of the Jews its originality and vigour.

Let us take, for instance, the address presented by Dr. James M. Black, chairman of the International Committee on the Christian Approach to the Jews. We hasten to say that there are admirable things in this address. There are also not a few points which suggest critical reflections about the missions to the Jews in general. Dr. Black says that he does not dare to leave the Jew to himself, and he asks : " How would you like to live your life and think your thoughts in the atmosphere of the Old Testament alone ? It is a dim land of uncertainty, compared with the assurance and joy of Jesus Christ."[2] But is it not a fallacy to think that the Jews live in the atmosphere of the Old Testament alone ? The Jews live in the atmosphere of rabbinical tradition at least as much as in the atmosphere of the Holy Scripture, and this tradition is not dim or uncertain. Does the Christian missionary not commit a mistake when he goes to the Jews with only the Bible in his hands and ignores or neglects the treasuries of Jewish " theology " ? This theology does not give the assurance and joy of Jesus Christ, but does it not constitute a *praeparatio evangelica*, as Greek philosophy did in the eyes of Clement and Origen ? Dr. Black, answering those who think that it is idle to impose a Western faith on the Oriental people, writes : " It is all rather comical ! The biggest bit of comedy lies in the fact that our Christianity, both in origin and thought, is entirely Oriental."[3] Our Christianity is undoubtedly Oriental in origin. But can we say that it has kept this character, that the Greek categories of thought and modes of expression have not overpowered the Jewish elements, and that, owing to its developments in the West, it has not assumed an appearance foreign to the whole Jewish being ? One of the main tasks of the Jewish evangelization of the Jews is to re-translate Christianity from Greek into Hebrew.

[1] Cohon, *The Jew and Christian Evangelization*, in *International Review of Missions*, vol. XXII, 1933, p. 471.
[2] *Christians and Jews*, p. 8.
[3] *Op. cit.*, p. 9.

We read further on : " Just in so far as any religion is concerned with truth about God and man, the terms ' Western ' or ' Oriental ' have no meaning. Truth is not local, but universal."[1] Yes, Truth is universal. But its local expressions or embodiments differ from each other. And, especially, the Jewish people differs from all other peoples. Not only has it its own psychological characteristics, but we believe that it has its own mission, that it still remains chosen by God, that it occupies a unique position in divine economy. Elsewhere Dr. Black writes : " I am bringing him [the Jew] the fruit and completion and crown of his own [faith]."[2] These affirmations ought perhaps to be qualified. The Gospel is the fruit and completion and crown of Judaism. But do missionaries bring to Jews the Gospel *as* the crown of their faith, when they consider as non-existent or unimportant the whole of the Jewish tradition of belief and worship which accompanies and supplements the Old Testament ? To bring to the Jews the crown of their faith means to show them the continuity between Christianity and the whole line of Jewish religious thought, rabbinical as well as Scriptural. Dr. Black says again : " If we are missionary then, we are only missionary as Paul and Peter and John were missionary."[3] Is this quite accurate ? Without insisting on the special Apostolic commission and *charismata,* we would point out that Paul, Peter and John remained Jews among the Jews as long as it proved possible. They were rooted in Jewish tradition. The first of them was a rabbi, educated at Gamaliel's feet. The second was, with James, the pillar of Judæo-Christianity. The third shows a deep knowledge of the Jewish theology of the " age of transition." All three used to attend the Temple, and Paul used to speak in the synagogues. It would be indeed a good omen for the Christian mission among the Jews if the Christian missionaries were only missionaries like Paul, Peter and John.

Thus, Dr. Black's address furnishes us not only with a clear view of some of the main deficiencies of the Christian Mission to the Jews, but also, as a consequence, with a definite programme of redress in these very points.

We do not wish to be unduly critical of the Christian missionaries in the Jewish field. Their difficulties are probably greater than those of missionaries in other parts. Orthodox circles are closed to them. The largest element of the Jewish

---

[1] *Op. cit.,* p. 9.
[2] *Op .cit.,* p. 11.
[3] *Op. cit.,* p. 11.

population is perhaps constituted by the " unsynagogued Jews " ; the young generations have been swept into . the streams of secular culture and are deeply indifferent to the restraints and ideals of Ancient Judaism ; such elements are out of touch with the missionaries. Nor can it be said that the Christian Mission to Jews receives (apart from the financial contributions which were, as we believe, considerable) much help from the normally constituted Christian congregations. On the contrary, Sunday school literature and pulpit common-places are often apt to arouse in the minds of the children a prejudice against the Jews, and do not facilitate a work of rapprochement. And the political conditions prevalent to-day in Continental Europe have compelled most of the missions to Jews to stop their work.

The average literature of the Mission to the Jews has been rather weak ; it often contains " padded " stories of conversions and distorted characterizations of Judaism. It exhibits crude propaganda, sanctimonious phraseology, an unimaginative outlook. By way of contrast, a learned and dignified presenta-tion of the Christian case may be found in the books of A. Lukyn Williams,[1] S. C. Kirkpatrick,[2] John Wilkinson,[3] Adolf Saphir,[4] David Baron,[5] Aaron Bernstein,[6] to quote only these few. The little book of Canon Herbert Danby,[7] coming from an eminent rabbinic scholar, deserves particular attention.

Among the leaders of Christian missions to Jews during these last years, we should mention the names of Dr. Conrad Hoffmann, Dr. James Black, Sir Leon Levison, The Rev. Frank J. Exley, The Rev. C. H. Gill, Dr. J. S. Conning, in the Anglo-Saxon world ; and, in Continental Europe, Otto von Harling and Hans Kosmala (Germany), Gyula Forgacs (Hungary), J. van Nes (the Netherlands), J. E. Lundahl (Sweden). These names are guarantees of a deep goodwill and of an enlightened outlook.

As one knows, the position of the converted Jew inside the Christian Churches of Germany has become extremely difficult. The Roman Church and the Confessional Church maintain the

[1] *The Hebrew Christian Messiah*, London, 1916, and *A Manual of Christian Evidences for Jewish People*, 2 vols., London, 1911. (We must admit that the very idea of a " manual of Christian evidences " makes us dubious!)
[2] *Through the Jews to God*, London, 1916.
[3] *Israel My Glory*, London, 1892.
[4] See the analysis, with large extracts, of his works and some of his sermons in G. Carlyle, *A Memoir of Adolf Saphir*, London, 1894.
[5] *The Ancient Scriptures and the Modern Jew*, London, 1900.
[6] *Some Jewish Witnesses for Christ*, London, 1909.
[7] *The Jew and Christianity*, New York.

right of the converted Jews to full membership in the Church. The State-subservient Church, theoretically, maintains their right, but qualifies it in practice with many restrictions. The Church of the German Christians excludes the Jews, rejects the Law of Moses and renounces the idea of any Christian mission to convert the Jews.[1]

THE MISSION OF THE CHRISTIAN CHURCH
TO ISRAEL

We have spoken until now of the Christian missions to the Jews in their empirical reality, i.e., as they have been and as they are. Will it seem presumptuous if we now try to sketch the Mission of the Christian Church to Israel as we conceive it and as we wish it to be ? We said " the Mission of the Christian Church to Israel " ; by this wording we signify that it is not only a question of some sectional mission to individual Jews, but of *the* Mission of the whole Church of Christ as such, to the whole community of Israel as such.

The Mission of the Christian Church to Israel will have to face two tasks : a theological task and a practical task.

A. *The Theological Task*

The first part of the theological task of the Mission consists in obtaining and formulating a true conception of the Mission itself.

One should, to begin with, be quite clear about the validity of the missionary approach to the Jews. It is noticeable that many of the Christian and Unitarian scholars who have a genuine knowledge of Jewish subjects show either a sheer indifference, or a reticent dislike, or an open hostility to the Christian missionary effort among the Jews. Thus, Travers Herford wrote to Hans Kosmala : " Anyone who seriously engages in a Christian mission to the Jews shows thereby that he does not understand Judaism. . . . And so long as he persists in that enterprise, he never will."[2] Another objection, of a more general character, comes from the Barthians. For the Barthians, the very idea of missions expresses the heathen *hybris*, the ungodly pride, of the Western Christians. We cannot offer Christ, because we must come and confess the ungodliness of our heathenish earthly existence. We may answer that Christianity is necessarily missionary, in the true

[1] A. Duncan-Jones, *The Struggle for Religious Freedom in Germany*, London, 1938.
[2] Quoted by H. Kosmala in the *International Review of Missions*, October 1940, p. 504.

sense that a Christian ought freely to give what he has freely received. Basil Mathews and Bernard Lucas, both of them specialists in racial-religious problems, are eager to draw a distinction between proselytism and evangelism ; they enthusiastically accept the latter and reject the former. But why ? G. E. Phillips quite rightly says : " In itself the term has no evil meaning. . . . It has incurred a two-fold deterioration, first from the bad things which have sometimes been done to induce people to change their religion, second, from a careless reading of Matthew xxiii. 15. The condemnation is not of the zeal which makes a proselyte, but of the waste of zeal upon making the proselyte more of a son of hell than yourselves."[1] H. Kraemer writes on the same subject : " The bad repute in which this word stands must not make us hesitant in using it with all frankness. . . . It is no mistaken form of proselytism, but it belongs to the very essence of obedience to God, that a Christian and a missionary should live by the ardent desire that all men will surrender to Christ as the Lord of their lives. Whosoever does not stress that, does not sufficiently consider the passionately prophetic and apostolic spirit of the Gospel."[2]

The validity of the Christian Mission to Israel once admitted, one should acquire a theological view of Israel's privileged function in the divine economy. Many Christians refuse to do it. A. Garvie, for instance, writes[3] : " I have heard Jewish missions advocated on the ground that God's chosen people have a special claim for consideration. Grateful as we may be for the legacy of Israel in the Old Testament and the divine revelation of which it is the human record, we must not abandon our Christian universalism. God has no favourites, individual or national . . ." We must certainly not abandon our Christian universalism, but this universalism does not exclude free election and special graces. Paul, desirous as he was of opening the doors of salvation to the Gentiles, believed in a primacy of Israel which would still be manifested in the future. The meaning of Israel's dispersion and sufferings in the modern world, the significance of Zionism, the Pauline doctrine of the grafting of the Gentiles on the Jewish tree, the " axis " rôle of Israel, so to speak, in the salvation of the nations, all this is an important part—which cannot be arbitrarily erased— of the theology of the Mission.

[1] *The Gospel in the World*, London, 1939, pp. 92-93.
[2] *The Christian Message in a non-Christian World*, London, 1938, p. 433.
[3] *The Jewish Problem*, in *International Review of Missions*, April, 1941, vol. XXX., p. 220.

Then we shall have to elaborate the theological presentation of the Christian *kerygma*, properly speaking, to the Jews—in other words, to build a theology of Christ for Israel.

It will necessarily begin as apologetics. We should not be afraid of this word, which the Church Fathers used. These apologetics will be centred around the person of Jesus. In theory, the normal way should be from the Old Testament to Jesus. In practice, the consideration of the person of Our Lord is usually the starting point of the process which leads a Jew to Christianity. The Jew not seldom " falls in love " with Jesus. As the most negative conclusions of modern criticism are often taken for granted by Jews (see the Jewish *Lives of Jesus*), one should insist upon the historicity of the Gospel narratives, while giving their due place to the ascertained results of scientific research. Certain features of the character of Our Lord—His absence of sin consciousness, His unique relation to the Father—should be emphasized. This cannot take the place of the direct experience of Christ in the soul, but it may prepare for such an experience. A missionary who has none of it and therefore cannot share it will be of little use.

We shall not always remain on the plane of apologetics. The theology of the Mission to Israel must develop into a biblical theology. By Bible, we mean here, according to primitive Christian use, the Old Testament. As W. Vischer puts it : [1] " Strictly speaking, only the Old Testament is ' the Scripture,' while the New Testament brings the glad tidings that now the content of that Scripture, the meaning of all its words, its Lord and Fulfiller has corporally appeared." The interpretation of the Old Testament has a capital importance for the Mission to Israel. The ancient Christian writers of polemics adopted the habit of reading into the biblical text everything they expected to find there and gave to their interpretations a " proof " value which no Jew could admit. Moreover, many Gentile Christians have ceased to see in the Old Testament a way of life and an approach to God. The theology of the Mission must react against these two defects. What will be our attitude towards Messianic prophecy ? So often now the tendency is to consider it as

---

[1] *Das Christuszeugniss des Alten Testaments*, I Band : *Das Gesetz*, Munich, 1935, p. 8 : " *Streng genommen ist eigentlich nur das Alte Testament ' die Schrift' während das Neue Testament die frohe Botschaft bringt, dass jetzt der Inhalt dieser Schrift, der Sinn all ihrer Worte, ihr Herr und ihr Erfüller leibhaftig erschienen ist.*"

a stumbling block rather than as a powerful buttress. We believe that the Messianic prophecy has not lost anything of its peculiar cogency. Indeed, we foresee, for the next future, a great revival of Messianic exegesis. But some principles should be always kept in mind. Messianic prophecies ought to be approached with a real interest for the theme in itself, not as weapons against Jews and infidels or crutches for a feeble Christian faith ; and a due regard ought to be given to their immediate temporal reference. Hebrew prophecy, besides, ought to be taken " as a whole." Stress should be laid not so much upon the text as upon the tendencies which were at work in giving it shape—not so much upon the evidence of particular short passages regarded in isolation as upon their convergence. And Jesus is the very centre of convergence. The scattered rays which gleam across the words of the prophets and rabbis are absorbed in the person of Our Lord. All these elements are brought together and realized in Him.[1] But Messianic prophecies will never be truly understood and received if the " prophetic word " is not spoken by the spirit of God in the soul of the reader.

Jesus, in His references to the Messianic texts of the Old Testament, assumes, with regard to their date, authorship and meaning, traditional views which have sometimes been discarded by modern scientific exegesis. Shall we say with Gore that the purpose of Jesus' quotations is " not to prove or disprove anything, to affirm or deny anything, but simply to press upon the Pharisees an argument which their habitual assumptions ought to have suggested to them ; to comfort them with just that question which they, with their principles, ought to have been asking themselves ? "[2] We fear that to explain Jesus' Messianic quotations thus is to explain them away. We would rather say that Jesus, without committing Himself to the habitual historical assumptions of which He was making use, safeguarded the truth of the new significance imparted by the Spirit to some texts of which the original meaning was different.

The theology of the Mission to Israel must also be a comparative, or rather " translating," theology. Kraemer says : " There is the obligation to strive for the presentation of the Christian truth in terms and modes of expression that makes its challenge intelligible and related to the peculiar

---

[1] See C. Briggs, *Messianic Prophecy*, Edinburgh, 1886 ; F. Delitzsch, *Messianische Weissagungen in geschichtlichen Folge*, Leipzig, 1890.
[2] C. Gore, *Bampton Lectures*, p. 198.

quality of reality in which they live. . . ."[1] He insists that such a presentation must be " a translation of meanings and not of detached words." This is only possible through the determined confronting of Christian and rabbinic theology. We have already tried to suggest how it could be done, especially in connexion with the Shekinah. The Talmud and the Zohar may furnish us with the Hebrew equivalents of many Greek-Christian terms and notions. Barth claims that, in the light of Christian revelation, all apparent similarities are dissimilarities ; points of contact are only to be found by antithesis. We deny this in respect of non-Jewish religions ; we deny it still more emphatically in respect of the religion of Israel. We stand here, as always, with the Church of the Fathers against Barth. Of course, there is the danger of an unreal syncretism. We do not know whether modern endeavours to bring Christianity and non-Christian religions together by affirming certain intrinsic affinities between them (as Reischelt and Saunders have attempted with Buddhism, Heiler and Appassamy with Hinduism, Wilson Cash and Levonian with Islam) are entirely successful in safeguarding the uniqueness and absoluteness of the Christian message. But the case of Israel is different from all other cases. The whole message of Israel is an authentic part of God's Revelation and can be, without the abolition of a single jot, brought together with the message of Jesus. Nothing of the true Jewish tradition—from Hillel to the modern Hasidism— needs to be altered in order to adjust itself to the Gospel : it needs only to be complemented. The Christian doctrines of the Word, the Son of God, the Messiah, the Mediator, the Holy Spirit, the Community are legitimate interpretations and extensions not only of Scriptural, but also of rabbinical Judaism. We have already said this at some length.

The theology of the Mission to Israel must go further than comparing and translating Jewish and Christian notions. It must establish a kind of fundamental theology of both Judaism and Christianity, a common ground as serving basis for the discussion on divergences. This may and ought to be done in co-operation with Jewish theologians. Such a theology would deal, for instance, with such problems as the Jewish ideas of the Word, the Messiah, the Atonement, etc., as they were found just before the parting of the roads, i.e., before the birth of Christianity. It would be a systematic and affirmative

The Christian Message in a non-Christian World, p. 303.

(not apologetic or polemic) theology. Oesterley and Box[1] have exactly indicated the nature of the work to be done : " Rich as Rabbinical Judaism has been in its later phases, it yet (so it seems to us) represents an essentially attenuated line of development. It is but one off-shoot from a larger stem. It sprang from a larger and richer Judaism which, to a greater extent than is sometimes supposed, held within itself the forces which afterwards diverged as Rabbinism and Christianity. The common meeting ground where these forces can be seen exhibiting themselves in combination (greater or less) is the field of the Apocryphal and Pseudepigraphical Literature of Judaism." The field of exploration should really cover the whole of the " age of transition," i.e., the interval between the Old Testament and Jesus. A special emphasis should be laid on Alexandrian Judaism. Though the motto " Back to Philo ! " be too one-sided, the theology which we have here in view should drink deeply of the water of life flowing from the Alexandrian springs. Would it be an irreverence towards modern Jewish theology to say that it seems, perhaps, to suffer from a kind of anæmia ? We are longing for a resplendent revival of Jewish theology (of which Buber and Abelson are probably precursors), and we believe that the new strength of Jewish religious thought will come from the old sources.

Finally, the theology of the Mission to Israel must incorporate itself more than heretofore in the general theological movement of our days. Provincialism and poverty should not be mistaken for autarkia or splendid isolation. Garvie writes[2]: " When induced to attend, as representative of the Congregational Churches, conferences on Jewish missions in Budapest and Warsaw in 1927, I was grieved to find how much division of effort there was, and how narrow in my judgment was the theological basis of much of this effort. For I hold that it would be a disaster if Jewish missions were bound for the most part to a less progressive theology than is current among Christian scholars and thinkers generally ; and I should desire an appeal broad enough to command a cordial response from all types of Christians." Let us give some details.

There is a dogmatic renaissance : it is enough to quote the names of Saint Thomas and Karl Barth. Has Judaism no contribution to make to modern theology ? Would, for instance, a theology of the Word and of the Shekinah be

---

[1] *The Religion and Worship of the Synagogue*, p. viii (of the 1907 edition).
[2] *The Jewish Problem*, in *International Review of Missions*, April, 1941, vol. XXX, p. 220.

without interest or fruitfulness ? Would a specifically Jewish-Christian christology not be a great achievement ?

There is at the present time an animated theological debate on ethics, society and culture. We find, among the main interlocutors of this debate, Berdyaev, Niebuhr, Maritain. Is there not a place for Jewish Messianism, for Zionist ideology, for the message of Buber ?

There is everywhere a " re-thinking " of the Mission idea. Kraemer's book, *The Christian Message in a non-Christian World*, is perhaps the best expression of this new missionary movement. Now, of the 455 pages of that book, only two are devoted to the Mission to Israel. The author (who, by the way, identifies Judaism with the Old Testament and neglects rabbinic theology) apologizes for the restricted space given to the subject and explains it by his lack of personal experience in this field. Those really responsible here are the missions themselves. If the missions to Jews were what they ought to be, if they had established in the eyes of the whole Christian world their proper significance and the originality of their message, they would occupy the first place in a survey of Christian missions.

There is a powerful liturgical movement not only in the Roman Church (chiefly among the Benedictines), but also in the German *Hochkirche*, in Swedish Lutheranism, in the Methodist and Reformed Churches, in the Church of England, in the Church of the Disciples of Christ, etc. Behind it, we find a theology of worship and of the sacraments. Why is so little attention paid to Jewish worship ? Why is the connexion between Jewish and Christian rites and prayers so generally ignored by Christian worshippers ? Why do Christian missionaries not endeavour to show the theological implications of the Jewish liturgy, e g., of Circumcision and Atonement ?

There is a revival of interest and studies in mysticism : let us mention, in England, the works of Von Hügel, Butler, Rufus Jones, Evelyn Underhill ; the new emphasis which the Roman Church lays on the doctrines of Saint John of the Cross ; the recent popularity of Saint Seraphim of Sarov and of the " prayer of Jesus " among the Russian Orthodox. But who endeavours to show the link between the Zohar or Hasidism and Christian mysticism ?

There is, finally, the " œcumenical movement " (Söderblom, Heiler, the conferences of Stockholm, Lausanne, Edinburgh, etc.). Are the promoters of this movement aware that no scheme of reunion can succeed if it is not vertical as well as horizontal ? Can the daughter Churches, i.e., the Christian Churches, become really reconciled if they make no step towards their mother, the Church of Israel ? We firmly believe that, in the plan of God, the mother will be—some day still far off— the centre and the instrument of unity. The Synagogue cannot be invited to take part in inter-Christian conferences. But cannot a thought be given to the Synagogue, in such assemblies ? We respectfully suggest to the organizers of future " œcumenical " conferences that the Christian Churches thus gathered together should elaborate a common " declaration of principles " or " declaration of position " with regard to Israel. The Churches should solemnly repent for their own past sins and the sins of some modern States against Israel ; they should outline a scheme of practical co-operation with the Jews ; they should also define the theological ground common to Christians and Jews, indicate the lines along which a dialogue could be held, and constitute some organization entrusted with the study of the problems of Judaism. Israel may have heard many individual Christian voices. Let Israel now hear the voice of the body of the Christian Churches met together.

B. *The Practical Task*

Under this heading, we shall examine two questions.

The first question is the relationship between service and message, between *diakonia* and *kerygma*. In speaking of the dispersion, we have already outlined what could be a Christian activity of help and service—a diaconal ministry—on behalf of the Jews. What connexion, if any, ought to be established between this ministry and the preaching of the Word ? Should we abstain from proclaiming the Gospel and simply be kind to the Jews ? This solution, understandable and sometimes advisable in certain individual cases, cannot be admitted as a general principle of the conduct of the Church. Goodwill is no substitute for the Gospel. On the other hand, we admit that, in respect to the Jews, the *diakonia* should always precede the *kerygma*. Let this be the first principle. There is a special reason for giving this priority to the *diakonia*. When Christians address people other than the Jews, they may begin with the message ; the Apostles themselves did so, in the days of Pentecost. The reason why we cannot do it now is that, since Christianity began, nineteen centuries have elapsed during which the Jews have suffered in greater or less degree at the hands of Christians. We have no right to approach the Jews now as if our hands were clean. We must first of all atone for our gross violation of the law of our Master and deserve the forgiveness and confidence of Israel. We shall speak of our faith only when we have proved our love. The second principle is that there should be no *kerygma* without not only a prior, but also a concomitant *diakonia* of some sort, though we must be careful never to make the acceptance of the *kerygma* a condition for sharing in the benefits of the *diakonia*. A third principle is that the *kerygma* should in some way shine through the *diakonia* and our personal life, so that the Christian preaching would consist only in naming and systematizing the realities which our action would have already made manifest to the Jews. (We are speaking here of the missionary attitude, not of the theoretical work of the theologian.) At the same time we should make it clear that we love the Jew not in order to win him over, but because we, as Christians, must unconditionally love him.

A few quotations will show that this standpoint is advocated by people whose opinion is authoritative on the subject. Rabbi Lyons says : " Treat all Jews with the humanitarianism of a Jesus and we shall love Him more for your example ; whereas we shall never be drawn to Him or to you for your theology. . . ."[1] Edwyn Bevan writes : " A Christian who believes in Jesus may see a Jew who gives in will and emotion such splendid effect to the truth of God's reality that he is humbled at the contrast of his own relatively poor action to what he believes to be a larger range of truth. . . . This would imply that the only legitimate form of propaganda for a Christian is in some way or other to say : Look . . . It may be, without speaking on the subject, by confronting them with Christianity in practice."[2] And O. von Harling : " The history of missions shows that the majority of Jews have been won through the witness of believing Christians in the congregation rather than through the preaching of missionaries. Jews meet the missionary—especially the Hebrew Christian—with the strongest suspicion and reluctance ; it is different in the case of the Christian through whom they are brought in contact with Christian life."[3]

The second question is specifically ecclesiastical. What shall we do with the Jew who wishes to become a Christian ? Shall

[1] Quoted by G. Hoffmann, *Modern Jewry and the Christian Church*, in *International Review of Missions*, vol. xxiii, 1934, p. 200.
[2] *Christian Propaganda among Jews*, in *International Review of Missions*, vol. xxii, 1933, pp. 499 and 483.
[3] *Missions to Jews to-day*, in *International Review of Missions*, vol. xxii, 1933, p. 352.

we advise him to apply for baptism to some of the numerous missions to Jews ? Or to be enlisted as a regular member of one of the existent Christian Churches ? Or what else ? We wish to say here and now only one thing on this subject. Generally speaking, we are very far from considering the adhesion of a Jew to one of the Gentile Christian Churches as an ideal solution. It may sometimes be the only possible one, but we do not think it either normal or desirable. The appearance and diffusion of a Jewish Christianity, inside the Church universal, is, as we believe, the only true solution. Of this we shall say more later on.

THE MISSION OF ISRAEL TO THE CHRISTIAN CHURCH

We uncompromisingly believe in the God-given Mission of the Christian Church to Israel. No less strongly do we believe in the God-given Mission of Israel to the Christian Church.

Cardinal Faulhaber, in the Advent sermons preached in the Church of St. Michael (Munich) in which he raised a noble protest against anti-semitism,[1] said : " After the death of Christ, Israel was dismissed from the service of the Revelation." This is, as we think, the standpoint of most Christians. And this is exactly the view against which we would warn every Christian interested in Jewish problems. If we share such a view, the strong words of Paul concerning Israel (Rom. ix.) become meaningless. Israel is nowadays used and will, to a greater extent still, be used in the service of the Revelation. The people of the Law and of the Prophets is perpetually sent (*missus, missio*) by God to the Christian Church in order to witness to certain truths and powers. The Synagogue does not organize missions to Christians, though there are conversions from Christianity to Judaism which deserve our attention ;[2] but the Jewish people remains entrusted with a universal message. Herbert Loewe said :[3] " God caused Christianity to spread and Judaism to survive in ever-increasing vigour, because He had need of both." If these words mean that the state of separation between Judaism and Christianity is a good thing in itself, we cannot admit them. But if they mean that, even in its present state of separation from Christianity

---

[1] *Judaism, Christianity and Germany*, Munich, 1933, translated from the German by G. Smith, London, 1934.
[2] See special note S.
[3] *Judaism and Christianity*, vol. I, p. 182.

(not because of it), Judaism fulfils a certain mission given from God, we fully subscribe to them. The present task of Judaism is to maintain certain affirmations of which Christians are in need no less than Jews and for the proclamation of which Israel has a particular authority. What are these affirmations?

(a) *The living and personal God.* Some Liberal Jewish writers have unhappily called Judaism an " ethical mono-theism." That abstract term, so uninspiring, misses the very essentials of Judaism—the warm and joyous relation to God. This faith in the personal and historical, objective and revealed God is valuable to counter-balance two dangers often met in hellenized Christianity : on the one hand, the substitution of the abstract God of metaphysics for the living God of Revelation ; on the other hand, a mysticism (neo-platonic in origin) of the absorption in the One and a possible forgetfulness of the otherness and personality of God.

(b) *The Scripture.* The deposit of the Old Testament has been entrusted to Israel. And Israel is still the keeper of the key to the Scriptures. We mean that the ancient rabbinical interpretation of the Old Testament is a very positive contribution of Judaism to Christianity—we would say more : it is the right approach to the understanding of the Old Testament. Like Jerome, the Christian Church should learn the Old Testament from the rabbis (we do not mean modern rabbinism, but the old masters of Israel). This may scandalize the scholars : is not the ancient rabbinic inter-pretation of the Old Testament hopelessly out of date ? From the historical and philological point of view, yes, quite certainly. But, from the spiritual point of view, we have still much to receive if we go to the Jewish Fathers. The pneumatological (we would not merely say, symbolical) interpretation of the Old Testament could perfectly co-exist with the strictest scientific exegesis of its letter and immediate meaning, if we only believe in the inspiration of the Scriptures. Such a spiritual re-reading of the Old Testament will perhaps be effected (we hope so) by the Judaism of to-morrow ; and it may have the consequence of making the Old Testament alive and fecund in the Christian Church, which at the present time it is very far from being. But would not the ancient Jewish interpretation of the Old Testament blind us to the latent mystery of Christ in the sacred texts of Israel ? No exegesis of the Old Testament is more messianically-minded than that of the primitive rabbis. Being able to name Him whom they could not name, we, under their guidance, would find Him hidden everywhere.

(c) *The Law.* The eternal principles of justice, duty and conscience have been entrusted to Israel. They have not been superseded by the message of Our Lord. The Gospel abolishes the Law only in the sense that it abundantly fulfils it. It is from Israel that we have received the thundering proclamation of the absolute exigencies of justice and moral law. Israel still shouts in the wilderness. The Churches, as institutions and under their human aspect, have sometimes been more ready than Israel to come to a compromise with successful injustice. The hearing of the Voice speaking on Sinai and the reading of the Tables of the Law given to Israel are the necessary safeguards against a distorted casuistry or against an anomism disguised under the name of spiritual freedom. Both casuistry and anomism have led many Christians of our day, in various Churches, to compromise with moral and social evil.

(d) *The Prophets.* " The bones of the Hebrew prophets still live in the Jews of to-day and have power to give life to the world in which they are being scattered " writes R. Smith.[1] The spirit of prophecy—to be found rather in the synagogue than in the Temple—is the oxygen necessary to the life of the Christian Church, if she is not to degenerate into clericalism and institutionalism. The saints, reformers, and mystics of the Christian Church have often fulfilled the task of the prophets. St. Francis of Assisi and St. Teresa, St. Seraphim of Sarov, John Wesley, George Fox, the Sadhu Sundar Singh were also prophets. But familiarity with the ancient Hebrew prophets, like Amos or Isaiah, maintains in the Christian Church a breath of that free and strong spirit which nothing can replace. This is not the only inheritance, but the continuous possession of Israel.

(e) *" Primacy of the Spiritual."* This phrase (*" primauté du spirituel "*) is borrowed from Maritain. The history of the Christian Church since Constantine, in Orthodox Byzantium and Orthodox Russia as well as in post-Reformation Germany, Elizabethan England, and Fascist Italy, has too often been the history of the subservience of the Church to the State. Judaism has always kept itself more independent of the temporal power. The Synagogue has been persecuted, but has not bowed to Cæsar. R. Smith says : " It may be that the

[1] *The New Captivity of Israel,* in *International Review of Missions,* vol. XXX, April, 1941, p. 230.

Hebrew genius will yet save mankind from the evils of nationalism, just because the Jews had been denied nationhood."[1]

(f) *Messianism.* The Jewish restlessness, its will to progress, its expectation of a Messianic future stir the Christian Church from slumber. The Messianic tension always present in Judaism may help Christianity to become less satisfied with things as they are, more conscious of its own Messianic and eschatological vocation.

(g) *Zionism.* The Christian Church has to learn that a new messianically-minded culture has begun and is to-day flourishing in the Land of the Promise. The Church has also to re-learn the hopes of the prophets and Paul about the magnificent future of an Israel endowed with the fullness of light. The Church has to re-learn how to think of Zion.

None of these points needs further development. They have already been expounded at some length in this book. They are mentioned here only as a *résumé*.

Let us listen again to some Christian pronouncements on this subject of Israel's Mission to Christianity. We shall quote three authoritative opinions.

First, C. H. Dodd : " . . . It may be well thought that the anti-semitism of the Church in later times was accompanied by a real impoverishment of ethical ideals. Some would say that at the present time the Church would gain from closer and more respectful relations with the Jews, who have preserved, in living tradition, elements of the prophetic ideal which belonged to Christianity at the first, but were overlaid by Greek metaphysics and Roman law."[2]

Next, the late Canon H. Goudge : " The great people of God's choice were soon the least adequately represented in the Catholic Church. That was a disaster to the Church itself. It meant that the Church as a whole failed to understand the Old Testament and that the Greek mind and the Roman mind in turn, instead of the Hebrew mind, came to dominate its outlook : from that disaster the Church has never recovered, either in doctrine or in practice. If to-day we are again coming rightly to understand the Old Testament and thus far better than before, the New Testament also, it is to our modern Hebrew scholars and in part to Jewish scholars themselves that we owe it. God meant, we believe, the Jews to be His

[1] *The New Captivity of Israel,* in *International Review of Missions,* vol. XXX. April, 1941, p. 230.
[2] *The Epistle of Paul to the Romans,* London, 1932, p. 181.

missionaries ; the first great age of evangelization was the Apostolic age, when the missionaries were almost entirely Jews ; no others could have done what they did. If to-day another great age of evangelization is to dawn, we need the Jews again."[1]

Finally, Conrad Hoffmann : " With Christ, Israel may again give to the world religious leadership, new religious truths, and profound spiritual experience, new vistas and new revelations of God."[2]

COMMUNION IN THE MESSIAH AND THE ECCLESIASTICAL COMMUNITIES — JEWISH AND CHRISTIAN

There is a Mission of the Christian Church to Israel. There is a Mission of Israel to the Christian Church. Will the Christian Church and Israel meet on the way and kiss each other ? Will they repeat one to the other the beautiful words which the Jewish-Christian writer of the *Odes of Solomon* ascribes to the Spirit of God : " Open your ears and I will speak to you. Give me your souls, that I may also give you my soul, the word of the Lord and His good pleasures, the holy thought which He has devised concerning His Messiah " ?[3]

The contents of this book have, perhaps, already given some idea of the meaning of its title—Communion in the Messiah. But we wish, at this point, to make this meaning clearer still.

We think that the word " conversion " should be avoided in reference to the acceptance of Christ by Israel. Conversion means to turn from a certain state to another state not only different from, but opposite to the precedent one. It implies that one is brought over from an error to a truth, either dogmatic (as in the conversion of the heretic or the unbeliever) or moral (as in the conversion of the sinner). Now the acceptance of Christianity by most of the believers in non-Christian religions—e.g., Hinduism—is a conversion in the full sense of the term. Such is not the case with Judaism. We say " Judaism," and not " the Jews." Many Jews, to become Christians, need a real conversion, either because they ought

---

[1] *The Calling of the Jews*, in the volume of collected essays *Judaism and Christianity*, London (Shears and Sons), 1939.

[2] *Christians and Jews*, p. 60.

[3] Ode 9. I reproduce the translation given by Rendel Harris in *An Early Christian Psalter*, London, 1909.

to undergo a moral change or because (like Saul before his " conversion ") they have personally denied or opposed Christ. But Judaism as such contains nothing opposed to the Christian faith. The negation of Jesus' Messiahship commonly associated with Judaism is super-added to the few articles of the authentic Jewish creed, but forms no part of it. This negation is by no means a Jewish dogma ; it is rather a *theologoumenon* which, although it is held by almost all Jews, is not thereby incorporated in the official message of Judaism. There is nothing, absolutely nothing, in Jewish belief that a Jew turned Christian ought to reject. Christianity is, in relation to Judaism, a completion and a fulfilment.

For the word " conversion " we would substitute " communion," giving it all the richness and also the indefiniteness of the Greek *koinonia* : sharing fellowship, common life, community. . . . A Jew who accepts (not only intellectually) Jesus as Messiah enters into communion with the Messiah *as Jesus*, and with the community of the followers of Jesus. Reciprocally, a Christian who becomes aware of the Jewish contents of his own faith and inwardly responds to this new awareness enters into communion with Jesus *as Jewish Messiah* and invisibly with the Messianic community of Israel, insofar as the Messiah displays an immanent activity inside it. Thus the Mission—the two-fold Mission—ends in communion.

What about the pious Jew who (without any guilt) has not accepted Jesus ? What about the pious Christian entirely unconscious of his Jewish inheritance ? Is there no communion between them ?

They communicate, to a certain extent, in the Messiah. This communion has two aspects : an obvious and a hidden one. The obvious aspect consists in the fact that both the Christian and the Jew hold fast certain beliefs, certain hopes and a certain charity objectively connected with the Messianic King, or His Father, or His reign. The hidden aspect consists in the immanence of the Messiah Himself under all the aspects of Messianic piety (and both Jewish and Christian piety are Messianic). The Messiah Jesus is Himself the substance of all Messianic faith, all Messianic hope, all Messianic love, all Messianic grace. A true Christian and a true Israelite communicate in the same Messiah. This communion is partial and implicit. God will make it some day total and explicit.

We hope that the title of this study has now been made quite clear. Every part of the book is an attempt to reach some aspects of the communion of Jews and Christians in one Messianism, therefore in the one Messiah.

What ought to be the practical relationship between the Church and the Synagogue ? As it is external and institutional, this relationship will necessarily be on a far lower plane than the inward relationship of communion which we have indicated. A fragment of a conversation between Bishop W. L. Rogers and a rabbi shows us at least what the beginning might be. " You and I, a Jewish rabbi and a Christian bishop, shall walk a long way together, hand in hand. I will go further, because to me Jesus lives so near God that I cannot see God for Him. You won't agree with me in all that, rabbi ?—No, he said. I cannot go that far. But I will start with you on the way."[1]

Martin Buber writes : " We both—the Church and Israel itself—know about Israel. . . . Every genuine holiness can acknowledge the mystery of another genuine holiness. . . . How it is possible that the mysteries exist side by side, this is God's mystery." But the Holy Spirit, the *pneuma agion* of the Christians and the *ruah-ha-kodesh* of the Jews, " is not Himself bound to this separateness." And Buber says with regret : " If the Church were more Christian . . . if Jewry were again Israel . . ."[2]

Claude Montefiore has written a sentence which may seem strange and paradoxical : " The purpose of Judaism was to produce Christianity ; the purpose of Christianity is to produce more Judaism."[3] But there is a deep truth in this apparent paradox. Judaism is the love of the Father ; therefore it was bound to produce Christianity, because only the Son loves the Father with a perfect love. Christianity is the love of the Son ; therefore it is bound to produce more Judaism, i.e., to share more and more the love of the Son for the Father. The third *Ode of Solomon*—we quote these poems with fondness, as they are so beautifully Jewish Christian—says exactly the same thing : " I love Him that is the Son, that I may myself be a son."

THE IDEA OF A JEWISH CHRISTIANITY

The Jew Trypho, of the famous *Dialogue*, asks Justin whether a man accepting Jesus as Messiah, but desiring to keep the Jewish legal ordinances, shall be saved. Justin

[1] *The Hebrew Christian Alliance Quarterly*, April-June, 1930, p. 39.
[2] " *Wir beide, Kirche und Israel selbst, wissen um Israel . . . Jedes echte Heiligtum kann das Geheimnis eines anderen Heiligtums anerkennen . . . Wie es Möglich ist, dass es die Geheimnisse nebeneinander gibt, dass ist Gottes Geheimnis . . . Wir fühlen . . . dass der Geist selber nicht in diese Scheidlichkeit eingebunden ist . . . Wenn die Kirche christlicher wäre . . . wenn das Judentum wieder Israel würde . . .* " *Die Stunde und die Erkenntnis*, Berlin, 1936, pp. 148, 151, 155, 165.
[3] *In Spirit and Truth*, symposium edited by G. Yates, London, 1934, p. 331.

answers that he will, unless he denies the possible salvation of Gentile converts not keeping the same ordinances. The whole problem of a Jewish Christianity is raised in this passage and receives, as we believe, the right answer. How did this principle work in practice ? How can it work nowadays ?

The first attempt[1] providing a connected story of the specifically Jewish section of the Christian Church has been made by Hugh J. Schonfield in his recent *History of Jewish Christianity from the first to the twentieth century*.[2] Schonfield retraces the history of the Nazarene group from the beginning, and, after the disappearance of this group, of the contribution and achievements of individual Jewish Christians. One may not agree with the historical standpoints of the author : he maintains, for instance, that James, Bishop of Jerusalem, was the leader of the local patriotic party, and that the Book of Revelation is a message from one of the deported Nazarene leaders to the Christian communities of Asia Minor ; but one will recognize that Schonfield has collected a very large and interesting amount of information.

The Church of Jerusalem was, of course, a Jewish Christian Church under the leadership of James. The views of R. Eisler (in *The Messiah Jesus*) concerning the election of James as High Priest by the people, are entirely unwarranted. When the armies of Titus approached Jerusalem, the Judæo-Christians retired to Pella, while the rabbinical leaders retired to Jabne ; political, and not religious, Jewish leaders undertook the defence of Jerusalem. Some ten or twenty years afterwards, we find, in the liturgy of the Synagogue, the first official traces of hostility against the Judæo-Christians. Into the daily blessings recited in the Synagogue was inserted a declaration, the *Birkat-ha-Minim*, which Samuel the Small wrote between A.D. 80 and 90. We cannot be certain of the original wording of this declaration, but we know that it was a curse against the *minim* or heretics ; according to Jerome, it contained an express mention of the " Nazarenes." This malediction was a kind of test, to detect the presence of the *minim* among the Jews ; for a Christian, or any " heretic invited to pronounce the Eighteen Benedictions," would probably omit that particular paragraph. This fact shows that, during the last twenty years of the first century, the Judæo-Christians still frequented the Synagogue. Another breach between

---

[1] See also F. J. A. Hort, *Judaistic Christianity*, London, 1894 ; F. J. Foakes Jackson, *The Parting o the Roads*, London, 1912.
[2] London, 1936.

Judæo-Christians and Jews occurred when the Jews decided on a Messiah other than Jesus. This happened in the time of Bar Kochba. Even then, the breach was not total, for neither was the Messiahship of Bar Kochba a matter of faith, nor did all the Jews accept his claims. An important factor in the estrangement between Judæo-Christians and Jews was the migration of the central authorities of Judaism to Babylon, before the end of the second century. The contacts with Christianity were, of course, fewer in Babylonia than in Palestine.

Even then it is almost impossible to draw the historical dividing line between Judaism and Christianity. There are still, in the second century, definite traces of Christian infiltration into the Synagogue. A certain Rabbi Eliezer was arrested for heresy (c. 100 A.D.) and strongly suspected of leanings towards Christianity. Several indications are given of the Nazarenes practising healing in the name of Jesus. Rabbi Akiba condemned those who whisper over wounds the words of Exodus xv, 26, We understand this condemnation if we realize that the last words : " I am the Lord that healeth thee " have the numerical value of the name Jesus. Epiphanios, bishop of Constantia, tells of the two following cases. The Jewish Christian Joseph, before his conversion, was dangerously ill. A Jewish elder came to him and whispered in his ear : " Believe that Jesus the Son of God was crucified under Pontius Pilate and that He will come again to judge the living and the dead." Another Jew, on the point of death, heard this whisper from one of the Jews standing by : " Jesus Christ, Who was crucified, the Son of God, will hereafter judge thee."[1] Travers Herford has given the most complete collection of references to Jewish Christianity in the Talmud.[2]

It is possible that there was an attempt to establish a kind of " Caliphate " in the family of Jesus. The first bishops of the Jewish Christian Church were drawn from this circle. According to Hegesippus, Domitian sent for two grandsons of Jude and interrogated them about the " kingdom " of Christ. As they proved to him that they were simple farmers, he dismissed them with some contempt, and " thus delivered, they presided over the Churches." In A.D. 107, another member of the family, a cousin of James, who was bishop of Jerusalem, was put to death by Trajan. Julius Africanus, in his letter to Aristides, mentions the *desposynoi* (heirs), venerated because

---

[1] H. Schonfield, *The History of Jewish Christianity*, p. 80.
[2] *Christianity in Talmud and Midrasch.*

of their relationship to Jesus and their Davidic descent, who came from the villages of Nazara and Kochaba.

Thirteen Jewish Christian bishops of Jerusalem are mentioned by Eusebius[1] before the revolt of 133 : they are Justus, Zaccheus, Tobias, Benjamin, John, Matthias, Philip, Seneca, Justus, Levi, Ephraim, Joseph, Judas.

The middle of the second century marks the transformation of the Jewish Christian Community of Jerusalem into a Gentile Church. In the new pagan city of Aelia Capitolina, from which Jewish Christians were barred, the Gentile Church constituted itself under a Greek Bishop, Mark. The importance of Jerusalem as an ecclesiastical centre declines more and more. The bishop of Jerusalem becomes only fifth in rank in the hierarchy of patriarchs.

The presence of the Gentile bishop in Jerusalem emphasized the break of the Christians from Judaism. At the dawn of Christianity the Jewish Christian Church had agreed that the full Jewish ritual practice should not be enforced among Gentile Christians ; but, in the second century, it is the Gentile Church who refused fellowship to Jewish Christians guilty of retaining any Jewish practices. Jewish Christianity is to be despised and considered as a sect. Parkes, speaking of the Jewish Christians, says : " There is no more tragic group in Christian history than these unhappy people."

A passage from *Shemoth Rabba* (36a) implies that Judæo-Christians in Palestine still practised circumcision in the fourth century. The Judæo-Christians of this period appeared either as Ebionites or as Nazarenes. Ebionism (from the Hebrew *ebion*, " poor ") was a definitely heretical sect which became associated with Essenism, the Elkesaite movement, the Gnosticism of the pseudo-Clementine literature, and which estranged itself from Judaism as well as from Christianity. Three main points mark the opposition between Ebionism and the teaching of the Christian Church : the Ebionites rejected the Gospels other than St. Matthew's ; they rejected Paul as an apostate ; they denied the divinity of Christ. On the other hand, the Nazarenes constituted a non-heretical form of Judæo-Christianity. They acknowledged the obligation of the Mosaic Law for Christians of Jewish descent, but allowed the Gentile Christians to omit these observances. They seem to have been, on the whole, quite a small body which did not win the support of the general Christian opinion. Irenæus thus refers to the Jewish Christians : " They practise circumcision,

[3] *Hist. Eccles.*, iv., 5.

persevere in the observance of those customs which are prescribed by the Law, and are so Judaic in their ways of life that they even worship Jerusalem as if it were the House of God."[1] Jerome writes to Augustine : " To this day in all the synagogues of the East there is among the Jews a sect called Minæi (Minim), which is condemned by the Pharisees. They are commonly spoken of as Nazarenes, and believe in Christ the Son of God, born of the Virgin Mary, the same Who, they say, suffered under Pontius Pilate and rose again. In Whom we, too, believe ; but while this sect desires to be both Jews and Christians, they are neither one nor the other."[2]

Isolated Judæo-Christians lingered on in Palestine for centuries, and perhaps still have some descendants there. According to H. Schonfield, there is, in the little Transjordian village of El-Husn, a small group of Arabs who keep Sabbath and circumcision, are vegetarians, reject image worship, govern their lives by the Sermon on the Mount, and look for the return of Christ. Schonfield identifies them with the historical Nazarenes.[3]

James Parkes makes, on behalf of Palestinian Judæo-Christianity, an apology to which we would subscribe with only a few reservations : " And they [the Judæo-Christians] on their side might well say—paradoxical as it may appear to us now---that the Gentile Church by its attitude made the acceptance of the Messianic claims of Jesus impossible to the Jew ; and that the perpetual statement of the Gentile leaders that the Jews continued to reject Christ was fundamentally untrue, because they were being offered Him only upon conditions which were false and impossible for a loyal Jew to accept —in other words, an attitude to the whole Jewish history and to the Law, which was based upon Gentile ignorance and misunderstanding, and was quite unsupported by the conduct of Jesus Himself."[4]

Before leaving the subject of primitive Judæo-Christianity, we must say that insufficient attention has been paid to the influence of converted Jewish priests on the development of Christian institutions. We shall come back later to this point.[5]

An unbroken stream of intermediate groups has continued to connect Judaism with Christianity during the Middle Ages and in modern times. These movements were initiated by

[1] *Adv. Haeres.*, I, 26.
[2] Ep. 89, 13, *P.L.* XXII, 924.
[3] *The History of Jewish Christianity*, p. 120.
[4] *The Conflict of Church and Synagogue*, p. 93.
[5] See special note N.

Christians of non-Jewish origin who attempted "to Judaize."
As we are concerned here with the problems of Christians of
Jewish origin, we shall postpone[1] the consideration of these
sects of Judaizing Gentile Christians.

The idea of a Jewish Christianity seems to have re-awoken
in the beginning of the 19th century among some Jews who
accepted Jesus. In 1813, forty-one Jewish Christians
constituted in London an association called *Beni Abraham*,
children of Abraham. In 1882, H. Stern founded in London
the Hebrew Christian Prayer Union. In 1866, the Hebrew
Christian alliance was started. The members of these groups
belonged to one or other of the Christian denominations.
Joseph Rabinowitz founded in 1882 the first Jewish Christian
community independent of any Christian denomination, and
more in the nature of a free Christian synagogue. The movement
started in Bessarabia. Rabinowitz himself came from Hasidic
circles and had accepted Jesus while in Jerusalem. His
followers named themselves " Israelites of the New Covenant."
Though baptized in Berlin, Rabinowitz refused to join any
Church or to attend any Christian temple where a crucifix
was displayed. His sermons, published in Yiddish, Hebrew
and Russian, were widely read. He died in 1899, and his
movement still has some devotees in Bessarabia.

The same idea of a Jewish Christian independent Church
has lately been defended in Galicia by Theodore Lutsky (or
Lucky), in Germany by Paulus Grün, in South Africa by
Philip Cohen, in America by Mark Levy. This last advocated
for Christian Jews the " Christ-given liberty to have their
children circumcized according to God's covenant with
Abraham, should they so desire, and to observe all the other
customs inherited from their fathers" and received a
favourable answer from the General Assembly of the Episcopal
Church of the United States (1907).

Lutsky, speaking of the Jewish convert who, because he
believes in Christ, gives up the Sabbath, said that he did not
condemn him, but was sorry for him and hurt to the depth
of his heart, for this convert, too, is a child of Israel and should
help to rebuild Jerusalem's walls.[2] Lutsky himself strictly
observed talmudic regulations. He died in 1916, and most of
his Hebrew-Christians reverted to Judaism.

The International Hebrew Christian Alliance, founded in
London in 1925, passed (1931) a resolution approving " the

[1] See special note T.
[2] Speech at the Jewish Christian Conference of Stanislavov, 1903.

principle of the establishment of a Hebrew Christian Church.'
But a revived Jewish Christian religious communion is not yet
within the realm of reality.

The historian of Jewish Christianity, Hugh Schonfield, is
himself looking forward to the revival of an independent
Jewish Christian community. Such a community would give
allegiance to Jesus as Messiah ; but, apart from this, it seems
that the faith accepted would be Jewish rather than specifically
Christian.

We think that the most important contemporary approach
to the formation of a Jewish Christianity has been the work
of Paul Levertoff. Born in Russia in 1879, Levertoff accepted
Christ when he was an eighteen-year-old-student. The war of
1914 found him in Leipsig where he had been appointed to
the chair of Hebrew and Rabbinics at the *Institutum Judaicum
Delitzchianum.* He came to England in 1913, was sub-warden
of St. Deniol's Library, Hawarden, and then was ordained to
the ministry of the Church of England and devoted himself
to the task, not of mission to the Jews, but of intellectual
contact and practical co-operation with them. He holds the
ideal of a Jewish Christian Community, which he conceives
as " . . . a Jewish branch of the Catholic Church in a congenial
Jewish traditional environment, where the essentials of
Christian Faith and worship are expressed, as much as possible,
in Jewish terms."[1] The originality of Levertoff's work lies
in three directions. Himself a scholar, unable to conform to
the obscurantism and weak pietism which have been regrettably
favoured by some Christian missionaries to the Jews, he
understood the importance of an intellectual appeal and the
necessity of expressing the theological concepts of Christianity
in Jewish terms (according to him, along the lines of the
Shekinah teaching and of Hasidic mysticism). Through his
numerous works[2], he has been a *Bahnbrecher*, a "way-opener,"
in that direction. Secondly, he has compiled a Jewish Christian

---

[1] Quoted by Olga Levertoff in *The Wailing Wall*, p. 119.
[2] Among which we shall quote : in Hebrew, *The Religion of Israel*, 1902 ;
The Son of Man, 1904 ; *The Life of St. Paul*, 1905 ; *The Confessions of St.
Augustine* (transl.), 1906 ; in German, *Die religioese Denkweise der Chasidim*,
1918 ; in English, besides his contribution to Gore's New Commentary,
Love and the Messianic Age, 1923 ; *Midrash Sifre on the Book of Numbers*,
1923 ; *St. Paul in Jewish Thought*, 1928 ; Werfel's *Paul unter den Juden*
(transl.), 1928 ; Dalman's *Jesus-Jeshua*, 1929, and *Orte und Wege Jesu*, 1930.
(transl.) ; *The Zohar on Exodus*, 2 vols., 1933 (transl.). See *Judaism and
Christianity. Essays presented to the Rev. Paul P. Levertoff, D.D.*, London,
1939 (Shears and Sons), edited by the present writer. This little volume is
not to be confused with the three volumes of the symposium *Judaism and
Christianity*, edited by E. Rosenthal (Sheldon Press), 1938.

liturgy of which a full description will be found elsewhere in this volume.[1] Finally, he has been able—a privilege more rarely given to a Christian of Jewish descent than to a Gentile Christian—to co-operate closely with the Jews for the defence of, and the help to, exiled Jewry in Britain ; he has always kept a passionate attachment to the idea of social and supranational justice of the Hebrew Prophets. One could hardly say that Levertoff has been able yet to gather around himself a regular congregation, still less a Hebrew Christian Church. But, through him, individual Jews have felt the call of the Messiah as he himself did. He has proved that a Christian Jew is not necessarily " de-Jewed." His most evident, though not deepest, achievement is best expressed if we say that he has lessened Jewish and Christian mutual prejudices and increased Jewish and Christian mutual interest.

Has history proved that Jewish Christianity is impossible ? Arguments in that direction have been advanced both by Christians and Jews. Lukyn Williams writes : " The history of the obscure and useless sects of Hebrew Christians in the first three centuries, so far as we know it, is not pleasant reading."[2] It may be so, partly : is it entirely the fault of the Hebrew Christians ? Has Jewish Christianity been so obscure ? Is the history of the Jerusalemite Church in the first century and at the beginning of the second completely unglorious ? Even if that were the case, obscurity does not constitute a crime. As to uselessness, Jewish Christianity has at least proclaimed and maintained a tradition. Rabbi Cohen writes : " Nineteen centuries have failed to produce a single example of a Jewish community accepting some form of Christianity and retaining its Jewishness."[3] To those who ask : " Why cannot Judaism welcome Jesus as its Lord and, at the same time, carry on its religious tradition ? " the Rabbi replies : " The answer to these questions is furnished by history. The past nineteen centuries have shown that such a fusion has been impossible." We think that the history of primitive Judæo-Christianity as well as a certain number of modern individual cases contradict this radical statement.

The very idea of a Jewish Christianity is disparaged by Canon Lukyn Williams not only on historical, but on theoretical grounds. Here are his arguments. It is proposed

---

[1] See special note V.
[2] *The Hebrew-Christian Messiah*, London, 1916, p. 212.
[3] *The Jews and Christian Evangelization*, in *International Review of Missions*, vol. XXII, 1933, pp. 476 and 477.

to separate the biblical from the rabbinic customs, to keep
the former while rejecting the latter ; but how will it be
possible to draw the line ? What about the dietary laws, for
instance ? On what principle will you go ? One of two
things will happen. If the Jewish Christian strictly observes
the customs, there is a danger that he will, little by little, be
led back into Judaism. If he is lax about the customs, the
tendency will be for him gradually to give them up, and then
we arrive at the present condition of things. The Jewish
Christians who attempted to retain their Jewish customs
have at last either become Jews or become merged with the
Gentiles. The learned historian of Jewish and Christian
controversies concludes : " After thinking it over, we find
ourselves compelled to believe that any attempt to bring about
a Hebrew Christian Church now is likely to end in failure and
do more harm than good."[1] We imagine that a believer in
Jewish Christianity would probably answer as follows : " I am
afraid that, in your objections, the central issue is obscured
by secondary problems. To a man of keen vision, these
difficulties, real as they are, will not seem insuperable. These
are only questions of adjustment, which have to be settled
according to places, persons, times and circumstances. If
a Jewish Christianity once comes into existence, the solution
will be given naturally by the needs of the moment :
demonstratur ambulando. Faith in God and the grace of God
will break down such inessential obstacles. When God grants
it, the Jewish Christian will be able to repeat to the Gentile
Christian the words of the Jerusalem elders to Paul : " Thou
seest, brother, how many thousand of Jews there are which
believe, and they are all zealous of the Law (Acts xxi. 20)."

In many countries, the nationalist spirit is making it
difficult for Jewish Christians to enter the national Churches.
This fact brings the idea of a Hebrew Christian Church much
nearer to-day. Israel Abrahams, far as he was from any
Jewish Christian ideal, wrote : " Some observers of the present-
day conditions (owing to the changes in Palestine) are of
opinion that a revival of the Judæo-Christian phenomenon
is not impossible."[2]

What practical forms could a modern Jewish Christianity
take ? Without advocating here any concrete step or
solution,[3] we may consider some possibilities.

[1] *The Hebrew-Christian Messiah*, p. 206.
[2] *Studies in Pharisaism and the Gospels*, 2 vols., Cambridge, 1917–1924, p. 57.
[3] Our only personal suggestions are indicated in the special note V.

A Jewish Christianity implies, as we have seen, something quite different from the individual adhesion to any present Christian mission or Church. It implies a Christian faith and a Jewish religious environment. Such a combination could .be achieved along two lines. We shall call the first way "un-synagogued Jewish Christianity" and the second "synagogued Jewish Christianity."

"Un-synagogued" Jewish Christianity means a Jewish Christianity which has broken its ties with the Synagogue. Such a Jewish Christian group might exist under two forms. It could be a special and autonomous branch of one of the present Christian Churches, e.g., of the Eastern Orthodox Church, or of the Roman Catholic Church, or of the Episcopal Churches in communion with Canterbury. The condition of this branch, having its own ritual, discipline, and theological tradition, would offer some analogies with the position of the Eastern Uniat Churches in the Church of Rome. Or the Jewish Christian group could become an independent Christian Church, like the Moravian and the Waldensian Churches.

"Synagogued" Jewish Christianity means a Jewish Christianity which keeps, as far as possible, its ties with the Synagogue. This way being much more complex and difficult than the preceding one, we shall devote much more space to it.

A few instances from modern religious history will help us to approach concretely the notion of a synagogued Christianity.

The Hungarian Rabbi, I. Lichtenstein, was a striking case of a Synagogue Christian in the last century. He began to quote the New Testament from his pulpit in Budapest, aroused some scandal, and publicly admitted his faith in Christ. He had to resign his office. But he refused to be baptized and, until his death (1909), remained a Christian within the Jewish community. He wrote a pamphlet *Judentum und Christentum*. Speaking of his first contact with the Gospel he said: "I looked for thorns and gathered roses."

When the converted German Jewish writer, De Jonge, tried to return to Judaism with "evangelical reservations" (*mit evangelischen Vorbehalten*), the rabbis of Berlin refused him (1907). This may be explained by the fact that he had previously broken with the Synagogue. If, instead of leaving the Jewish community, he had remained inside it with his

" evangelical reservations," would the rabbis have expelled him ? De Jonge died in 1920, after having returned to Judaism. We do not know whether he kept the " evangelical reservations " till the end.

A movement was started in Central Europe about ten years ago by G. Lazlo and Dr. Foeldes under the name of " Alliance of Jews who believe in Jesus." This movement, which spread chiefly in Hungary, included Jews connected with the Church, but also Jews connected with the Synagogue. The latter keep the observance of the Sabbath with the Jewish community ; they are united to the Church Christians by a personal allegiance to Jesus. Lazlo's book *Spires, Bells and Dreams* has given expression to the idea of this movement.

These three instances perhaps make clearer to us the meaning of " synagogued Christianity." Here we have Jews who accept faith in Christ, but do not wish to secede from the Synagogue. This attitude may lead to several eventualities, which we shall examine in turn.

A comparatively simple case would be that of a whole Synagogue community accepting Christ. This community would become *ipso facto* a Jewish Christian Synagogue. Such a case may, in our day, seem purely hypothetical. But we suppose that several Christian communities of the first and second century started in this manner. The same phenomenon might occur again if a Christian movement ever developed inside Judaism.

Far more delicate is the case of an individual Jew or of a small group of Jews who would believe in Christ and at the same time keep their membership in a synagogue community. A Nicodemite attitude of prudent silence might, of course, avoid difficulties. But we are thinking of the case of a Jew who, without being provocative and without trying to under-mine the community, would not hide, when challenged, his own attitude to Christ. If this man faithfully adheres to all Jewish rites, observances and beliefs, including the hope of the Messianic Kingdom, and adds to them his own acceptance of Jesus as personal Messiah, is this incompatible with any binding creed or canon of Judaism ? It is not for us to answer, although we do not know of any Jewish dogma or universally admitted statute which would preclude such a possibility. The practical difficulties would be, of course, very great. But would there be a legal Jewish ground for an excommunication or expulsion from the community ?

But this case implies other and no less delicate questions.

If the " synagogued " Christian does not feel any need for Christian Church membership, specific Christian worship, and Christian sacraments, he will be fully satisfied with what the Synagogue gives him and what he himself keeps individually in his heart. But, if he feels the need of something else besides the Synagogue, what is he to do ? He will, perhaps, turn to some Christian Church to supply him with what is lacking. We know Jews who often attend meetings of the Society of Friends, and it is true that Quakerism, by its silent worship, absence of ritual, undogmatic frame of mind, makes this *koinonia* particularly easy, and may play a great part in building bridges between Judaism and Christianity. Or this complement of his faith may be found in Churches in the stricter meaning of the word, e.g., in Episcopalian or Protestant Churches. Or perhaps some " synagogued " Christians will follow the example of the Jewish Christians of Apostolic times who added private gatherings to their regular attendance at the Temple and Synagogues. The transformation of Jewish rites into sacraments, as it was achieved by Jesus and His disciples, might perhaps be attempted again in circumstances not dissimilar from the original ones. Baptism, of which Buber says it is still practised " with a high and gladsome passion "[1] in Hasidism, would once more take on a new Messianic meaning. Once more the *kiddush* or the *seder* could become a Lord's Supper. Would attempts be made, or not, to link this additional group (and perhaps house) worship with the historical Apostolic succession ? One can imagine numerous and much diversified modes of this " Jesus-ward movement from within." Only a very strong feeling for the true Jewish treasures and for the recovery of Jesus as the Jewish Messiah could make " synagogued " Christians equal to the difficulties which they would inevitably experience from the Jewish and the Gentile sides alike.

Questions of terminology are not unimportant in connexion with a re-awakening of Jewish Christianity. Non-Jewish terms, associated (for the Jews) with distasteful historical recollections, constitute a very serious obstacle between Christianity and Judaism. Could they not be removed by Jewish Christians ? Centuries of use have made these Greek words sacred for us, Christians of Gentile descent, but there is no reason to enforce them upon Jews. Why should a Jewish Christian use the Greek word " Christ " (*Christos*) instead of

---

[1] *Deutung des Chassidismus*, p. 25 : ". . . *von den Zaddikim mit hoher und freudiger Leidenschaft geübt . . . ."*

the Hebrew " Messiah "—which means exactly the same—or, to revive an historical name of the Jewish Christians, " Nazarene " ?   Why should he speak of the " Church " (*ecclesia*) instead of the Hebrew *qahal* or *habnrah*, which stand for religious community ?   The terms used by the first Christians themselves were quite fluid.   Their nomenclature displays no final or hardened terminology, but informality and variety of expression.   They called Jesus not only Christ or Messiah, but the Lord, the Son, the Servant, the Nazarene, the Prophet, the Saviour, the Coming One ; they called themselves not only Christians, but Disciples, Brethren, Friends, Believers, Saints, Nazarenes, Galileans ; they called the Church congregation, fellowship, flock ; where we say " Christianity," they used the beautiful word " the Way."[1]   These questions have their importance, but they are not essential.

We would like to say again that we are not pleading here for any particular form of Jewish Christianity : we are merely considering possibilities.   We do not know whether there will be a Jewish Christian revival nor, if there is one, what forms it may assume.   But we wish to emphasize two points.

In the first place, we are convinced that a Jewish Christianity, under some form, is desirable for the good of the whole Christian Church.   On this point, let us quote Conrad Hoffmann : " In the event of a Jewish movement towards Christ, and there are signs of such . . . we should help such a movement to remain Jewish and Hebrew rather than endeavour to divorce it from Jewry. . . . The possibility of a new Church evolving out of such a movement must be anticipated.   We must be prepared to accept such into the Christian Church family and even perhaps be ready to profit in a spirit of humble gratitude by the new light which may come to our Jewish neighbours as they discover their long expected Messiah. . . ."[2]

Secondly, we believe that the development of a Jewish Christianity is inseparably linked with the development, among Christians, of a new œcumenical consciousness. Therefore it is useless and even dangerous to think of a future Jewish Christianity in too precise categories.   Jewish Christianity, if it grows, will grow and evolve with the re-united Church which the present œcumenical movement is

---

[1] See Harnack, *Mission und Ausbreitung des Christentums,* 4th edit., I, pp. 410 ff. ; or Book III and Excursus I in earlier editions, and English translations of the same work ; and Henry J. Cadbury, note XXIX : *The Titles of Jesus in Acts,* in *The Beginnings of Christianity,* edited by F. Foakes Jackson and Kirsopp Lake, vol. V, London, 1933.

[2] *Christians and Jews,* p. 60.

trying to restore ; without the Jewish seed, the œcumenical organism will not grow, and, isolated from an œcumenical Christianity, Jewish Christianity will remain a sect—unless it develops entirely within the Synagogue, fecundates it and brings it into real spiritual contact with the Church. Jewish Christianity will find its natural place in a re-united Christianity. These two "processes of affirmation" are complementary. As Berdyaev writes : " The universal Church has not been entirely actualized in the visible historic Church. . . . Beyond the diversities of Christian confession, the one universal Church is in process of affirmation, and of this fact we may become aware even while we still remain faithful to our own confessions."[1]

[1] *Freedom and the Spirit*, pp. 336 and 356.

PART EIGHT

Having reached the end of these studies, we should like to add to them, as a theological conclusion, a few short and simple notes on some of Saint Paul's utterances concerning Israel, in the Epistle to the Romans.[1]

" I would not, brethren, that you should be ignorant of this mystery " (xi. 25). According to Paul, the fate of Israel is a *mysterion*, a thing kept secret by God and hid from our understanding till it be revealed to us. The Jewish problem is not entirely within the reach of the ordinary human intellect. It cannot be deduced by arguments. Its solution can only be " given " and " received." Now Paul considers that he has obtained a special revelation of God on this subject, and he will communicate to us at least a part of it. The letter to the Romans should be the basis of all Christian approach to Judaism. And we must share Paul's desire that the knowledge of this mystery should be diffused as widely as possible. The Christian masses have not yet been penetrated by the Pauline revelation about Israel.

Saint Paul chiefly draws our attention to four aspects of Israel's mystery : it is a mystery of election, of rejection, of incorporation, and of restoration.

Israel has been elected, chosen by God. " What advantage has the Jew ? . . . Much in every way " (iii. 1–2). Definite privileges were granted to the Jewish people. Paul recites (ix. 4–5) the privileges of the Jews, which point forward to the coming of the Messiah : they are Israelites, bearers of the sacred name ; theirs is the Sonship (as the first-born), theirs the Glory or manifestation of the divine Presence ; theirs the Covenants made with the Patriarchs and Moses ; theirs the promises and the Patriarchs who received them ; and—as a climax—theirs, according to the flesh, is the Messiah. These privileges were a free gift and a favour.

---

[1] See the English Commentaries on Romans by Sanday and Headlam, 1900; Gore, London, 1900; Dodd, London, 1932; Boylan, Dublin, 1934. Sadler's Commentary (London, 1888) may appear antiquated in some respects, but we find it, from a theological point of view, very rich and inspiring. Among continental Commentaries, see Lagrange, *Epître aux Romains*, Paris, 1931 ; Althaus, *Der Brief an die Römer*, Göttingen, 1932 ; Lietzmann, *An die Römer*, Tübingen, 1933. The famous Commentary by Barth is useless for our purpose ; by applying to the Christian Church all that is said of the Jewish people, it explains away the problem of Israel.

Israel, as a corporate whole obtained them whatever might be the behaviour of individual Israelites.

Since the death of Jesus, it may seem that Israel has forfeited all privileges and been rejected. But it is not so. "Has God cast away his people? God forbid" (xi. 1). We shall see that this apparent rejection is neither total nor final.

The alleged rejection is supposed to be a consequence of the repudiation of Jesus the Messiah by the Jews. But can we say that the Jews, as a whole, repudiated the Messiah? This unqualified statement is not supported by history. If most of the Jews refused to identify Jesus with the Messiah, they never intended to repudiate the Messiah as such. Moreover, if Jewish conversions were few after A.D. 70, this is not true of the earlier period. The bulk of the Christians were Palestinian or *diaspora* Jews and, even in the Gentile Churches founded by Paul, a Jewish element was not lacking. Harnack considered that the synagogues of the *diaspora*, a network which furnished the Christian propaganda with centres and courses of development, formed the most important presupposition for the rise and growth of nascent Christianity. A corporate adhesion of Israel to the message of Jesus would hardly have been possible ; men can follow in masses a military chief or a political leader (and Moses was partly that), but they cannot accept in masses the call to a personal change in life, the call to perfection. Have the Gentiles accepted Christ? Was the "Christianization" of the Roman empire after Constantine a true conversion? Are the "Christian" nations of to-day really Christian? Gentiles cannot condemn the Jews for not having done what they failed themselves to achieve. And, as we have just said, an important Jewish minority accepted Jesus. If we link the so-called rejection of Jews by God with the repudiation of Christ by the Jews, we must say that the rejection cannot be total, since the repudiation itself was not such.

"God hath not cast away His people which He foreknew" (xi. 2). Who are the people of whom Paul speaks? Does he perhaps mean that the Gentile Christian Church, the new Israel, has taken the place of the ancient Israel and become the only heir of the promises? Or does he mean that the Hebrew Christian Remnant—"at this time also there is a remnant according to the election of grace" (xi. 5)—is now the true Israel? Or do the Remnant and the Gentile Church together constitute Israel, the people whom God foreknew?

These interpretations are excluded by the affirmations : " All Israel shall be saved " (xi. 26), " This is My Covenant unto them, when I shall take away their sins " (xi. 27), and " For the gifts and calling of God are without repentance " (xi. 29). The unbelieving Israel will be saved as well as the Remnant and the Gentile disciples, and it will be saved as Israel, in virtue of the promises. Once more, the rejection of Israel is neither total nor final.

But how are we to explain the partial and temporary rejection ? How is it that, the elect having obtained what Israel sought for, " the rest were blinded " (xi. 7) ?

According to Paul this state of things is due to God Himself : " As it is written, God hath given them the spirit of slumber " (xi. 8). He has himself hardened their hearts and closed their eyes. But this rejection is a mystery of grace and mercy, not of judgment and condemnation. " Have they stumbled that they should fall ? God forbid " (xi. 11). This mystery has several aspects. In the first place it illustrates the predominance of grace over righteousness. Let us suppose that Israel as a whole had accepted Christ. They would have received their reward and inherited all the blessings of the Covenant. Then their salvation would have been the outcome of their righteousness. God permitted their repudiation of Christ in order that, righteousness having failed, Israel might share in the free mercy extended to the Gentiles, and that all men might be saved by grace : " If it be of work, then is it no more grace " (xi. 6) and " God hath concluded them all in unbelief, that He might have mercy upon all " (xi. 32). Another aspect of the mystery of rejection is that the stubbornness of the Jews resulted in the accession of the Gentiles to Christ. As Paul and Barnabas told the Jews in the synagogue of Antioch in Pisidia, it was necessary that the Word of God should be first spoken to them ; since they did not receive it, Paul and Barnabas turned to the Gentiles. If the Jews had accepted the Christian message, none of the Apostles would have troubled at first about the Gentiles. They would certainly, later on, have carried the Mission into heathen territory, for God did not make the conversion of the Gentiles dependent on any such condition as the unbelief of the Jews. But the whole process of evangelization of Gentiles would have been postponed and diminished in importance. The Jewish refusal rendered Paul free for the Gentile Mission ; so it happened that " the Gentiles, which followed not after righteousness, have attained to righteousness, even the righteousness which is of faith," while " Israel, which followed after the law of righteousness, hath not attained to the law of righteousness " (ix. 30–31). " Through their fall, salvation is come to the Gentiles " (xi. 11). There is still another aspect of the mystery of rejection. The call of the Gentiles was destined, in the mind of God, " to provoke them (the Jews) to jealousy " (xi. 11). What kind of jealousy ? If the Gentile Christians, by their life and conduct, exhibit manifestly the grace of God promised to—and not yet obtained by—Israel, the splendour of this grace will act upon the Jews as a stimulus and incite them not to envy, but to a holy zeal ; they will change their minds and accept Christ ; their hearts will burn for Him more than they would have done if the Messianic grace had not been thus manifested, and they will surpass the Gentiles in fervour. This divine intention makes sadly clear the reason why Jews do not come to Christ. Is our Christianity such as to provoke them to a sacred jealousy ? Their adhesion to Christ is indefinitely retarded by our unfaithfulness, our coldness, our divisions. The hour of this adhesion, to a great extent, depends on us.

Let us now turn to what we have called the mystery of incorporation, i.e., the consideration of Israel as *corpus mysticum*.

Paul, speaking of the Jews, says : " They are beloved for the fathers' sakes " (xi. 28). The notion of the " merits of the fathers " is an important tenet of Jewish theology. In Deuteronomy, x. 15, we find : " Only the Lord had a delight in thy fathers to love them, and He chose their seed after them, even you above all people, as it is this day." According to the Talmud, the prayers spoken by Elijah on Mount Carmel were not heard, but, when he called Yaweh the God of Abraham, Isaac and Jacob, then at once he was heard ; Moses could stand up and speak for the justification of the Israelites forty days and forty nights without being heard, but, when he mentioned the dead, God heard him. The congregation of Israel, commenting on Canticles i. 5 (" I am black, but comely "), is supposed to say : " I am black through mine own works, but lovely through the works of my fathers." Again the Talmud compares Israel, supporting itself on the fathers, to the living vine which grows out of a dry and seemingly dead stock.[1] We have already emphasized the

---

[1] See Weber, *Jüdische Theologie auf Grund des Talmud*, pp. 293 *ff* ; and the detached note : *The Merits of the Fathers*, in *A Critical and Exegetical Commentary on the Epistle to the Romans* by W. Sanday and A. Headlam.

importance of the binding of Isaac in the Jewish idea of atonement. Thus the whole of Israel is a mystical body. God cannot forget that every Israelite is a child of the Patriarchs. " As concerning the Gospel, they are enemies . . ." (xi 28), but " as touching the election " they remained beloved because of their fathers.

The mystical body of Israel is the true olive tree on which the wild olive branches, i.e., the Gentile Christians, have been grafted, so that they partake " of the root and fatness of the olive tree " (xi, 17). " Thou bearest not the root, but the root thee " (xi, 18). Jeremiah had already said of Israel : " The Lord called thy name a green olive tree, fair and of goodly fruit . . ." (Jer. xi. 16). The metaphor of the grafting of a new branch on the tree is employed by the Rabbis to express the attachment of heathen elements to Israel. Rabbi Eleazar ben Pedath (third century), commenting on Genesis xii. 3, said : " What is the meaning of the text : ' And in thee shall all the families of the earth be blessed ' ? The Holy One (blessed be He !) said unto Abraham : ' Two good shoots have I to engraft on thee, Ruth the Moabite and Naomi the Ammonite.' "[1] We have been grafted on the tree like Ruth and Naomi. We are members of the mystical (i.e., invisible, but real) body of Israel, members by grace in the Chosen Community.

The mystical body of Christ has become one of the favourite themes of modern theology. One realizes now more than ever before all the wealth of this Pauline and Patristic notion. The *corpus mysticum Christi* is not a metaphor ; it is an organic and invisible reality. But the theology of the Body of Christ should be linked with a theology of the mystical Body of Israel. This is one of the deepest and most beautiful tasks of a " bridge theology " between Judaism and Christianity.

The idea of our membership in Israel has an immediate application in all the modern questions concerning Jewry. If we seriously admit the mystical bond which ties us, as Christians, to the community of Israel, if we feel ourselves true Israelites, our whole outlook may be modified, and our lives of practical action as well.

Lastly, we must consider the mystery of the restoration of Israel. " Blindness in part has happened to Israel, until the fulness of the Gentiles be come in. And so all Israel shall be saved, as it is written : There shall come out of Zion the Deliverer and shall turn away ungodliness from Jacob."

[1] *Yebamoth*, 63a ; *Yalkut*, Gen. 65.

(xi. 25–26). " Now if the fall of them (the Jews) be the riches of the Gentiles ; how much their fulness ? (xi. 12)." " If the casting away of them be the reconciling of the world, what shall the receiving of them be, but life from the dead ? " (xi. 15).

There may be difficulties about the times and circumstances of this restoration. Some have speculated wildly upon it. But the general ideas are clear. Israel will be restored to the lost privileges of the ancient people of God ; in Paul's words, Israel here cannot possibly mean the whole Church, Jews and Gentiles considered as one, but the whole Jewish people. The details are known only to God. We can quite understand that, for some modern theologians, this preferential treatment extended to the Jewish nation as such is rather embarrassing. Dodd writes : " From our standpoint, with a far longer historical retrospect than Paul could have dreamt of, the special importance here assigned to the Jews and their conversion in the forecast of the destiny of mankind appears artificial."[1] But Paul reminds us that the destiny of Israel is a " mystery " —" lest you should be wise in your own conceits " (xi. 25). Paul associates these events with some new and extraordinary manifestations of grace, of which Israel will be the minister. It will be still greater than the triumph of Zion announced by the Prophets ; it will be " life from the dead." What does this mean ? Is it an allusion to the resurrection of the body ? Or does it foretell some immense revival, such an overflowing of mercies as will bring life to an almost spiritually dead world ?

The words of Paul to the effect that all this will happen when " the fulness of the Gentiles be come in " (xi. 25) may possibly allude not to a mass conversion of the Gentile world, but to a perfect fulfilment by Israel of all the spiritual possibilities with which the Gentiles have been endowed. Israel would then concentrate and unify in itself all the spiritual forces. It would bring to the old Creation of God, to the House divided, this Unity which mankind is seeking for. The Zohar says : " Israel will one day sing a complete song comprising all other songs."[2]

These words bring to mind Hosea's prophecy (ii. 15) : " And I will give her vineyards from thence, and the valley of Achor for a door of hope : and she shall sing there, as in the

---

[1] *The Epistle of Paul to the Romans*, p. 182.
[2] *Vayelech*, 286a.

days of her youth, and as in the day when she came up out of the land of Egypt."

Then the true self of this strange people, always provocative and afflicted, stiff-necked and broken, so old and so youthful, victim of the envy of the " Nations " and also of its own frenzy, irritating and endearing, always sinner and always forgiven, will be revealed to all. They will recognize in it all that which, since the Choice and in all vicissitudes, it has never ceased to be : the first-born Child, the Son—Israel the Beloved.

SPECIAL NOTES.

A. JEW, HEBREW, ISRAELITE

" Jew" (*iehoudi, ioudaios*), in the strict sense of the word, designates persons belonging to *Judah.* Later on the term became a national name (*to ethnos ton ioudaion*) in contrast to Gentiles. This was already the case in Maccabæan times and in the writings of Josephus ; it is also in general use in the New Testament, but rather in the mouth of Gentiles than Jews. The expression " Judaism " (*ioudaismos*) occurred in Gal. i. 13, 14, with the meaning of the " Jews' religion."

" Hebrew " (*Ibrith, Hebraios*) is derived either from the patronymic *Eber* (Gen. x. 21) or from a verb or preposition which means " coming across " (the Red Sea ? the Jordan ? the Euphrates ? or some land boundary ?). This word is purely secular and gave place, from the seventh century onwards, to " Jew," which has some theocratic connotation.

" Israel " (*Ysrael*) probably means " God persists." It became the name of Jacob, and the people who acknowledged him as their ancestor called themselves the " children of Israel " (*bene Yisrael*) in Old Testament times.

Eusebius of Cæsarea, in the beginning of the fourth century, invented a division of Israel into two categories : the faithful " Hebrews " and the rebellious " Jews." These last produced such characters as Korah, Dathan, Abiram, Saul, etc., while the Patriarchs and the prophets were ascribed to the former—and transferred to the Church. The word "Jew" became a term of abuse. In the controversy between Nestorians and Chalcedonians, the Nestorians are called " Jews." The synod of Ephesus writes to " Nestorius the new Jew." Gregory the Great accuses him of *judaica perfidia.* With equal fervour, the Monophysites called the Chalcedonians "Jews." Severus of Antioch expresses his dislike for the *Henotikon* of Leo by calling it " Jewish." A letter of St. Augustine refers to Christians who call themselves " Jews " and says that, though Christians are the " true Israel", they nevertheless should abstain from using this name (*Ep.* 196, *P.L.* xxxiii. 894).

B. MARTIN BUBER

No name is more important for knowledge and appreciation of modern Judaism. The grandson of the rabbinic scholar, Salomon Buber, from Lemberg, he was born in Vienna (1878), where he began his career as editor of the Zionist journal *Die Welt* and as a disciple of Achad-Ham. He edited, with Franz Rosenzweig, the periodical *Der Jude* (1916–1924). Also with Rosenzweig he began the publication of a new German translation of the Hebrew Bible

(1926). He was professor at the University of Frankfort am Main till 1933, when he became professor at the University of Jerusalem. His chief books are : *Daniel, Gespräche von der Verwicklichung*, 1919; *Ekstatische Konfessionen*, 1909 ; *Die judische Bewegung, Aufsätze*, 2 vols., 1900–1920; *Vom Geist des Judentums*, 1916; *Die Chassidischen Bücher*, 1927 ; *Das Kommende*, 1936 ; *Ich und Du*, Engl. translation : *I and Thou*, 1937 ; *Die Stunde und die Erkenntniss*, 1936 ; *Die Frage an den Einzelnen*, 1936 ; *Zion als Ziel und als Aufgabe*, 1936. According to Buber, the three highest points of Judasim are : prophecy, primitive Christianity and Hasidism. These three interests are reproduced in Buber's whole activity as Bible translator, Zionist leader, philosopher, theologian and mystic. The new stream of spiritual life noticeable to-day in Judaism is in great part the result of Buber's effort. He may be for contemporary Judaism (and for Christianity as well) almost a new Philo. Lev Shestov places Buber side by side with Kierkegaard and Nietzsche. Berdyaev writes in the Russian periodical *Put* (1933, No. 38, p. 91), that Buber's books " must be received as eminent manifestations of the religious thought of Europe."

See H. Kohn, *M. Buber, Sein Werk und seine Zeit* (1930), and W. Michel, *M. Buber, Sein Gang in die Wirklichkeit*.

C. CRITICISMS OF PHARISEES IN THE TALMUD

The Talmud enumerates seven classes of Pharisees. The first five classes consist of fools or hypocrites. They are : (1) the " shoulder Pharisee," who ostentatiously wears his good actions upon his shoulder; (2) the " wait-a-little Pharisee," who always postpones help to his neighbour until he has performed some legal observance awaiting him ; (3) the " bruised Pharisee," who bruises himself against the walls as he runs to avoid looking at women ; (4) the " pestle Pharisee," who walks with head down like the pestle in the mortar; (5) the " ever reckoning Pharisee," who is always calculating by what good works he may counteract his negligences. It is in connexion with such types of Pharisees that the Talmud uses the words " destroyers of the world " and " Pharisaic plagues." To these abuses the Talmud opposes the two true types of Pharisees : the " God-fearing Pharisee " after the manner of Job, and the " God-loving Pharisee " after the manner of Abraham.

See the Talmudic references given in the *Jewish Encycl.*, art. " Pharisees," vol. IX, p. 665.

D. CLAUDE MONTEFIORE

Claude Goldsmith Montefiore (1858–1938), whose name is so often quoted in this book, deserves a special notice as scholar and theologian. Son of the surgeon and philanthropist Nathaniel

Montefiore (1819–1883), grandnephew of Sir Moses Montefiore (1784–1885) to whom Palestine and Jewry in general owe so much, he was educated at Balliol, where he came under the influence of Jowett and T. H. Green. The inspired leader of English Liberal Judaism, he did more than any other Jewish scholar (Buber excepted) to build bridges between Judaism and Christianity and to help the re-discovery and "recovery" of Jesus by the Jews. Among his numerous writings, we shall especially mention : *Liberal Judaism ; Outlines of Liberal Judaism ; The Place of Judaism among the Religions of the World ; Hibbert Lectures on the Origin and Growth of Religion as illustrated by the Religion of the Ancient Hebrews ; The Old Testament and After ; Rabbinic Literature and Gospel Teachings ; Some Elements of the Religious Teaching of Jesus according to the Synoptic Gospels ; Bible for Home-Reading ; Judaism and St. Paul.* In collaboration with his close friend, the eminent Jewish scholar Israel Abrahams (1858–1925), he published *The Synoptic Gospels* and *Aspects of Judaism*, and in collaboration with Herbert Loewe *A Rabbinic Anthology.* In conjunction with Abrahams again he founded and edited *The Jewish Quarterly Review.* He was an authority on questions of education and a well-known philanthropist.

See L. Cohen, *Some Recollections of Claude Goldsmith Montefiore*, London 1940.

E. THE QARAIM

The *Qaraim* were originally known as Ananites, from the name of their founder Anan ben David, of Baghdad (about 760). The Exilarch Anan, who led the schism, seems to have been influenced partly by a feeling of revolt against the Baghdad rabbis, partly by Islam, partly by the underlying Sadduceeism which had not yet died out and which advocated adherence to the written Word and rejection of oral tradition. Many rabbinic controversialists, like Saadya, simply identify Qaraim and Sadducees. Besides the *Sefer ha-mitsvoth* ("Book of Commandments") written by Anan, there is a vast Qaraite theological literature ; we shall mention, in the ninth century, Benjamin, Daniel al-Kumisi ; in the 10th century, Abu Yusuf al-Karkasani, author of the *Book of Luminaries*, David ben Boaz, David al-Fasi ; in the 11th century, Joseph al-Basir ; in the 12th century, Judah Hadassi, who concentrates all the streams of Qaraite thought ; in the 15th century, Elijah Bashyazi, whom the Qaraites call " the late Decisor " ; in the 17th century, Elijah Yerushalmi. Constantinople and Jerusalem were important centres of Qaraite learning during the Middle Ages ; at the beginning of the 13th century most of the Qaraim migrated (whence and why history remains dubious) to the Crimea ; they were also found in Lithuania, Volhynia and Galicia, and mixed freely with the Tartars. The most prolific writer of the "Taurido-Lithuanian period " is Simha Isaac ben Moses (+1766). Cairo and

Damascus had considerable Qaraite colonies. The Russian Government treated the Qaraim with benevolence and occasionally played them off against the Rabbinists. The Russian Qaraim were controlled by a supreme spiritual board which had its headquarters in Eupatoria. The 19th century produced some eminent Qaraite scholars, *e.g.* Isaac ben Salomon (+1826), Joseph Lutski (+1844), and especially Abraham Firkovitch (+1874), who discovered in the East archæological materials showing the early origin of the Qaraim. Firkovitch's results were assailed by the criticism of other Jewish scholars ; the latter even pointed to various forgeries. The solution of the problems involved must be left to the future. The Qaraite preacher, Samuel Pigit (+1911) published some valuable sermons. In 1911 the Qaraite students of the University of Moscow initiated a neo-Qaraite movement and founded a monthly journal ; but this attempted revival proved a failure. From the 17th century onwards Christian scholars took an interest in the Qaraim, opened a correspondence with them and visited their centres (among the 17th and 18th century scholars, reference should be made to Rittangel, Peringer, Warner, Wolf).

See J. Fürst, *Geschichte des Karäerthums*, 3 vols., Leipzig 1862–1869, and S. Poznanski, *Die Karäische Literatur der letzten dreissig Jahre* (1878–1908), Frankfort a.M., 1910.

The present fate of the Russian Qaraim (12,894 in 1911) is unknown. Some 2,000 Qaraim were living in Galicia, Turkey and Palestine.

F. THE SAMARITANS

The time and circumstances of the final rupture between the Jews and the Northern Israelites remain obscure. According to Josephus, the schism was occasioned by the marriage of Manasseh, brother of the high-priest Jaddua, to the daughter of the Persian Governor of Samaria, Sanballat ; unwilling to accept the demands of the Jerusalem clergy to the effect that he should divorce his wife or renounce his priesthood, Manasseh obtained from his father-in-law a high-priesthood in connexion with a new Temple on Mount Gerizim. According to other accounts, the rupture dates from the days of Alexander the Great. John Hyrcanus destroyed the Gerizim Temple in 128 B.C. The Gospels witness to the traditional hatred between Jews and Samaritans. Samaria experienced intellectual and religious revival in the fourth century under the leadership of Baba Raba and of the theologian Marqah. Whether a second Samaritan Temple was built, and destroyed in the fifth century, remains uncertain. Under the Muslims the Samaritans had some periods of literary activity (11th and 14th centuries). There are still to-day a few hundred Samaritans who cling to the old Mount and to the old faith. The Pentateuch is their one sacred book. They highly extol Moses (above Abraham), not only as law-giver, but as mediator and intercessor. Their chief festivals are still celebrated near the site of their former Gerizim sanctuary. They expect a Messiah or rather Restorer (*Taheb*), who ranks in importance below Moses. They sacrifice lambs on the Passover and still have a priesthood (Aaronic till 1623, since then, from the tribe of Levi) and a high-priest. Christian scholars (Scaliger in 1584, Huntingdon in 1671, Marshall *c*. 1775, Ludolf *c*. 1685, de Sacy in the last century) were in contact with the Samaritans. A full collection of Samaritan liturgical texts, edited by A. Cowley, was published in 2 vols. by the Clarendon Press in 1909.

See J. Montgomery, *The Samaritans, the Earliest Jewish Sect: their History, Theology and Literature*, Philadelphia 1907 ; J. Thomson, *The Samaritans, Their Testimony to the Religion of Israel*, Edinburgh 1919 ; M. Gaster, *The Samaritans, Their History, Doctrines and Literature* (The Schweich Lectures of 1923), London 1925.

G. WAS JESUS A RABBI ?

R. Bultmann (*Jesus and the Word*, translated from the German by L. Pettibone Smith and E. Huntress, London 1935) suggests that Jesus, being a scribe received the necessary scribal training and passed the requisite scribal tests ; it is at least clear that Jesus actually lived as a Jewish rabbi. It is true that his intercourse with sinners, prostitutes and publicans was alien to the practices of a rabbi : " However, we cannot doubt that the characteristics of a rabbi appeared plainly in Jesus' ministry and way of teaching." There is evidence that Jesus was known to Jewish tradition as a rabbi of the Tannaic period ; the Talmud refers to Jesus' disciples in the technical terms applied to the pupils of the rabbis (*talmidhe Jeshu ha-Notsri*, Aboda Zara 16b—17a and Sanhedrin 43a). Jesus is well acquainted with Hillel's Golden Rule (Lk. x. 25 & 28). The Gospels and the Talmud show a similarity in debates about particular points of practice, such as the Sabbath, fasting, tributes, etc.

None of these considerations affords any proof that Jesus was a rabbi. The differences between Jesus and the rabbis are more striking than what they had in common. The great difference between Jesus and the rabbis consists in their methods ; that Jesus speaks with authority, while the rabbis quote authorities. The rabbi proclaims : I declare what Scripture and tradition have to say. Jesus uses a more simple and more authoritative formula : I say unto you. This also differentiates Jesus from the prophet, who, being a mere messenger of God, introduces his message by the formula : Thus saith the Lord.

See *Jesus as Teacher and Prophet*, by C. Dodd, in *Mysterium Christi, Christological Studies*, by British and German theologians, edited by G. Bell and A. Deissmann, London 1930.

H. TALMUDIC DIALECTICS

The Talmud lays down definite rules and methods for the investigation of truth, chiefly for the exact determination of the meaning of the Scriptures. There are three collections of such rules, namely : (1) the seven rules of Hillel ; (2) the thirteen rules of Rabbi Ishmael ; (3) the thirty-two rules of Rabbi Eliezer ben Jose ha-Gelili. Akiba also formulated some hermeneutic rules. Many of these rules run parallel with Western logic, *e.g.*, the rule of " conclusion," argument *a minori ad majus* or *a majori ad minus*, which Mielziner calls " the Talmudic syllogism " (M. Mielziner, *The Talmudic Syllogism or the Inference of Kal Vechomer*, in *Hebrew Review*, I, Cincinnati 1880), or the rule of analogy, or the proof by the context. Some rules, like the limitation of the general by the particular and *vice versa*, or " a standard from two passages of Scripture," have more Jewish originality. The *pilpul* (from the verb *pilpel*, " to spice ") is a method of explanation by distinctions and differentiation of the concepts. It is extremely ingenious and complicated and offers evident similarities to the technique of the formal syllogistic disputation in Western scholasticism. To the deductive methods of the *baal pilpul*, " master of disputation," was opposed the methods of the *baal shemut*, "possessor of the tradition," which consisted rather in collecting, arranging and preserving the sentences of the ancient Doctors.

See H. Hirschfeld, *Halachische Exegese*, Berlin 1840, and *Hagadische Exegese*, Berlin 1847 ; A. Schwartz, *Die Hermeneutische Analogie*, Vienna 1897 ; *Der Hermeneutische Syllogismus*, Vienna 1901.

I. JEWISH CREEDS

The first attempt to systematize and formulate the contents of the Jewish religion was made by Philo of Alexandria. In his work on the *Creation of the World*, 61, Philo enumerates five chief tenets of Mosaism : (1) God is, and rules; (2) God is one ; (3) the world was created ; (4) creation is one ; (5) God's providence rules creation. The Decalogue, the Shema, and the daily liturgical prayer : " True and established is Thy word for us . . ." were often considered as summaries of the faith. More technical words have been elaborated by Saadia, Judah ha-Levi, Bahya, Ibn Daud and Hananiel ben Hushiel. The most popular creed is that of Maimonides, the thirteen articles of which are as follows :

1. I firmly believe that the Creator (blessed be His name !) is both Creator and Ruler of all created things, and that He alone has made, does make and will make all the works of nature.

2. I firmly believe that the Creator (blessed be His name !) is one ; and there is no unity like His, in any form ; and He alone is our God who was, is and ever will be.

3. I firmly believe that the Creator (blessed be His name !) is not a body ; and no corporeal relations apply to Him ; and nothing exists that has any likeness to Him.

4. I firmly believe that the Creator (blessed be His name !) was the first and will be the last.

5. I firmly believe that the Creator (blessed be His name!) is the only one worthy of adoration and that no other being deserves our worship.

6. I firmly believe that all the words of the Prophets are true.

7. I firmly believe that the prophecies of Moses our teacher (peace on Him!) were true; he was the first of the Prophets, both of those who preceded him and those who followed him.

8. I firmly believe that the Torah which we now possess is the same that was given to Moses our teacher (peace on Him!).

9. I firmly believe that this Torah will not be changed and that there will be no other Torah given by the Creator (blessed be His name!).

10. I firmly believe that the Creator (blessed be His name!) knows all the actions and thoughts of men, as it is said (Ps. 33, 15): He has made the hearts of them all and considered all their works.

11. I firmly believe that the Creator (blessed be His name!) rewards those who keep His commandments and punishes those who transgress them.

12. I firmly believe in the coming of the Messiah; and, although he may tarry, I hope every day for His coming.

13. I firmly believe that there will be a revival of the dead when it will please the Creator (blessed be His name and exalted His memory for ever!).

Joseph Albo reduces the creed of Maimonides to three fundamental articles: (1) Existence of God, one, incorporeal, eternal, sole object of worship; (2) Revelation of God through Moses, the Law and the Prophets; (3) Retribution manifested in the Resurrection and the Judgment.

These three principles are the essentials of the religious instruction given to children and of the confessions of faith to be recited by proselytes (modern texts composed by Büdinger, Stein, Einhort, etc.). We have already given the articles of faith adopted by the American Liberal Rabbis.

All these creeds—including the thirteen articles of Maimonides—lack the authoritative sanction of a supreme ecclesiastical body. They cannot be considered as final or binding as the three great Christian creeds or the Moslem *Kalimat.* Creed-building was never intense among the Jews, because race and birth, not profession (except in the proselytes), admitted to the fellowship of Israel; moreover Judaism required deeds, rites or moral duties, as much as beliefs. The above-mentioned creeds have nevertheless been, to a certain extent, incorporated in the liturgy, and carry great weight.

See Schechter, *The Dogmas of Judaism*, in *Studies in Judaism* (1896), pp. 179–221.

J. BAT KOL

" After the death of the last three prophets, Haggai, Zechariah and Malachi, the Holy Spirit departed from Israel; but the *Bat Kol* was yet heard " (Talmud, Tos. Sotah XIII. 2). *Bat Kol* means

" daughter of the sound " ; this mysterious term might allude to the echo, or perhaps to the resonance of the music of the spheres which the Talmud mentions (*Yoma* 20b). But, more probably, *kol* must be understood as a voice, and then *bat kol* signifies the daughter of a voice or simply a daughter voice, *i.e.* a voice which has to be distinguished from the usual voice. Practically in rabbinic literature the *bat kol* is a divine or heavenly voice heard without any visual manifestation. It is the " voice from heaven " frequently alluded to both in the Old and New Testaments. The *bat kol* differed essentially from the inspiration of the Prophets ; it was physically heard ; the rabbis identified it with the Holy Spirit, even with God. But it could not be possessed like the Spirit ; therefore the Spirit could depart from Israel, *i.e.* not rest on it, and yet speak to Israel by means of the *bat kol*. The Voice used to make its announcements through the Scriptural passages.

See *Jewish Encycl.*, vol. II., art. *Bat Kol* ; and S. Louis, *Ancient Traditions of Supernatural Voices : Bat Kol*, in *Trans. Soc. Biblical Archæology*, IX. 18.

K. JEWISH MESSIAHS

The opening of the Christian era saw in Palestine a number of pretenders to Messiahship. We learn from Josephus about Theudas, about the Egyptian who gathered 30,000 people on the Mount of Olives, and about a third pretender who prepared to lead the people into the wilderness ; in these three cases the Messianic followers were killed by the Roman soldiery. Menahem, under Agrippa II, was successful in capturing the fortress Antonia, but jealous colleagues assassinated him. Bar Kochba, who did not style himself Messiah, but was hailed as such by the " sages," gathered an army of half a million men, was proclaimed king and held Jerusalem for three years ; the Romans defeated and killed him in 135. The results of this adventure discouraged personations of the Messiah till the fifth century : then there appeared in Crete a certain Moses who led a crowd of enthusiasts into the sea, promising to take them dry-shod to the mainland ; many were drowned, the others rescued, and Moses disappeared. Abu Isa (seventh century) fought against the Arabs, was slain in battle, and gave his name to the sect of the Isavites. One of his disciples, Yugdan, was also considered as Messiah and immortal. A few minor Messiahs arose in the West. David Alroy (12th century), hero of Disraeli's novel *The Wondrous Tale of Alroy*, was of far greater importance. Coming from Persia, he collected a large following, proclaimed himself Messiah, and raised the standard of revolt against the Sultan. He was killed in a battle, but his cult continued for many years. Abulafia (13th century) is better known as a cabbalist than as a Messianic pretender ; he came to Rome, where he attempted to convert the Pope to Judaism, escaped from the imprisonment in which his boldness had involved him, proclaimed himself Messiah in Sicily, announced the millennium for 1290, and then disappeared.

Some minor pretenders—Botarel of Cisneros, Jacob Carcasoni, Nissim of Avila, Asher Lammlein (whose eschatological teaching was accepted by many Christians)—mark the transition between the Middle Ages and the 16th century. David Reubeni arrived at Venice in 1524, coming mysteriously from the East ; he claimed to be brother of an Oriental king, begged the assistance of the Pope and the King of Portugal in a war with the Sultan, was considered by the Jews as a semi-divinity, then became compromised in the stormy adventures of his disciple Molkho ; he went with him to Germany, where they attempted to convert Charles V to Judaism, and were arrested. Reubeni was taken to Spain and seems to have died at the hands of the Inquisition. Solomon Molkho is a no less extraordinary figure. A Christian of Jewish descent and stirred by Reubeni's influence, the gifted young man Diogo Pires reverted to his ancestral Judaism under the name of Molkho. Having left Portugal for Turkey, he collected around him people who considered him as a prophet and as almost divine ; then he came to Rome, had visions, foretold events which subsequently occurred, won the Pope's favour, and became " the Jewish Savonarola." But his own Jewish enemies secured his arrest by the Inquisition as a renegade Christian. Condemned to be burned, he was, by the Pope's orders, hidden within the papal apartments and smuggled out of Rome. He thereupon rejoined Reubeni and they started on their unlucky German journey. Put into chains and carried to Mantua, Molkho was again tried by the Inquisition and sentenced to death. He rejected a pardon offered him on condition that he returned to Christianity. He obtained (1532) the martyr's crown which he had longed for all his life. He published (1529) a collection of addresses under the title *The Book of Wonder*. Isaac Luria (+1572), Hayyim Vital (+1620), Abraham Shalom (c. 1574) were also looked upon as Messiahs.

The most influential of all the pretenders was Shabbathai Sebi (c. 1621–1676). Born at Smyrna, noted for his physical beauty, he acquired a considerable reputation as a cabbalist and revealed himself as the Messiah. The rabbis excommunicated him. He went to Constantinople and Salonica, wandered about the Orient, spent two years in Cairo, reached Jerusalem and announced the opening of the Messianic Age for 1666. This prophecy was promulgated throughout the whole world. When the pretender returned to Smyrna, his journey took the form of a triumphal progress. The local Jewish community acknowledged him as their sole ruler. Even from the North Sea ports, tributes poured in upon the " King of Kings." He was hailed as the Messiah in many synagogues. Some Christians themselves believed in his mission. Prophets arose everywhere and blessed his name. The Sultan imprisoned him in Constantinople and, later on, in Abydos. When he was removed to Adrianople he embraced Mohammedanism, without abandoning his Messianic claims. He became one of the Sultan's doorkeepers and founded the Judæo-Islamic sect of the Dönmeh, which still exists. He fell into disgrace and died at Dulcigno. Most Jews repented bitterly of their support of the movement.

Half a dozen petty Messiahs (*e.g.* Querido, Cardoso) succeeded Shabbathai. Jacob Frank (1726–1791), born in Poland, claimed to be the re-incarnation of all the former prophets and Messiahs. The Frankists opposed the Talmudists and found friends in the Roman hierarchy. Frank accepted baptism. He was nevertheless imprisoned for thirteen years on a charge of heresy. Liberated by the Russian invasion, he lived—latterly as the baron of Offenbach—in various capitals, with a vast income supplied by his adherents. Moses Hayyim Luzzato (1707–1747), a cultured, mystical and wealthy Italian poet, who died in Palestine, was one of the last men whom any considerable section of Jewry accepted as Messiah.

It would be a great mistake to consider all these people as impostors. Frank was perhaps the only unmitigated charlatan. Shabbathai himself seems to have been, to a certain extent, a genuine seeker of God. We must remember that some of these men were hailed as Messiahs against their own wish by their enraptured followers. Neither Molkho nor Reubeni ever claimed Messiahship. Moreover there existed a belief in an Ephraimitic Messiah or a Messiah ben Joseph who was to be the forerunner of the Davidic Messiah. Among the Messianic pretenders, there were many who did not claim to be more than forerunners. Jewish Messianism is an extensive and collective notion ; it is easy to conceive oneself as having a share in Messiahship without being the Messiah Himself. Such was the position of Isaac Luria and Hayyim Vital, these evidently sincere mystics. Luzzato was a rather pathetic victim of his own delusions, with some attributes of genuine saintliness.

Little has been written on the general subject of the Jewish Messiahs, though there are detailed studies on the individual pretenders. As early as 1697 Johannes a Lent published a *Schediasma historicophilologicum de Judaeorum Pseudo-Messiis.* The articles *Pseudo-Messiahs* by G. H. Friedmann in the *Jewish Encycl.,* vol. X, and *Messiahs (Pseudo)* by A. M. Hyamson in *Hastings' Encycl. for Rel. and Ethics,* vol. VIII, give a résumé of the subject.

See : on Molkho and Reubeni, E. Adler, *Auto de Fé and Jew,* London 1908 ; on Shabbathai, A. Freimann, *Sammelband kleinen Schriften über Sabbathai Zebi und Seine Anhänger,* Berlin 1912 ; on Frank, H. Graetz, *Frank und die Frankisten,* Breslau 1868 ; on Luzzato, *Autobiografia di S. D. Luzzato,* Padua 1882.

L. THE EXPERIENCE OF THE SHEKINAH AND CHRISTIAN MYSTICISM

The experience of the Presence (Shekinah) in Jewish mysticism finds equivalents in almost all religions. The "feeling of Presence" has been much studied by religious psychology. There are in Christian mysticism some definite equivalents of the Shekinah experience. This last could perhaps be translated, in the technical terminology of the Christian mystics, as an "intellectual vision" (distinct from "imaginative vision") of God or Christ. "Intellectual vision" is defined as "an intuitive and supernatural knowledge . . . of things, or even of corporeal things, but abstracted from all sensible form." (A. Farges, *Mystical Phenomena*, transl. from the French by S. Jacques, London 1926, p. 339.) St. Teresa writes: "Jesus-Christ seemed to be by my side continually, and as the vision was not imaginary I saw no form" (*Life*, ch. XXVII, 3) and: "She was conscious of His being at her right hand, although not in the way we know an ordinary person to be beside us, but in a more sublime manner. . . . This Presence is, however, quite as evident and certain and indeed more so than the ordinary presence of other people" (*Interior Castle*, ch. VIII, 4). A Poulain quotes these passages as instances of intellectual vision (*The Graces of Interior Prayer*, transl. from the French by L. Yorke Smith, London 1912, p. 318). The experience of the Shekinah may have been often accompanied by other mystical phenomena as imaginative visions, supernatural hearing, luminous effluvia, ecstacy, etc. Some mystics made of the divine Presence the centre of their life. In the 17th century, the saintly and simple-minded Brother Lawrence, author of the beautiful little book *The Practice of the Presence of God*, states that the quest for this Presence is the all-sufficient meditation—the one that he practised. St. Francis de Sales, in his *Introduction to the Devout Life*, and Rodriguez, recommend definite methods of putting oneself in the presence of God.

M. THE SEAT OF MOSES

Jesus and the first Christian generation seem to have taken the view that the scribes, Pharisees and priests were entrusted with a divine mission and even with certain *charismata* related to it. They were, therefore, entitled to the respect and docile attention of the believers. Jesus says: "The scribes and the Pharisees sit in Moses' seat. All therefore whatsoever they bid you observe, that observe and do . . ." (Mt. xxiii. 2–3). One remembers also John xi. 51: "And this spake he [Caiaphas] not of himself; but, being high-priest that year, he prophesied that Jesus should die for that nation"; and Acts xxiii. 5: "Then said Paul: I wist not, brethren, that he was the high priest; for it is written: Thou shalt not speak evil of the ruler of thy people." Christians, in their attitude to the ancient Jewish priesthood and scribal tradition, should not forget these passages. A Christian can see a sure assistance granted by God to the Synagogue in the fact that, during so many centuries of Jewish history, Israel has kept intact the deposit of the Old Testament and surrounded it with such veneration.

The Jewish idea of the " seat of Moses " is connected with the belief in the transmission of the Tradition by Moses to the Elders and their successors, up to the present time. This seat or chair of Moses is symbolically represented by the *almemar* or *almemor* (corruption of the Arab *al-minbar*, " chair," " pulpit "), an elevated platform in the synagogue, on which the desk stands for reading the lessons from the Scripture. Ibn Danon (15th century ; quoted in Neubauer and Diver, *The Fifty-Third Chapter of Isaiah according to the Jewish Interpreters*, vol. ii, p. 203) says : " Our Rabbis, the doctors of the Talmud, deliver their opinions by the power of prophecy, possessing a tradition concerning the principles of interpretation, so that their words are the truth."

N. JEWISH AND CHRISTIAN PRIESTHOOD

We find striking analogies between the ministry of the Synagogue and the ministry of the Christian Church. In the Apostolic age, the ordination of rabbis was practised by the laying of the hand, (*semika*) of three elders (*zekenim*) on the new rabbis. There was a threefold ministry of the synagogue, analogous to that of the Christian Church. The head of the local synagogue, *rosh-ha-keneset*. in Greek *archisynagogos*, corresponds to the bishop; the elders, *zekenim*, in Greek *presbyteroi*, correspond to the priests ; the minister, *hazzan*, in Greek *hyperetes*, corresponds to the deacon. " The use of these titles would seem to come down from a time when the village synagogue and the local Church were in fact identical. Thus it seems reasonable to hold that the Palestinian Churches were from the outset modelled on the synagogues, and in places identical with them, and that the original president at the local Eucharist was, in the absence of an Apostle, an elder analogous to the Jewish *arkhisynagogos*." (W. L. Knox, *St. Paul and the Church of Jerusalem*, p. 87. In spite of its promising title, the book of James Donald, *Ministering Members in Synagogues and Churches in the First Century*, Glasgow. 1935, is entirely disappointing and does not even touch the subject of the connexion between synagogue and church ministries.)

Harnack has suggested that the word " apostle," with its technical meaning, was adopted by the Jews before it was used among Christians. On the name and function of these Jewish " apostles," we have valuable information from Jerome (. . . *Usque hodie a patriarchis Judaeorum apostolos mitti*, etc., in Commentary on Gal. i, Migne *P.L.* XXVII, 311), Eusebius (*In Esaiam*, XVIII, 1 ; Migne *P.G.*, XXIV, 213), and Epiphanius (Panarion XXX). The ethnarch or patriarch (Hebr. *nasi*) of the

Jews, recognized by the Romans from the second to the fourth century, when the leadership of the Jews passed to the Exilarch of Babylon, had official representatives entrusted especially with the collection of financial contributions from the Jews outside Palestine. They were, nevertheless, not merely collectors but legates from the patriarchs with extensive powers. These envoys of the Jewish Patriarchate were called in Hebrew *shelihim*, in Greek *apostoloi*, in Latin *apostoli*. One of the *shelihim*, Joseph of Tiberias, became a Christian and was given the rank of *comes* by Constantine. Some scholars (Harnack, Juster) think that the institution of the *shelihim* goes back to the fall of Jerusalem. It is even maintained that it may be traced to the Persian period. There is an incontestable link between the idea of the *shelihim* and that of the apostles commissioned by Jesus. The *Mishnah* said: " He who is sent by a man is as he who sent him " (*Berakoth*, V. 5). This equation of the person who " sends forth " with those who sent forth is common to the late Jewish " apostolate " and the mission of the Twelve : " He that receiveth you receiveth me " (Mt. x. 40). All this suggests that the Twelve originally chosen by Jesus were actually called *shaliach* or *shelihim*.

(See the article "Apostle" in the *Jewish Encycl.* ; F. Gavin, *Shaliach and Apostolos* in the *Anglican Theological Review*, January, 1927 ; F. Foakes Jackson and Kirsopp Lake, *The Beginnings of Christianity*, London, 1933, vol. V., pp. 48-52.)

The book of the Acts says (vi. 7) that " a great multitude of priests " received the faith. It is probable that such priests were naturally asked in Christian gatherings to " give the blessing " and, later, to officiate at the Eucharist, because of their sacrificial priestly status. After the destruction of the Temple the Eucharist became the service substituted for, and fulfilling, the abolished sacrificial worship of the Temple. The link between the old and the new covenants would thus be constituted by the Aaronites, first priests of the Christian Church. (See P. Levertoff, *Synagogue Worship in the First Century*, in *Liturgy and Worship*, London, 1932.)

Priesthood has not completely disappeared from Judaism. The Synagogue still recognizes people of sacerdotal descent, the *kohanim*, or priests, and the Levites, and gives them a position of honour. Though they have nothing to do with the organization of the synagogue services, which are led by the *hazzan*, or with preaching and judging, which belong to the rabbi, they are called up first to read the Law and occasionally bestow the priestly blessing.

O. BAAL SHEM TOB

Israel ben Eliezer, named also *Baal Shem Tob* ("the good Master of the Name," a Master of the Name being a man who is supposed to work miracles through the name of God) or *Besht*, was born about 1700, of poor parents in some unknown place in Poland. Left an orphan, he was taken care of by the community, studied in a *heder* (talmudical school), served as synagogue employee and teacher in several villages, and married twice, but lost his wives. He soon became famous as a moral teacher and as a healer. Having settled in the small town of Miedzyboz, he began to preach to the lower classes and incurred the hostility of the Talmudists. " All that I have achieved," he said, " I have achieved not through study, but through prayer." He was the very type of righteous man, the *zaddik*, as the Hasidim conceived it. He was, writes Schechter, " the incarnation of a theory and his whole life the revelation of a system." His intercourse with the innkeepers, then despised as the publicans were in the time of Jesus, furnished a silent protest against the haughty attitude of the rabbis ; he himself, for a while, kept a village inn. He saved the soul and the life of a prostitute whose relatives tried to kill her. He taught that friendly intercourse with sinners is more important even than prayer. His distinguishing traits were mercy, joy and contemplation. He supplied his lack of scholarship and oratory by the telling of beautiful parables. Once he heard a voice in heaven declaring that he had forfeited his share in the future life ; he exclaimed : " Blessed art Thou, O God ! Now indeed can I serve Thee out of pure love, since I may not expect reward in the future world ! " This proof of his love for God won him a new divine declaration, annulling the first one. When he died (in 1760) many legends clustered around him and glorified his name. He wrote nothing.

The first source for his biography is Baer ben Samuel's *Shibbe ha-Besht* (1814). A. Kahana published *Rabbi Yisrael Baal Shem*, Jitomir 1900.

See L. Ginzberg, art. *Baal Shem Tob*, in the *Jewish Encycl.*, vol. II.; P. Thémaulis, *Les Merveilles du Besht*, Paris (Lipschutz) ! and the bibliography on Hasidism which we have already given.

P. JUDAISM AND SOME FRENCH CATHOLIC CIRCLES

Judaism has, to a remarkable extent, found understanding and sympathy in some French Roman Catholic circles during these last years, chiefly among the Catholic intellectuals influenced by Maritain. Léon Bloy had opened the way with his book *Le Salut par les Juifs*. Charles Péguy knew and loved through his idealist friend Bernard Lazare ; he saw that the Jews are " d'une fidélité inébranlable à la mystique de l'amitié " (*Notre Jeunesse*, IV. 219) ; he wrote also : " Tout le monde est malheureux dans le monde moderne. Les Juifs sont plus malheureux que les autres " (*Notre Jeunesse*, IV., 216). Jewish hope helped him to understand that " c'est d'espérer qui est difficile " (*Le Porche du Mystère de la deuxième Vertu*, V.) and that the parables of hope " sont le cœur peut-être et le couronnement des évangiles " (*Le Mystère des Saints Innocents*, VI. 94). (See E. Mounier, M. Péguy, G. Izard, *La pensée de Charles Péguy*, Paris, 1931.) Maritain, whom we have quoted at

length on anti-semitism, was a disciple of Bloy; he had learned
from his master that " l'histoire des Juifs barre l'histoire du genre
humain comme une digne barre un fleuve, pour en élever le niveau."
His wife Raïssa Maritain, herself a Jewess by birth, wrote *Histoire
d'Abraham ou la Sainteté dans l'état de nature*.

The great poet Paul Claudel has more than once expressed
profound thoughts about Israel. In his drama *Le Père humilié*,
Oriane says to Pensée de Coûfontaine, daughter of the Jewess
Sichel and symbol of the Ancient Law : " Est-ce pour fermer les
yeux que vous êtes venue à Rome ? " Pensée answers : " Montrez-
moi la Justice, et cela vaudra la peine de les ouvrir. . . . Vous autres,
vous voyez, qu'est-ce que vous faites donc de la lumière ? Vous
qui dites que vous vivez. qu'est-ce que vous faites de la vie ? . . .
Ce Dieu, c'est nous qui vous l'avons donné. Ah, je le sais, s'il y a
un Dieu pour l'humanité, c'est de notre cœur seul qu'il était capable
un jour de sortir ! . . . Qu'en avez-vous fait ? Est-ce pour cela que
nous vous l'avons donné ? . . ." In the symposium *Les Juifs*
(pp. v.-vii.) Claudel has published three letters on Israel, from which
we quote : " L'étude continuelle que je fais de la Bible m'a pénétré
de l'importance exceptionnelle d'Israel au point de vue de Dieu
et de l'humanité. C'est Israël, avec un courage héroique et une
audace intellectuelle qui serait inexplicable sans une vocation
d'en haut, qui a toujours maintenu, contre les séductions de la
Grèce, l'idée d'un Dieu personnel et transcendant, supérieur à toutes
les superstitions du paganisme. Et c'est précisément le paganisme
renaissant sous la forme la plus basse et la plus hideuse qui vient,
une fois de plus, se heurter à cette pierre inébranlable. . . . J'ai
renoncé maintenant à toute expression fictive et je vis à genoux
dans l'éblouissement sans cesse accru des Livres Saints. C'est un
émerveillement qui ne cesse de croître à mesure que j'y attache mon
attention, mon cœur et ma pensée. Quelle gloire pour Israël d'avoir
été choisi comme rédacteur et dépositaire d'un tel message ! "
Claudel wrote these last lines to a Jewish friend on Jewish Passover
day.

Such books as *Le Mystère des Juifs et des Gentils dans l'Eglise*,
by Erik Peterson, *Situation du Sionisme* and *Quand Israel aime Dieu*,
by Jean de Menasce, *Sur les Ruines du Temple* and *Juifs et Chrétiens*,
by the Jesuit Bonsirven, show that some Catholics from Paris
understood Israel better than the convert, René Schwob, who
displays an astonishing ignorance and lack of sympathy in *Moi Juif*
and *Ni Juif ni Grec*, and begins an essay entitled " Etre chrétien "
(in *Les Juifs*, p. 317) with these words : " Je n'aime pas les Juifs."
O. de Ferenczy, author of *La Question d'Israel* and editor of the
journal *La Juste Parole*, interested himself in the fight against anti-
semitism, and was a link between the Parisian circles and the
pro-Jewish Catholic Austrian writers who published the symposium
Die Erfüllung (Vienna, 1937). A Catholic "Association of the
Friends of Israel" seemed to the Roman authorities somewhat

too zealous, and it was censured in a document from the Holy Office (September 5th, 1928). The young Barthian Protestant writers from Paris follow the same trend of ideas as Maritain and Claudel on Jewish problems. Denis de Rougemont has aptly described the Jewish mystical mind which seeks for the knowledge not of " causes," but of " intentions": it does not want " utiliser les choses, mais distinguer en elles les intentions divines, pour les offrir en holocauste spirituel au Créateur" (in *Les Juifs*, p. 152).

See also *Colloque avec Salomon*, by A. Schmidt, in the French Barthian periodical *Hic et Nunc*, nos. 9–10.

Q. YIDDISH AND NEO-HEBREW LITERATURE

Jewish literature of the nineteenth and twentieth centuries has not yet received the attention it deserves, notwthstanding its cultural and spiritual importance not only for Jewry, but for the whole world. Among the writers in Yiddish (*Judisch-Deutsch*) we shall mention the realist and humorist Sholem Asch. Neo-Hebrew, developed from biblical Hebrew, has already a magnificent literary tradition. We shall mention *The Lyra of the Daughter of Zion* by Micah Lebensohn (+1852), the profoundly moving poem *Compassion* by Abraham Lebensohn (+1878), father of Micah; the *Eternal People* and *The Wanderer through the Paths of Life* by Peretz Smolenskin (+1885); *The Sins of Youth*, confessions of a Jew in the sixties, by Lilienblum (+1910); *On the Hills of Zion, I have desired Thee* and *If I forget Thee*, poems by Menahem Dolitzky (+1931) which have become folk-songs. Micah Ber-ditchevsky (+1921), Judah Steinberg (+1908) and Hillel Zeitlin have expressed in their writings the glow and tenderness of Hasidism. J. L. Peretz (+1915) had kept alive in Yiddish this Hasidic element through his novels *Modern Melodies, From the Mouth of the People*, and *The Soul of Hasidism*. The awe-inspiring poem *This too is God's Chastisement* by Tchernikhovsky recalls the pogroms of the first Russian Revolution (1905); other works of the same writer, *Nocturno, Wood Magic, Deianira, Before the Image of Apollo*, express the struggle between a love for pagan ideals and the absoluteness of Judaism; he says to Apollo: " I come to thee—dost thou know me ? I am the Jew, and between us is an eternal conflict. . . . The skies and the sands of the desert are too short to span the breach between the Torch of my fathers and the faith of them that worship thee."

Zionism is partly a product of modern Jewish literature. *The Love of Zion* by the poet Judah Gordon (+1892) opened a new world to the Russian Jew of the fifties and revealed to the arid Ghetto the intoxicating joy and beauty of Palestine : " We were one people, we will remain one ! We have shared joy and grief these two thousand years, since we were dispersed. And, from nation to nation, young and old we will go." Hayim Nachman Bialik (+1934) is the greatest poet of contemporary Zionism ; his

Songs of Splendour unite an intense introspection with a tremendous emotional appeal; he wrote of himself: " I am neither poet nor prophet; I am but a hewer of wood—hewing the wood in the forest of Jewish tradition." Joseph Brenner and Shmaryahn Levin must also be mentioned. The monumental *Thesaurus totius Hebraitatis* in ten volumes by Eliezer ben Yahuda is the capital contribution of modern Palestine to linguistic studies.

See J. Klausner, *A History of Modern Hebrew Literature* (1785–1930), translated from the Hebrew by H. Danby, London 1932.

R. JUDAISM AND PHILOSOPHY IN MODERN TIMES

The history of modern philosophy and psychology is simply crowded with Jewish names : e.g., Salomon Maimon, Herz, Cassirer, Husserl, Max Scheler, Lasson, Brunschvicg in general philosophy; Meyerson in logic ; Max Dessoir in esthetics ; Adler, Charlotte Bühler, Freud, Koffka, Munsterberg, Stern in psychology ; Durckheim, Levy-Brühl, Simmel, Steinthal in Sociology; Gomperz, Munk, Freudenthal in the history of philosophy. But, if there are many Jewish philosophers, one can hardly say that there is a Jewish philosophy. An attempt has been made to exhibit the philosophy of Bergson (1859–1940) as a re-emergence of Philonian thought. This is mere fancy ; Bergson descends from Maine de Birau and Ravaisson ; moreover, his remarks about Judaism ("Israel and its stern God were not close enough together for Judaism to be a mysticism . . ." *The Two Sources of Morality and Religion*, trans. by R. Andra and C. Brereton, London, 1935, especially p. 205) show a complete lack of knowledge.

Among recent "technical philosophers," Hermann Cohen (1842–1918), leader of the Marburg School of Neo-Kantism, affords the rare example of a Jew who tries (in his *Religion der Vernunft aus den Quellen des Judentums*, 2nd ed., 1929) to express his Judaism through philosophy. He found correspondences between Kantian rationalism and Jewish dogmatic soberness, between Kant's ethical stress and the Torah, between the " categorical imperative " and the thunders from Sinai. Schleiermacher had already remarked that of every three educated Jews at least one was a Kantian. Cohen evolved a special theory of the Messiah. He conceives the Messiah as being essentially the Suffering Servant or Substitute, not indeed for the guilt of men, but for their punishment and earthly suffering, By substitution (*Stellvertretung*), certain persons bear the sufferings of others and so influence them that they win them back to God ; those "substitutes" may be regarded in their totality as the Messiah, a title which refers not to one person, but to the Jewish nation or, more truly, to all them that share Israel's task. (See A. Lukyn Williams, *A Modern Jewish Philosopher on the Doctrine of the Messiah*, in *The Church Quarterly Review*, April–June, 1936.)

We should perhaps hesitate to call Buber, Rosenzweig and Shestov philosophers in the technical sense of the word, but they are the representatives of a specifically Jewish thought. Martin Buber's philosophy is best expressed in *I and Thou*, which we have analysed elsewhere. We consider him as the only real Jewish philosopher alive to-day. Franz Rosenzweig (+1929) unfolded a general conception of the world in his book *Der Stern der Erlösung* (The Star of Salvation, 1921). Besides an explanation of life grounded upon the three notions of creation, revelation and salvation, and upon the immanence of a *logos* or system of forms in the universe, Rosenzweig has some profound views on Judaism as the religion of hope, on marriage as the symbol of salvation for which the loving soul is thirsting, and on the relationship between Judaism and Christianity. The absolute essence of God or the eternal Truth is like a star ; the fire of the star, or eternal life, corresponds to Judaism ; the rays of the star, or the eternal way, correspond to Christianity. Rosenzweig believes in the " possibility of hastening the kingdom by prayer." The most profound critique of Rosenzweig's work is that by the Jewish Christian philosopher S. Frank (*Mistitcheskaia philosophia Rosentzveïga*, in the Russian periodical *Put*, No. 2, 1926). The Russian philosopher Lev Shestov (+1938) was a Jew by descent and never joined the Christian Church ; he was nevertheless deeply Christian in his thought and even a Christian maximalist. He became a link between Hebraic prophecy and the " existential philosophy " of Kirkegaard and Berdyaev. The urgent dilemma— Athens or Jerusalem ?—on which he insisted is a major moment of the dialogue between Jews and Christians. Shestov, more than anybody else, has emphasized the contrast between these two conceptions of life, Hebrew and Greek (*Athènes et Jerusalem. Un essai de philosophie religieuse.* Translated from the Russian by B. de Schloezer, Paris 1938). The " I believe, O Lord ; help my unbelief ! " of Jerusalem has, says Shestov, been superseded by the " I believe, O Lord, but, if it be possible, I would like to know " imported from Athens. We must choose between these two formulas, and Shestov wishes that the Jerusalemite *credo ut vivam* should prevail over the Athenian *credo ut intelligam*.

(See H. Schoeps, *Geschichte der judischen Religionsphilosophie in der Neue Zeit*, Band I, Berlin 1935 ; A. Lichtigfeld, *Twenty Centuries of Jewish thought* ; L. Roth, *Jewish Thought in the Modern World*, in *The Legacy of Israel*, pp. 433–473.

S. CONVERSIONS TO JUDAISM

Jews claim that Judaism is not a militant religion and does not strive to bring outsiders into its fold. Nevertheless there have always been and there still are conversions to Judaism. The talmudic *ger*, the *proselytos* of the New Testament, the *epelus* of Philo were Gentiles who accepted the Jewish religion ; the Old Testament also refers to them, though only in periphrases. Judaism made many conquests among Romans of the upper classes. There were also " half-converts " who embraced Jewish monotheism and morality without, however, submitting to circumcision or ceremonial laws ; they seem too have been more or less identical with the " God-fearing " and the " proselytes of the gate " (though this last name originally designated one under Jewish civil jurisdiction). The technical term for " making a convert" in rabbinical literature is " to bring one under the wings of the Shekinah." After the Hadrianic rebellion a complete procedure of reception came into use ; it included examination before a board, circumcision, baptism and instruction. Many of the earlier rabbis (e.g., Rabbi Eliezer) took an unfavourable view of proselytes ; on the other hand Rabbi Eleazar ben Pedat (*Pes.* 97b) saw in Israel's dispersion the divine purpose of winning proselytes. Women seem to have predominated among converts or half-converts to Judaism : e.g., Fulvia, wife of the senator Saturninus, and Poppæa Sabina, mistress and second wife of Nero. Titus Flavius Clemens and his wife Flavia Domitilla, cousins of the emperors Titus and Domitian, embraced Judaism ; the consul Flavius Clemens was executed, under Domitian's orders, and Domitilla banished to an island. This case is rather complex, for this branch of the imperial Flavian house was inclined towards Judaism and at the same time towards Christianity ; is the Domitilla whom Dion Cassius (*Hist.*, 67, 13) ranges among the " many who had followed Jewish customs and laws " the same Domitilla whom Eusebius (*Hist. eccl.*, 3, 18) describes as a Christian martyr ? It is rather strange that the Domitilla chapel in the catacombs of Rome is arranged on a Jewish pattern.

(See Bertholet, *Die Stellung der Israeliten und der Juden zu dem Fremden*, 1896, and Grätz, *Die Jüdischen Proselyten im Römerreiche*, 1884.)

The little kingdom of Adiabene, in Mesopotamia, embraced Judaism during the first century. Some Arab tribes, e.g., the Dhu Nuwas and the Kenites, did the same before the sixth century. The kingdom of Khazars (South Russia) accepted the Jewish faith in the seventh century. That many converts came from the ranks of the Christians appears from the prohibition of conversion to Judaism issued by the Councils of Orleans and the code of Alfonso X (which made it a capital crime). Bishop Bodo, chaplain of the Emperor Louis the Pious, was converted to Judaism under the name of Eleazar. In more recent times, a Polish nobleman, Count Valentine Potocki embraced Judaism under the name of Abraham and was burned at the stake at Vilna (1749) ; Potocki's friend, Zaremba, also became a Jew, as well as his wife and child, and went with them to Palestine. Lord George Gordon (1751–1793), the agitator of the " Gordon riots," was converted to Judaism and conformed strictly in all respects to the Law ; he retired for a while to the house of a Birmingham Jew. Warder Cresson (1798–1860), a Quaker from Philadelphia, became a proselyte to the Jewish faith. He explained his remarkable change in a book called *The Key of David*, and dated " Philadelphia, 5612 " (i.e., 1852). Having assumed the name of Michael Boaz Israel, he became the first American consul in Jerusalem, where he died in 1860.

Between 1868 and 1929, 6,310 Christians adopted Judaism in Vienna. In 1928, 58 persons adopted Judaism in Budapest. In 1925, 23 Christians adopted Judaism in Warsaw. According to S. M. Melamed, no fewer than five thousand Gentiles are received each year in the Jewish communities of America through inter-marriage (*The Reflex*, September, 1929, p. 16). In Europe, many cases of conversion to Judaism are rather cases of " return " (Lord Melchett, for instance). There are, however, cases of purely ideological conversions. Nahida Ruth Lazarus (+1928), wife of the German philosopher Moritz Lazarus, was a convert to Judaism and wrote on Jewish questions.

An interesting pamphlet, *Jewish Views on Jewish Mission* (London, 1933), contains the documents of a controversy on this subject raised seven years ago between Rabbi Mattuk and C. Montefiore. Montefiore's position is as follows :—If he cannot tell what forms the " Mission of Israel " may assume in the future, he expects Liberal Judaism to act as a beacon. a leaven and a ferment ; he does not dismiss the idea that Liberal Judaism might become the world religion. While not seeking to win adherents by unworthy means, he would leave the gates freely open, not make the approach difficult, and render what is seen and heard within increasingly intelligible and attractive. (See Montefiore, *The Old Testament and After*, p. 568.) In 1927, the Central Conference of American Rabbis published a *Manual for the Instruction of Proselytes* the foreword of which says: "Judaism is a world religion . . . The supreme task of Israel has been first to receive and develop our faith, and then to make it known to the people of the earth."

In 1926 a book was published in Paris under the title *Le Sanctuaire inconnu* (The unknown Sanctuary). In it A. Pallière related how he was converted to Judaism from Roman Catholicism. Pallière's book has been translated into English, German and other languages ; its author is now ministering as lay preacher in the temple of the Liberal Israelite community in Paris. He was a friend and pupil of the famous rabbi Elie Benamozegh, of Leghorn, an apostle of the universality of Judaism who advocated the admission of the Gentiles, not to the Mosaic covenant, but to the Noachite covenant (the commandments given to Noah by God) and saw in Noachism the ground of a future world-religion. Like his master, Pallière acknowledges Christianity as divine and places its mystery side by side with that of Judaism. Having the privilege of knowing Aimé Pallière not only by his books, but by personal acquaintance and friendship, we venture to say that, in Judaism, he probably had the sense of approaching nearer to Jesus, and we can witness to the deep " Christian " impression which his preaching in the synagogue of the *rue Copernic* is apt to make upon Christian hearers.

T. JUDAIZING MOVEMENTS WITHIN CHRISTIANITY

A not very important, but continuous judaizing stream has always existed among Christians of non-Jewish descent. We know little about the *Insabbatati, Passagii,* and judaizing sects of the 12th and 13th century in Southern France ; but the little we do know points to their strange and quite considerable influence. A strong judaizing sect, the centre of which was Novgorod, spread in Russia during the 15th century ; they rejected the Trinity, the Messiahship of Christ, the Church, the Sacraments, and gave greater honour to the Old Testament than to the New Testament. In the 18th century, Uklein. the founder of the Russian sect of the *Molokani,* adopted for himself certain Jewish dietary laws. Sundunkov regarded Christ as inferior to Moses, and established the sect of the *Subbotniki* (Sabbatarians), who observe the Jewish Sabbath, the Mosaic rites, and are scarcely distinguishable from Talmudic Jews. In 1846 Nicholas Ilyin founded the sect of the Jehovists, a kind of Old Testament Christianity. About the middle of the 18th century. John Glas and Sandeman founded in English-speaking countries a small sect (" Glasites "), who refrain from blood and things strangled. The Seventh Day Adventists and Baptists judaize in so far as they are Sabbatarians. John Roe founded in England (1822) and America the sect of the Christian Israelites who keep the whole Mosaic Law, while subscribing to the Gospel, and try to gather together the twelve tribes of Israel. William Croody established in America (1896) a " Church of God and Saints of Christ," which is a Negro Church confessing Christ, keeping the Sacraments, and observing the Jewish calendar and festivals. In 1894, the Szeklers of Transylvania, a Sabbatarian sect founded at the end of the 16th century by Thomas Pecsi, who translated Jewish liturgical books into Hungarian, joined the Jewish religious community. They observe all Jewish ritual laws. Whether these "Aryans " who have adopted the Jewish faith should be made subject to the Jew-laws is a problem now troubling the Hungarian authorities (*Jewish Chronicle,* Nov. 29, 1940).

(See L. I. Newman, *Jewish Influence on Christian Reform Movements,* New York, 1925 ; K. Grass, *Russische Sekten* in *Religion in Geschichte und Gegenwart,* V ; L. Gray *Judaizing* in Hasting's *Encycl. of Rel. and Ethics,* vol. VII).

U. A JEWISH CHRISTIAN LITURGY

(Outlines of the Eucharist composed by Dr. P. Levertoff)

This Hebrew Eucharist has been, for the last ten years, regularly celebrated at St. George's, Bloomsbury, at Holy Trinity, Bethnal Green, and at St. Michael's, Golders Green. The Hebrew and English text of this liturgy can be obtained at St. George's,

Bloomsbury. The liturgy is entitled : *The Meal of the Holy King*
(a term from the Zohar). The rubrics say that the holy ark, containing the rolls of the Book, should stand at the right hand of the
altar. In point of fact, as the service is held in Anglican churches,
the rubrics are not applied.

At the opening of the service the congregation sings a beautiful
Hasidic hymn : " Friend of my soul, father of mercy, draw me to
Thee in Thy gracious majesty ; may Thy love be sweet to me, Light
of the world, great in Thy beauty, my soul is sick with love for
Thee ; heal it, O Lord, with Thy light. Shower upon me all of
Thy pity ; shew mercy to the son of Thy love ; Thy power I long
to see and extol Thee. My Beloved, give me Thy peace ; may Thy
glory enlighten the earth ; with Thy grace let my countenance
shine." After the initial blessings and thanksgivings, the priest
recites the *Shema*, the confessions of faith in the One God. An
adapted *ahabah* begins as follows : " Thou hast loved us with an
everlasting love, with great and exceeding pity hast Thou pitied
us. Thou hast chosen us in the Messiah before the foundation of
the world, that we should be holy, without blame before Thee in
love . . . ." There follows a Christian variant of the synagogue
Eighteen Benedictions. After a collect for the day. the priest reads
the *parasha* (synagogal section from the Law), the prophetic lesson,
the Epistle, the Gospel. The recitation of the Creed is followed by
the hymn taken from the early liturgy of St James: " Let all mortal
flesh keep silence. . . ." Then an *anaphora*, including the *trisagion*,
the institution words and an *epiclesis* ; this anaphora is partly
inspired by the liturgy of St. John Chrysostom, partly taken from
Isaiah (" A child is born unto us, a Son was given unto us. . ."
and passages about the suffering Servant). Confession (Psalm li)
and Absolution follow. The priest sings Psalm xxiii—the Shepherd
Psalm. After the communion, all recite the Lord's Prayer. A
fragment of the Hallel is said. Then a dialogue begins between the
priest and the congregation : " Ye who cleave to the Lord your
God, ye are all alive to-day. I am my Beloved's, and my Beloved
is mine." The dialogue goes on, in antiphonal sentences from the
prologue of the Fourth Gospel and from Isaiah liii. The Aaronic
blessing closes the service.

A detailed analysis of the sources of this liturgy has been given
by the German liturgiologist, P. Schorlemmer, in Friedrich Heiler's
Quarterly Review *Eine heilige Kirche*, Munich, April–June, 1934.
Dean Carpenter, of Exeter, has written the following appreciation
of Levertoff's liturgy : " Learned scholars, Dr. Oesterley, Dr.
Nairne, Dr. Cooke, testify that it is made from early Jewish and
Christian liturgical sources ; it contains the essentials of the
Christian Eucharist ; it is reverent and, as sung with the haunting
lilt of Hebrew melodies, it is exquisitely beautiful. . . ." (Editorial
of *Theology*, January. 1935.) W. K. Lowther Clarke, in *Liturgy and
Worship* (London, 1932), p. 816, says : " The beauty and the

impressiveness of the rite are beyond praise. . . . But, when every-thing has been said in favour of Dr. Levertoff's rite, which has elements of greatness, it remains a " fancy Liturgy," an archæo-logical reconstruction without roots in history." Its materials have certainly roots in history. It is true that the arrangement of the materials is the result of an individual endeavour and not the fruit of a long collective liturgical experience. But how were the historical liturgies (e.g., sacramentaries, Prayer-Book) fixed in the first place ?

V. JEWISH LEARNING FOR CHRISTIAN STUDENTS

A student who wishes to specialize in Hebrew or rabbinics finds appropriate courses in Universities. We think that something should be done for the Christian ministers, missionaries, theological or other students who wish, not to become specialists in Hebrew philology or history, but to become acquainted with Judaism and practical Jewish problems. Theological or missionary Colleges could receive visits from itinerant lecturers to deliver short courses of lectures on Jewish questions. A more detailed course, including, e.g., modern Jewish history and literature, Jewish worship, com-parative theology (Jewish and Christian), modern Jewish social problems, could be organized in some theological or missionary centres, not for the purpose of producing missionaries, but to give a deeper introduction to Jewish questions to any " lover of Zion " who would like to know Judaism or to prepare for some work connected with the Jews. Such initiation would be given by a kind of " group leader " rather than by a " professor," and should imply friendly practical contacts with Jewry, its religious and social activities.

We will try to formulate a dream. We hope that the day will come when a few Jews and Christians, and possibly a few Moslems, could form a small community in Jerusalem and share in a common life of prayer, religious study, and varied service to society. This humble settlement, which would have a likeness to an Indian Ashram, could perhaps become a useful instrument of God in Palestine and even outside.

Finally, the Student Christian Movement and the Young Men and Women Christian Associations could try to establish closer spiritual contact with the Jewish religious organizations for Youth.

W. JEWISH AND CHRISTIAN UNITED WORSHIP IN A SHELTER (1941)

The following account is abridged from the Article *Sirs, ye are Brethren*, published in the *Church Times* of March 14, 1941 :—

This shelter, in the neighbourhood of Oxford Street, is in the parish of St. Mark's, North Audley Street. It is the night refuge of larger numbers of Christians and Jews. When it was first filled, after the coming of the German bombers, the vicar of St. Mark's, the Rev. Kenneth Thorneycroft, visited its depths to say night prayers. But because there were a great many Jews among the shelterers, a spokesman came to Mr. Thorneycroft and asked if a Jewish rabbi might be asked to say the prayers to which Jewish ears are accustomed. So it was agreed that on Monday nights there should be a combined service to which both Christians and Jews could come, when prayers would be used which both could follow and use with conviction and sincerity. The English priest and the Jewish rabbi would take each his own part, and would give alternate talks.

The one open space in the shelter, where dances are usually held and darts played, was filled with benches. A hymn-sheet was handed round. Six of the familiar A. and M. hymns were included, but here and there a verse was omitted so that the Jewish brethren could join in with an untroubled mind. " The day Thou gaveth, Lord, is ended," was given in its entirety, but " Abide with Me " was without its last verse, and there was no doxology at the end of " All People that on Earth do Dwell." All the Jewish men had by this time covered their heads, some with hats, some with hand-kerchiefs, and the rabbi with a black skull cap. Night prayers were said by Mr. Thorneycroft, his congregation continuing to sit with bowed heads.

Then the rabbi finished the service. The ancient prayers of Christendom were followed by the still more ancient prayers of the Jews. A synagogue hymn was sung to music reminiscent of, and yet hauntingly different from, Plainsong. The Canon of the Jewish Prayer Book was closed fourteen hundred years ago, and this song was probably of far more ancient origin :

" He is my God—My Redeemer liveth—and a rock in my travail and time of distress.

" And He is my banner and my refuge, the portion of my cup on the day when I call."

Soon the rabbi was calling to those who had lost a relative in death during the past twelve months, and two men stood forward. Swaying rhythmically backwards and forwards they repeated the Mourner's Kaddish.

The rabbi's address was the preparation for the Feast of Purim. The religion of the English people stood in as great a jeopardy from Nazi-ism, in the last resort, as did the religion of the Jews, he said. They faced a common evil together. They were given in that shelter a common place of prayer. All knew the ancient words, " See how joyful a thing it is, brethren, to dwell together in unity."

A last hymn was sung. The blessing was given. Outside the siren hooted, and the guns began to boom.

Y. JEWISH WORSHIP IN A CAMP OF INTERNEES, ISLE OF MAN (1940)

The following is taken from the article *Judaism comes to the Isle of Man. A religious revival*, published in the *Jewish Chronicle of* November 29, 1940 :—

" In the ordinary camp on weekdays there are more worshippers than in the Great Synagogue, London, on Sabbath. Prayers are said with an ardour that has become rare since the destruction of Jewish life in Eastern Europe. It is surprising what a large number of internees brought their own Tallis, Teffillin and prayer-books with them. It is a still greater miracle how the Synagogue Committees found ways and means of providing the forgetful with these requisites. Long before the appearance of books and newspapers, sufficient copies were available of the Pentateuch in many editions.

" The scene when Tisha b Ab occurred was typical. The event overshadowed the whole camp life. Many internees fasted ; the social centres were closed ; there was no music ; the Orthodox sat by candlelight and intoned the Lamentations of Jeremiah. They sat by the waters of the Irish Sea and wept, as the exiles wept by the waters of Babylon.

" Every Sabbath leaves it mark on camp life The Ark is set up with unimaginably modest equipment. Cardboard and ink are skilfully used to suggest the stone plates with the initials of the Ten Commandments. Ornaments for walls and windows, seven-branched candlesticks and Magen David are made of paper. The worshippers forget they are refugees and internees ; they are ' in Shool ' and welcome loudly the approach of Princess Sabbath. There could be no intenser Sabbath feeling in any Community."

Z. JUDAISM AND CHRISTIANITY AS REPRESENTED IN ART

The attitude of the late Middle Ages to Jews is well illustrated by some specimens of Christian art of the 13th century. Statues of the Church and Synagogue adorn the porch of Strasbourg Cathedral. The Church wears a crown and holds a chalice which she has taken from the Synagogue. The Synagogue, with her head downcast and her eyes veiled, still grasps a broken banner and a fragment of the tables of the commandments. In the Jesse-tree miniature, from the 12th century Bible at Lambeth Palace, the Synagogue is being exhorted by Moses and Isaiah, but a hand from Heaven draws a veil over her eyes. The miniature of the " Bible of Olivares," which was preserved among the treasures of the Casa de Alba, in Madrid, make a striking contrast with the anti-Jewish allegorical representations described above. In 1422 Don Luis de Guzman, Grand Master of the military Order of Calatrava, asked Rabbi Moses Arragel to undertake a translation of the Bible into Spanish, with a commentary thereon. Arragel was helped by some Friars. One of the miniatures illustrating the text shows the inside of a synagogue. In the frontispiece, Arragel himself, wearing the Jewish badge, presents his work to the Grand Master, while Knights of the Order are seen feeding hungry Jews or attending to sick ones. Right and left of the frontispiece, the presence of two Friars, a Dominican and a Franciscan, gives the finishing touch to the scholarly and irenic volume ; this miniature expresses a complete and detailed programme of co-operation between Jews and Christians.

We should mention two modern works. One, by Solomon J. Solomon, exhibited in the Royal Academy in 1904, now in the Harris Museum and Art Gallery of Preston, and reproduced in the first volume of *Judaism and Christianity*, shows Moses supporting the dead body of Jesus. The body, wearing the crown of thorns, is reposing on the knees of Moses, who holds in his hands the tables of the law. The other work is " Law and Love," a stained glass window in the Chapel of Westminster College, Cambridge, completed in 1921 by Douglas Strachan and reproduced as frontispiece to Vol. II of *Judaism and Christianity* ; in the hands of Law is the roll of the Commandments, in those of Love the chalice of sacrifice.

INDEX

Abelson 35, 70, 78, 79, 89, 90, 98, 99, 187
Abraham 214
Abrahams 4, 20, 33, 94, 205
Achad-Ham 163
Adam Kadmon 70
Akiba 48
Ambrose 14
Amoraim 46
Anatolio 21
Anti-semitism 152–156
Apostolic Church Order 10
Apostolic Constitutions 10
Arragel 25
Art (Judaism and Christianity as represented in) 242–243
Atonement 89–96, (Day of) 130
Augustine 1, 16–17
Autos-da-fe 17
Averroes 19
Avicebron 19
Avicenna 19

Baal Shem Tob 142, 230–231
Barnabas (Epistle of) 13
Barth 57, 109, 110, 112, 115, 116–118, 150, 186
Barthianism and Missions 182
Bat Kol 224–225
Bede 20
Berdyaev 100, 111, 120, 151, 210
Bergson 234
Besht *See* Baal Shem Tob
Bialik 165, 233–234
Biurists 56
Bloch xii
Bloy 231
Box 22
Branscomb 3
Brierre-Narbonne 93
Brunner (C.) 38
Brunner (E.) 111
Buber (M.) 2, 27, 40, 57, 104, 116, 117, 141, 147, 158, 165, 169, 187, 188, 218–219, 235
Buber (S.) 218
Bultmann 112
Buxtorf 27–29

Cabbala 24, 25, 67
Callenberg 173
Calvin 26
Caro 20, 47
Casuistry (Jewish) 61–62
Chrysostom 1, 14
Chwolson 34
Claudel 113, 232
Clementine Recognitions 13
Cohen 234
Communion in the Messiah 195–197
Conversions of Jews to Christianity 176–178
Conversions to Judaism 235–237 ; *See* Proselytes and Judaizing Movements
Cournos 39, 119
Creeds (Jewish) 223–224
Cyprian 1, 13

Dalman 34, 60
David del Bene 22
De Jonge 39, 206–207
Delitzchianum (Institutum Judaicum) 175
Diakonia and Kerygma 189–191
Dialectics (Talmudic) 222–223
Dialogue 1–3
Diaspora (Jewish) 148–160, 212
Didache 10
Didascalia 10
Dodd 194
Dogmas (Judaism and Christian) 96–98

Ebionites 200
Edersheim 33
Einstein 39, 177
Eisler 102
Eliezer ben Yahuda 165, 234
Ephrem 14
Epistle to the Romans (exegesis of the) 211–217
Erasmus 22
Eschatology 109–111
Eschelbacher 37

Exegesis (Jewish) 53–57
Existential Thinking 108–109

Fathers (Patriarchs) *See* Merits of
   the Fathers
Fathers (Jewish) 45–50
Faulhaber 191
Ferrer 18
Feuchtwanger 150
Filson 13
Foeldes 207
Frank, J. 227
Frank, S. 235
French Catholic Circles (Judaism
   and) 231–233
Freud 234

Gamaliel 5, 48
Gamaliel (the Second) 46
Gaonim 46
Gematria 53–54
Glory 84–88
Goodwill Movements 157
Goudge 194
Graetz 35
Guillaume 22

Harling 40, 167
Harnack 212
Hasidism 140–147, 233 *See* Baal
   Shem Tob
Haskalah 29
Hebrew (meaning of the word) 218
Hebrew Christian Alliance 202
Hellenism 71–75
Herzl 163–164
Hesed 135
Hess 163
Hilary 14
Hillel 47–48
Hippolytus 1
Hoffmann 194–209
Horodetzky 147

Isaac (binding of) 91
Israel *See* Mystery of Israel
Israel (Community of) 149–150
   See Mystical Body
Israelite (meaning of the word) 218

Jabotinsky 163
James (Apostle) 11
Jerome 16
Jerusalem and Christianity 171
Jerusalem (Primitive Church of)
   198–200
Jesus 3–6; attitude of modern
   Judaism towards 35–40; Jewish
   prayers used by 132–133; as
   a Zaddik 147; and Old Testa-
   ment prophecies 185; titles of
   208–209; as a rabbi 222
Jew (meaning of the word) 218
Jewish Christianity (modern) 202–
   210 *See* Liturgy
Johnson 95
Judah ha-Levy 20, 46, 140, 160
Jude 11
Judaeo-Christianity (Primitive)
   9–12, 198–201 *See* Priesthood
Judaizing Movements 238
Justin Martyr 1, 197

Kavanah 135
Kerygma 184, diakonia and, 189–
   191
Kiddush 128, 208
Klausner 7, 37–38
Kosmala 181, 182
Kraemer 188

Law *See* Torah
Lazaron 119
Lazlo 207
Lectionary (Synagogue) 51
Leo Hebraeus 47
Levertoff ix, 8, 34, 51, 70, 84, 114,
   141, 203–204, 230, 238
Levita 23
Levy (J.) 38
Levy (M.) 202
Liberal Judaism 29–32, 42–43, 103
Lichtenstein 206
Liturgical Movement and Judaism
   188
Liturgy (Jewish Christian) 238–240
Loewe 33, 191
Love in Jewish piety 138
Lucky *See* Lutsky
Ludwig 39
Lukyn Williams 1, 13, 204
Lull 20

Luria 49, 90
Luther 21, 26
Lutsky 202
Luzzato 227

Maimonides 19, 20, 23, 46, 83, 86,
    118 See Creeds
Manasseh ben Israel 29
Maritain (J.) 153, 155, 156, 193,
    231–232
Maritain (R.) 232
Martini 18, 21
Martyrologies (Jewish) 48
Marx 154
Marxism 119–122
Masorah 51
Mattuk 160
Mediation 90–93
Melamed 35
Memra 52, 78–81, 98, 111
Mendelssohn 29, 56
Merits of the Fathers 214–215
Merkabah 64
Messiah 92, 100–105, 111
Messiahs (pseudo-) 225–228
Messianism 100–126, 194
Middle Ages (Judaism in ·the)
    17–22
Mission of the Church to Israel
    182–191
Mission of Israel to the Christian
    Church 191–195
Missions to the Jews 172–182
Mitsvah 135
Molkho 226
Montefiore (C.) 7, 8, 31, 57, 74, 76,
    86, 89, 99, 103, 178, 219–220, 237
Montefiore (M.) 220
Montefiore (N.) 220
Moravians and Judaism 174–175
Moses (seat of) 228–229
Murder (ritual) 153
Mystery of Israel 211–217
Mystical Body of Christ 215
Mystical Body of Israel 158–159,
    215
Mysticism (Jewish) 63–70, 188
    See Hasidism

Nahmanides 79, 84, 86
Nazarenes 200–201

Neo-Hebrew Literature 233–234
Nicholas of Lyra 21
Notarikon 54

Obedience (Messianism and) 111–
    112
Oecumenical   Movement   and
    Judaism 188–189, 209–210
Oesterley 45, 99, 132, 187
Old Testament and the Mission to
    Israel 184
Orthodox Judaism 44

Palestine (Judaism and) 162 ;
    Communal settlements in, 186
Pallière ix, 237
Parables (rabbinic) 56
Parkes 1, 7, 13, 201
Parousia 110, 113, 115
Passover 130–131
Patristic times 1–17
Paul 6–8 See Epistle to the Romans
Peace Army in Palestine 170
Peguy 151, 231
Pharisees 3–6, 219
Philip (Acts of) 13
Phillips xi, 183
Philo 74–75, 79, 187
Philosophy (Jewish) 234–235
Pico della Mirandola 23–24
Piety (Jewish) 134–140 See
    Mysticism and Worship
Pinsker 163
Pius (the Eleventh, pope) 159
Posquières (Isaac of) 66
Prayer Books (Jewish) 127
Priesthood (Jewish and Christian)
    229–230
Prophecies (Messianic) 184–185
Prophets 193
Proselytes (Jewish) 235–236

Qahal 209
Qaraism 43, 220–221
Quakerism and Judaism 173–174,
    208

Rabbinowitz 202
Rabbis 45, 49
Rashi 47, 49

Reformation and Judaism 26
Refugees (Jewish) 157–160
Remnant 122–125
Renaissance and Judaism 22–26
Rendel Harris 12, 13
Reubeni 226
Reuchlin 24–25
Robertson 4
Rosenstock 3
Rosenzweig 3, 57, 99, 235
Rougemont 233

Sabbath 128–129
Saboraim 46
Sacraments (Christian) 128, 208
Sadducees 5
Saintliness (Jewish) 139
Salvador 35
Samaritans 43, 221–222
Schechter 29, 35, 141, 147
Schoeps 3, 39
Scholasticism 19
Schonfield 18, 19, 198, 199, 201, 203
Schweitzer 100, 107, 108, 109
Scripture 50, 57
Sefirot 66–68
Servant (Suffering) 93–96, 101
Shabbatai Sebi 226–227
Shekinah 52, 65, 81–87, 88, 98, 138–139, 149, 186, 187, 228
Shema 132
Shestov 235
Sholem Asch 40, 233
Shulhan Aruch 20, 47
Silver 38
Simon 27
Smith 193
Socialism (Jewish religious) 119
Solomon(Odes of) 12, 195
Soloviof x
Sonship (Divine) 80–81
Spinoza 27, 28–29
Spirit (Holy) 77, 87–89
Strack and Billerbeck 34

Tagore 113
Talmud 27, 57–63 See Dialectics
Tannaim 45

Targums 52
Tefillah 137
Tertullian 1
Teshubah 136
Testament of the Twelve Patriarchs 12
Testimonies 13
Theatre (Jewish) 163
Theology (Jewish and Christian comparative) 185–188
Thomas Aquinas 19, 118
Toldoth Yeshu 18
Torah 7, 60–61, 193
Tradition in Judaism 41–45
Travers Herford 4, 6, 182
Trinity 70, 77, 80
Trumpeldor 163
Tryphona (Dialogos pros) 1, 15–16
Tsimtsum 67
Turner 5, 10, 11

University of Jerusalem 165–166

Vischer 114, 184

Walker 3
Wasserman 150–151
Wechssler 73
Weizmann 165
Werfel 8
Word See Memra
Worship (Jewish) 127–134, United Jewish and Christian W. in a shelter 240–241, Jewish W. in a camp of internees 241–242 See Liturgy

Yemenite Jews 44
Yetsirah 65–66
Yiddish Literature 233–234

Zaddikim 144–147
Zangwill 150–159
Zionism 160–171, 194, 233–234
Zohar 67–70
Zwingli 26